The Bargain Book for Savvy Seniors

How to Save on Groceries, Utilities, Prescriptions, Taxes, Hobbies, and More!

Wood, Gayle K

Publisher's Note

The editors of FC&A have taken careful measures to ensure the accuracy and usefulness of the information in this book. While every attempt was made to assure accuracy, some Web sites, addresses, telephone numbers, and other information may have changed since printing.

This book is intended for general information only. It does not constitute medical, legal, or financial advice or practice. We cannot guarantee the safety or effectiveness of any treatment or advice mentioned. Readers are urged to consult with their personal financial advisers, lawyers, and health care professionals.

The publisher and editors disclaim all liability (including any injuries, damages, or losses) resulting from the use of the information in this book.

Love the Lord your God with all your heart and with all your soul and with all your mind and with all your strength.

Mark 12:30

Contents

Contents

Antiques

Search out a quality auctioneer

One of the best places to find antiques is at an auction. You can find auction listings in many places, including the classified ads of your local newspaper. But once you're ready to jump in with your wallet, attend auctions only conducted by reputable auction houses. Check with the Better Business Bureau, your state's auctioneer licensing office if you have one, or your county or state consumer protection office.

The National Auctioneers Association (NAA) is another resource for auction listings and other information. Only members can post an auction on their Web site, ensuring each one is run by a reputable auctioneer. Visit them at *www.auctioneers.org*. Once you've been to an auction house you like and trust, you can get on their mailing list to receive notices of upcoming events.

Do your homework — don't overpay

The last thing you want is to come home from an auction with something you spent too much money on. So do your homework, especially if you're looking for a specific item. That means knowing what similar pieces sell for, either at retail or through other auctions.

Get the auction catalog ahead of time, if possible, and study the goods. Find out if you can preview the auction — which allows you to inspect items from an hour up to a week beforehand. Talk to the auction staff about items you're interested in. They sometimes will discuss value. Bring along an expert or pay for a dealer's advice — whether it's someone who knows cars or antique china.

Then, based on all this homework, set your bidding limit. Many auction authorities say don't pay more than half the retail price of any item.

Know which bargains are best

The best bargains at auctions range from flatware to furniture, according to Leslie Hindman, auctioneer, author, appraisal show host, and CEO of Eppraisals.com. She believes these are the top 10 bargains you'll find.

- Upholstered furniture — If a battered sofa or chair was made well in the first place and has good "bones," a

Auctions — a bargain bonanza

Visit an auction, and you could step into a warehouse full of repossessed luxury automobiles, a room gleaming with antiques, or a small country barn piled with tools and Americana. You're there because you want to buy something — and you want a bargain. You could spend a quarter, or a quarter of a million, adding to the growing total of more than $200 billion a year spent at auctions.

The number one reason half of all Americans attended a live auction last year was the excitement of getting a good deal. Auctions give people the chance to sell their terrific treasures for a retail price — more if bidders get excited and push each other to higher bids. But it's also possible the most precious item will be overlooked, and you'll be the one who buys it for pennies on the dollar.

relatively inexpensive reupholster job can turn it into a magnificent piece of furniture.

- Chandeliers — They're hard to display, so if you can recognize the potential grandeur of a hanging chandelier while it's sitting in a heap, you have the advantage on those who can't.

- Dinner services and stemware — Demand for fine china is low because of changing entertainment customs and an abundance of department store dishes. Find a pattern you like, and it will probably be a steal.

- Silver flatware — Another overlooked bargain because most people don't think of looking for silver at an auction.

- Monogrammed objects — If it has value as an antique or family heirloom, what does it matter that they're not your initials?

- Old books — Not usually a popular item at auctions, boxes of 10 to 20 books, sometimes containing rare finds, are often sold for less than the bookstore price of just one.

- Jewelry — Many people don't want someone else's personal items, and nothing is more intimate than an engagement ring, wedding band, or engraved brooch. This can mean incredible bargains for someone who just appreciates quality.

- Minor contemporary works of art — If the artist is not well-known, it's not unusual for paintings to sell for no more than the price of the canvas alone.

- Large-scale furniture — Anything bigger than 8 feet often won't sell despite the advent of 12-foot ceilings and huge great rooms where large pieces are just the ticket.

- Box lots — Knickknacks and other miscellaneous articles are often put in boxes and sold as one lot. Look for the one item that makes taking home the whole box worthwhile.

Don't get burned by a purchase

Auction items are purchased "as is." That means, of course, no warranty, no returns. Now if you're buying table linens, it's no big deal. But anything electrical or mechanical can be a dicier issue. You can often find appliances, power tools, and other such items at country auctions for much less than retail. A good deal isn't a good deal if you spend more on repairs than you would buying new. That's when it is more important than ever to be knowledgeable about the item, or bring along someone who is.

10 ways to determine value

The value of antiques, fine art, or collectibles is determined by what someone is willing to pay. An auction is a good place to find that out. How should you decide if something is worth buying? Here are the criteria that many auction experts believe you should use.

- Authenticity — Is it real?

- Condition — What shape is it in?

- Rarity — How many others are there?

- Provenance — Who owned it before? Does it have a traceable history?

- Historical significance — Was it there when something important happened?

- Size — Bigger isn't always better. Can you move, display, or wear it conveniently?

- Medium — An oil painting is worth more than a drawing, which is worth more than a print.

- Subject matter — What is it a picture of? Some scenes are just more pleasing than others.

- Fashion — Collecting has trends, just like women's clothing and the stock market.

- Quality — Where does it rank towards being "the best of its kind"?

Know before you go

If you're interested in a specific type of item — a pie safe, for instance — and an auction ad claims they'll be offering a "large selection of pie safes," don't hesitate to call before attending. One person's idea of a large selection may not match yours. You don't want to spend time and effort getting to an auction just to find out you and your competition are all bidding on a single item. No bargains there.

Learn basics before you jump in

Don't attempt a swan dive your first time off the auction diving board — you may belly flop. Instead dip your toe in the water by going to several auctions without intending to bid on anything. You can watch, learn, and get comfortable in the environment.

If you're lucky, your auctioneer might spend time educating the crowd on auction practices. According to the National Auctioneers Association (NAA), good auction staffs want people to keep coming to their auctions, so they are eager to answer questions.

But it's all too easy to make an expensive mistake. It's best to figure out your own high bid beforehand, and then stick to it when the bidding gets hot. And keep these other factors in mind.

- Learn the "hidden" charges like buyers' premiums (usually 10 to 15 percent commission to the auctioneer, auction house, or gallery), shipping charges, sales tax, etc. You'll have to add any or all of these on to your winning bid. Suddenly that good deal may not sound so good.

- Know if it's cash only. Many auto and police auctions are.

- Realize there may be a "reserve price" — the lowest price the seller will accept. Usually auctioneers are not allowed to reveal it, but the bidding can start at this minimum or bid up to it. If this amount is over your limit, stay out.

- Take every one of your bids seriously because you can't back out. Many people get swept up in the excitement and bid past their limit.

- Look for the rules of the auction on the bidder card or on posters or handouts. They may reveal the use of "house bidders" planted to drive up prices. If so, be extra careful not to overbid.

Unless the rules dictate a bidding increment, feel free to jump the bid less than the auctioneer is asking — a $5 or $10 increase instead of $50, for instance.

Smart strategies for better bidding

Bidding at an auction is a little like playing poker. You'd like to know the other bidders' intentions, and at the same time keep your own strategy secret. It helps to watch your opponents during the bidding. Many experienced auction buyers also use the preview and registration periods to pick out and "read" potential competitors.

During the auction, some experts prefer to stand at the back of the room so they can look over the entire crowd. Others say it's best to sit at one of the front corners, where you can turn slightly and see almost everyone's face but still be visible to the auctioneer. Then you can see facial expressions and pick out the subtle bidding movements some bidders use — not everyone bids by shouting and waving their arms. You can also make sure the auctioneer isn't running up the bid on his own.

It also helps to spot the professional dealers in the audience. They'll be the serious-looking

> A few tools will make your auction experience a lot easier. You never know when you'll have to peer into dark corners, check a measurement, or identify a tiny marking. Carry these in a small satchel, large purse, or fanny pack, and you'll be prepared for anything.
>
> ✓ flashlight
> ✓ tape measure
> ✓ magnifying glass
> ✓ screwdriver
> ✓ pliers
> ✓ notebook and pen

bidders buying lots of items. Dealers have a good idea of how much something will bring at retail, so they will try to get it for 50 to 75 percent of that in the auction. If you want an item badly enough, you can go just a little higher and still be less than retail.

Don't let the dealers trick you, though. They may quit bidding or say things to make you think an item isn't worth it, and then sneak back in after you've dropped out.

Save $$ — avoid a bidding war

All it takes is two determined potential buyers and you have a bidding war — which translates into an inflated price for the item. Avoid getting into a bidding war where you'll probably start offering dollar amounts way beyond your original limit.

- Don't express blatant enthusiasm over any item during the auction preview that could alert others to your find and increase the competition.

- Try to bid calmly and thoughtfully. Shouting, arm waving, or constantly holding your paddle in the air is not necessary — or wise.

- Neither is letting on that you want an item, no matter what. Bidding early and ferociously just makes others believe the item is worth bidding on.

- And offering your maximum amount early on means the price can only get higher as others join the bidding, leaving you out of the running.

Most professional auctioneers move an average of one item every minute. That's not a lot of time to dither, but plenty of time to join the fray without calling attention to your intentions.

Pine furniture — an auction bargain

When you look for an antique bargain at an auction, think about pinewood furniture. Long considered the low end next to mahogany, cherry, maple, and even oak, pine is gaining prestige as a nice-looking wood. One of pine's best features is its affordability. A 1900 pine cupboard will cost much less than one made of oak or cherry, for example. Pine's neutral color blends well with furniture from other woods, and it hides dust better than darker woods. It's also more comfortable, as you can tell by sitting on a pine chair seat, compared to one made from mahogany or oak.

Bottom feeders grab bargains

A great way to catch auction bargains is called "bottom feeding." An item that either didn't sell or didn't get the seller's reserve price is called a passed lot. You can place a private bid on that item immediately after it is taken off the block. It can be a little more work and take some time, since the auction house must contact the seller. But if the seller is willing, you could walk away with a great buy.

Appliances

Buy major appliances at half price

Why break the bank on a new dishwasher or refrigerator when you can get it at less than the wholesale price? Rental stores offer great prices on previously rented appliances. They are not brand new, but usually they have been thoroughly reconditioned. If they have any scratches or dents, let those flaws lend themselves to a bigger discount.

Discounts depend on how long the appliances were leased. You could buy an appliance with a longer rental history at a 50-percent savings, but even those with very brief rental histories can be purchased at savings of at least 20 percent.

Appliance rental centers like Rent-A-Center, a company with thousands of locations nationally, have a steady flow of appliances available for sale, and most have been used fewer than seven months. Major rental services refurbish appliances returned to them by renters, so what you purchase looks and acts like new.

Most previously rented appliances come with full manufacturers' warranties and may come with generous loaner-during-repair guarantees from the rental stores themselves.

Start your search for a major appliance at rental and rent-to-own stores in your area. It may be your best shot at the bargain you've been hoping for.

A bargain you can't afford to miss

You can save lots of money by buying a floor model — a new appliance that's been on display. Eventually, they're moved along as clearance items, complete with their original warranties.

Start your search for floor models before they reach the clearance area. Keep your eyes open for appliances on display in the showroom. Notice their condition. If you see any signs of wear, let the sales clerk know you're interested and make him an offer. Even if he says no, he may tell you when to check with him again.

Prowl for scratch and dent sales

A new appliance at a huge discount with a full warranty is a fantastic bargain. One little bump, bang, or ding in a retailer's warehouse may be all it takes to change an immaculate refrigerator, dryer, or food processor into a scratch-and-dent item. And, lucky for you, that item will probably find its way into a clearance section or outlet store and sell for a fraction of the suggested retail price.

Think about it. What if the side panel of a new chest freezer has a long scratch? Where do you plan to keep the freezer? In your garage or basement? A scratched freezer will keep things frozen as well as its perfect twin.

Scratch-and-dent appliances are worth prowling around for, but make sure you prowl in the right places. Many retailers have departments dedicated to the sale of returned and blemished items. Others have their own outlet stores. Sears is one of the best known for bargains at its outlets, but Sears isn't alone. Try Home Depot, Lowes, or Circuit City — any retailer that carries appliances. Call the retailers in your area to see what they do with scratched-and-dented, blemished, returned, or clearance appliances.

Other places to look include appliance rental and thrift stores. Don't overlook free newspapers, shoppers, and bargain bulletins. People who deal in scratch-and-dents often advertise there.

Smaller appliances, like mixers, blenders, irons, and coffeemakers, used as display models may end up in clearance at department stores because shoppers have handled them. Be sure to understand the sale conditions of scratch-and-dent items. They're often sold "as is" but usually come with a full manufacturer's guarantee.

Solid savings at liquidation outlets

Appliance manufacturers worldwide use outlets to sell products that move outside normal sales avenues. For example, factory outlets carry appliances with minor imperfections, closeouts, discontinued models, floor models, overruns, returns or exchanges, even one-of-a-kind demonstrators used at trade shows.

Because inventory is fleeting and prices low, plan to shop for a class of appliance, like side-by-side refrigerators, rather than a specific model.

Everything is essentially new and comes with full manufacturer's warranties. Imperfections are always minor and don't affect performance.

Examples include Sears outlets and regional chains, like ApplianceSmart with stores in Minnesota, Ohio, California, Texas, and Georgia.

Hunt for last year's prize

Discontinued models are to appliances what last year's models are to new cars. The "new" have arrived. The "old" have lost their luster. But they're still brand new — and dealers want to rid them from their stockrooms. It's time to make a deal.

The easiest way to flush discontinued models out of hiding is to ask the salesman if he's got any in stock. If he does, set your sights on a bargain.

Since markups on major appliances are typically15 percent, 30 percent on smaller ones, aim for saving that much or more.

Plan now to save later

The next time you're in the market for a new appliance it will probably dawn on you that you've seen the very item you're looking for on sale within the past 12 months. If only you could remember when.

Appliances, and almost everything else, have their own sale seasons. Some items, like air conditioners, are seasonal, so you can count on end-of-season savings. And just like cars, appliances have times of the year when the newest models are introduced. Last year's models are sold at a bargain to make room for the next generation. You can also count on seasonal clearances of overstocked and surplus items.

Consider how many years your appliances are likely to survive in light of these industry statistics.

- Refrigerators — 15 to 20
- Stoves — 17 to 25
- Microwaves — 10
- Dishwashers — 7 to 12
- Garbage disposals — 5 to 10
- Trash compactors — 7 to 12
- Washers — 10 to 13
- Dryers — 10 to 15

One fact to remember that will help you decide is how much they've improved over the years. They're quieter, easier to operate and clean, and more energy efficient.

Savvy shoppers learn the seasonal ebb and flow of the appliance industry and shop accordingly. Timing your appliance shopping right will save you a bundle, so mark your calendar.

December is a great month to make plans, not shop. You'll rarely find good deals on appliances unless you can wait until the week between Christmas and New Year's.

While some sales span two or three months, waiting for the arrival of particular months works best. Your patience will assure you of the very best bargains.

January is a good month for appliances, in general. In February, focus on air conditioners. You may not need one then, but it's a great time to buy.

With the arrival of March comes sales on washers and dryers. Spring is a good time for televisions and VCRs — especially May.

July is another good month for finding an air conditioner on sale, but you're likely to find big discounts on other appliances, too. One of the best times of year to go appliance shopping is late fall — October and November.

Land a deal through the classifieds

Classified ads are a great place to find deals on used appliances. When people move or remodel, they worry about what to do with the appliances they're replacing. Keep your eyes peeled for deals in the appliance section, as well as the moving, garage, and yard sale sections.

Another strategy is to place an ad in the "wanted" section. You could say, "I'm looking for a good, used, large-capacity washer-dryer combo." Offer to pick it up yourself. This might be all it takes to stir someone who has an appliance stored in his garage or a desire to upgrade to a newer model.

Make ads work for you

Think of all the reading you do to keep up with the ads you get in the mail. Here's how to make your time worthwhile.

Retailers want your business. One of their appeals is the "price-match guarantee." They'll match or beat their competitors' prices. Price matching is especially attractive when the competitor with the washer on sale is across town, and the price matcher is nearby.

Here's what to do. Take the ad for the appliance, including the brand name, model number, price, and dates of the sale, to your more conveniently located retailer. The manager wants the sale, but he's a businessman. He'll make sure you're comparing "apples with apples." The price match won't work if you're comparing a Hotpoint washer with a Maytag.

Once you've agreed on a price, it's your turn to make sure it's apples for apples. If the competitor offered free delivery, insist that your appliance be delivered for free, too.

Beware of wholesale clubs

BJ's, Costco, Sam's, and other wholesale clubs may be a boon to bulk shoppers, but they're not convincing as a bargain source for major appliances.

In the first place, you must pay an annual membership fee of $35 to $45 for an opportunity to shop there. Some of these warehouse giants only allow members to enter the store for browsing and price comparing.

What's more, availability of major appliances at these stores ranges from sparse to fair and varies from one locale to another. And if you can't haul your purchase home yourself, delivery is extra.

If you are a member, don't assume warehouse bargains are better than sales at other retailers. Shop around.

Select 'bells and whistles' with care

Appliances can do amazing things. Take coffeemakers. All of them can brew a fine cup of coffee, but some models do more — like brew a pot while you're still in bed, adjust the coffee's strength and temperature to suit your tastes, allow you to draw a single cup while you're waiting for the pot to fill, and even grind your coffee beans. Unfortunately, these bells and whistles come at a premium price.

Most appliances come in three versions — basic, mid-grade, and high-end. With this in mind, be on your guard when you shop. Ask yourself these questions:

- What do I need this appliance to do?

- How easy is it to operate?

- Is it an energy-efficient model?

- Does it have the safety features I need?

- Are other features, like digital controls, programmable timers, and self-cleaning options, important to me?

The deciding factors in the purchase of any appliance should be cost, usefulness, user-friendliness, and safety. If the basic model does what you need it to do, buy it. You'll be delighted with your appliance and your savings.

Many people who buy up-scale models rarely use the high-tech features. These extras often do little more than complicate the operation process.

One extra you shouldn't overlook is the automatic shut-off feature on appliances with heating elements. Have you ever left the house only to be plagued with doubt as to whether or not you turned off your iron, coffeepot, or curling iron? An appliance that shuts itself off relieves you of that worry.

Appliance manufacturers have done their job and deserve your business if they've made their products easy to use. Don't ignore the owner's manual, but its main purpose should be as a trouble-shooting guide, not as a map through a maze of complex directions. The ordinary operation of most appliances should be almost intuitive.

When to buy an extended warranty

Extended warranties are an expensive option offered for all big-ticket appliances. They're insurance policies covering repairs once the manufacturer's warranty lapses. They've long been a cash cow for vendors because so few policyholders actually take advantage of them.

Most consumer experts don't recommend extended warranties except for products notorious for frequent breakdowns and repairs — a problem not characteristic of time-tested, tried-and-true major appliances.

But to give extended warranties a fair hearing, follow these steps.

- Investigate the repair history and overall reliability of the appliance and brand name in question. It's easy to find this information online or in consumer magazines. Who wants a lemon, regardless of the warranty's coverage?

- Know who's covering the warranty. Third party warranties are the least reliable. Those from the dealer, if it's nearby, are better, but manufacturer's warranties are the best. Once you've mailed in the product registration card, the manufacturer is likely to contact you about extending your warranty. Ponder which of these three is most likely to remain in business throughout the life of your appliance, and which will be easiest to track down when you need help.

- Know what the warranty says. What's covered? Parts? Labor? Does it mention exclusions and deductibles? Are you responsible for getting estimates and second opinions or for shipping your appliance to a repair center? Will it pay for clothes burned in a faulty dryer or food ruined in a malfunctioning freezer? Does it provide for a loaner while your appliance is out of commission?

If you have a warranty, whether it's the manufacturer's original or an extended plan, keep all paperwork where you can find it. Without it, your warranty will be useless when it comes time to make a claim.

Perhaps the best insurance for appliance repairs is the "cookie jar" installment plan. It involves dividing the amount you'd pay for a warranty into weekly or monthly increments and setting it aside in an appliance-repair account. The funds in this account will be yours to use long after the extended warranty lapses, and you'll have it available for service and repairs on any of your major appliances — or replacement of less-expensive, smaller appliances.

Keep appliances in tip-top shape

Your appliances need tender loving care to keep them healthy. Follow this simple maintenance routine, and you'll keep them going strong for many years.

Kitchen appliances need a checkup about twice a year. Begin with your refrigerator.

- First, open the doors and check the gaskets that seal the cooling compartments. They should form an airtight seal against the frame. If they're cracked, have them replaced. Otherwise, just wash the gasket and frame with warm, soapy water.

- Clean the cooling fan and condenser coils. They're usually underneath, or in back of, your refrigerator. Use a brush designed especially to clean these delicate parts. Accumulated dust reduces your refrigerator's efficiency.

- Replace your icemaker filter every six months. It removes odors that make ice taste and smell badly.

- Check the walls of your freezer for frost buildup. If you have it, there's trouble in your self-defrosting system. To remove excess frost, defrost the freezer. Don't scrape it out with a tool.

Next, tend to your stove. Check the drip pans and broiler pans. If they're too dirty to clean, replace them. Replacements are inexpensive and easy to find. Don't cover drip pans with aluminum foil. It keeps ovens from venting properly and can short-circuit electric stoves.

Take a good look at your dishwasher. Clean or replace the filter. Dirty or damaged filters affect the dishwasher's pump and motor seals. Make sure the little holes in the spray arms are open and free of debris. Check for rust on the dishwasher's racks and repair or replace them if they are rusty. Tiny pieces of rust can damage the water pump.

You can give your old appliance a new life and help the environment, too, by recycling.

Few people know recycled appliances are the second largest source of recycled metal, particularly steel. What's more, manufacturing steel from recycled scrap only takes a fourth of the energy required to make it from virgin ore.

If you need help recycling an appliance, call 1-800-YES-1-CAN or 1-800-937-1226. Someone there can direct you to an appliance recycler near you.

Now head to your laundry room. Investigate these things on your washer twice a year.

- Water fill hoses for signs of leaks and aging. Even little leaks can have disastrous effects on your house. Replace those hoses every three to five years.

- Water dripping into the tub when it's turned off. This is a sign of a bad water inlet valve.

- A level washer on a well-supported floor. If either of these isn't up to snuff, the washer's own weight and movement contribute to that horrible banging during rinse cycles, not to mention the early death of your machine.

Twice a year, get rid of dryer lint buildup by cleaning the vent that leads outside your house. Dryer vent brushes from 10 to 20 feet long make this messy job a cinch. If you notice the vent tube between the dryer and the wall is white vinyl, replace it. These no longer meet code. Rigid aluminum vent pipe is best.

Download missing owner's manuals

You've inherited or purchased a great pre-owned appliance. The problem is no paperwork came with it — including the owner's manual.

Just brush the dust or scrape the frost away from the placard with the model number on it, write it down, and get ready to spend a few minutes in front of your computer.

Some manufacturer's Web sites, like *www.maytag.com* or *www.geappliances.com*, offer downloadable manuals, some free of charge. Other sites, like *www.livemanuals.com*, provide free online manuals for a variety of manufacturers and appliances.

Art

Art that won't cost an arm and a leg

Look for interesting pieces of high-quality art at an art museum sale. By keeping an eye out for sales and shopping around for the best values, your home will be adorned with a classy collection of art in no time. Whether you visit in person or online, an art museum may be the best place to find art that will enhance your home without enhancing your credit card bill.

Visit your local art, natural history, or science museum to see what artwork is available for purchase. For the more technologically inclined art fan, many museums have Web sites where you can shop online.

The Art Institute of Chicago has an impressive collection of canvases, framed artwork, matted prints, posters, and wall decor available for purchase online. Once you've accessed their site at *www.artic.edu*, follow the links to the museum shop where you can browse not only art, but books, jewelry, stationary, and home furnishings.

A similarly impressive collection can be found at *www.metmuseum.org*, The Metropolitan Museum of

Art's official Web site. Click on The Met Store link to check out posters, panels, framed prints, and even sculptures.

The Online Shop for the Museum of Fine Arts, Boston, also has some gorgeous matted prints and other reproductions based on artwork from their exhibits at *www.mfa.org/shop*. Make sure to check out their sale section where products have been marked down by as much as 65 percent.

Learn from the experts

Many auction houses offer lectures, courses, and other programs to help collectors learn more about various aspects of art and collectibles. Sometimes they're free. Sometimes you'll have to pay a small fee. Contact an auction house near you for more information.

How to find the perfect poster

You can find great posters and prints online at reasonable prices. These sites are good places to look for replicas of your favorite artwork.

- *www.postercheckout.com*

- *www.art.com*

- *www.AllPosters.com*

- *www.postershop.com*

- *www.easyart.com*

Before you buy a framed poster, check out framing prices at arts and crafts stores, like Hobby Lobby and Michaels. You may find it's cheaper to have the prints framed locally or to frame them yourself. Also, when you calculate the cost of the print, include fees like shipping and handling before you commit to the purchase.

Framing on a dime

So you got a great deal on that piece of art. Now don't break the bank framing it. Here are a few cheap alternatives to having a piece of art professionally framed.

- Find a frame shop where you get a discount for doing some of the work. Most of the time, they'll even supervise and give help when you need it.

- If you have your own miter saw, save money by building your own frame. Just leave the matting to the professionals, since it tends to be more complicated and requires special tools.

- Check out yard sales in your area. If you know the measurements of the print, you might find a used frame at a rock-bottom price. That still leaves assembly, matting, and maybe even glass, but ultimately the total cost will be lower.

Priceless but not pricey

Don't pay a fortune for expensive prints when you can get the same effect from a replica you framed yourself. If you're looking to bring the great masters into your home, you can find them at craft stores, museum shops, and stationary shops in the form of note cards, post cards, posters, and more. A grouped display of framed post cards by your favorite artist can have great impact. And a $20 poster will look like a million bucks with the right mat and frame. So, drive on past the auction house, and head straight for the nearest poster shop.

- Keep costs down by buying your supplies a-la-carte and letting the professionals do the rest. Look for your mat, frame, and glass at craft stores where pieces are sold separately in standard sizes.

- Enjoy arts-and-crafts? There are tons of ways to keep your framing expenses down when you're willing to get a little crafty. Check out craft magazines to learn how to make one-of-a-kind frames using household items and things from nature. For more ideas, browse Web sites like *www.diynet.com* and *www.hgtv.com*.

You really can do it yourself

One determined bargain hunter had a plan to frame between 20 and 30 pictures, and he knew it would cost him a fortune to have them all professionally done. He decided to go to a frame shop where they let customers do the work in exchange for waiving the labor costs. The employees helped him pick out the frame, the matting, and the glass. Then they charged him a one-time fee of $8 to use their equipment and supplies.

He and his wife came to the shop three nights in a row to work on the framing. Because the pictures were all different sizes, the labor costs the couple would have paid ranged from $25 to $80 per picture. At the end of the project, the two of them had saved more than $1,000 in labor charges. Since the $8 equipment charge was a one-time fee, they saved more money with every picture they framed themselves, and they even had fun in the process.

Auto

■ New cars

Homework pays off in better deals

The last person you should ask about the price of a new car is a car salesman. To him, uninformed shoppers equal big commissions and huge profits. So, do some homework and save your money. Position yourself to be the one who decides how much you'll pay for your next car.

You can find information on autos, options, and accessories in books and online. Sources like the Kelly Blue Book, Edmunds.com, and Consumer Reports offer car shopping pointers, detailed  descriptions and comparisons of every new vehicle, definitions of terms, and, of course, prices.

Begin your quest with one basic question — how much does the car I want really cost? If you call a dealer and ask, the first figures you'll hear will be "sticker price" or "MSRP" (manufacturer's suggested retail price). But the hunt for a great deal has to start with "dealer invoice" — the price the dealer pays for the car. Dealers hope to keep that a secret, so you'll have to find it yourself. Plan to bargain up from invoice, not down from MSRP.

Next, figure out the amount they plan to make on this car. It will typically be between 10 to 20 percent. You can find the actual "profit factor" by dividing the dealer's cost (which you've dug up) by the MSRP, then subtracting that amount from 1. Knowing this percentage will let you figure for yourself how much you'll allow the dealer to profit from the sale. If you're generous, offer him 3 percent. That would be a $750 profit on a $25,000 automobile.

If you have access to a computer, visit auto manufacturers' Web sites. There you'll unearth special offers, promotions, and rebates being offered on select models. These mean added bonuses and price reductions.

Finally, construct your bid and start shopping. If you'd like to spare yourself the discomfort of face-to-face negotiations with a salesman, visit dealers' Web sites and make your offer online. Or visit sites such as Autobytel at *www.autobytel.com* or AutoWeb at *www.autoweb.com*.

Wise up to your loan options

Save up to pay cash for a car, and you'll save yourself thousands of dollars in interest charges. But if you have to finance it, you can save by arranging for a loan before you even enter the dealership. That way, you can choose your own terms and not feel pressured to take the dealer's financing.

It helps to have your credit score in hand so you can prove you're eligible for the best rates. If your score is on the low side, you may want to take steps to improve it before you apply for a car loan.

Loan sources range from credit unions to banks to online lenders. If you have a computer, that's one of the easiest places to begin shopping. Lenders like E-LOAN at *www.eloan.com* and CapitalOne at *www.capitaloneautofinance.com* are great sources of competitive loans. Application is free and rates are guaranteed for 30 to 45 days.

Some lending services actually send your loan inquiry to several banks that respond with bids for your business. One example is LendingTree.com at *www.lendingtree.com* or 800-411-8733.

One benefit with online lenders is that you won't have application fees or hidden finance charges. But if an online loan isn't right for you, or you just want to use the Web to gather information, then visit your bank or credit union next. Let them know you've been shopping for a deal, and you're familiar with interest rates.

After you find some possible loans, you can plug the rates, fees, and length of payment term into an online calculator. One place to check is *www.myfico.com* under Calculators. It will help you get a true picture of how much you'll pay for your car and what it's going to cost each month.

After you have your financing squared away, you can confidently negotiate with the dealer to get the best price on your new car.

> Make the best deal of your life without negotiating. These seven easy steps can save you thousands on your next new car.
>
> ✓ Do your homework ahead of time.
> ✓ Find a loan before you talk to a dealer.
> ✓ Decide on options before you visit the showroom.
> ✓ Take your time and shop around.
> ✓ Obtain bids from several dealers.
> ✓ Get top dollar for your trade-in.
> ✓ Time your purchase right.

Know your score for better rates

"Your credit score isn't good enough for our low rates."

That's one line slick salesmen might try against you to get your money. If you don't know any better, they've got you over a barrel. You'll pay too much.

But walk in with your credit report in hand — touché! It's an advantage, even if you find it needs repair. Once you know your score, you can do something about it.

Your credit report is available from the major credit reporting agencies. A new law states you can order one for free once each year.

- Equifax *www.equifax.com* 800-685-1111

- Experian *www.experian.com* 888-397-3742

- Trans Union *www.transunion.com* 800-916-8800

Shop around to save $$

Does saving hundreds, even thousands, of dollars appeal to you? Then visit, call, or inquire online for prices from at least five dealerships. Don't be shy about telling them you are price shopping. Get them to bid against each other.

Gain an added advantage by approaching each dealer with your research in hand. Have the dealer's invoice. That's your point of beginning in the bidding process.

Make sure their bids include all sale-related costs, such as taxes and destination fees. And get them in writing.

Beware of ad appeal

Dealers give bargains to customers who've done their homework, shopped the Web, and know what's up at rival dealerships. The secret to getting what you want is to stay focused when you enter the showroom.

If you've done your homework and settled on a particular car, don't sabotage your efforts by listening to other sales promotions and slick advertising. Rebates, financing, or other models on the lot are more distractions to watch out for.

Your goal is to leave in the car you came to buy, not one you buy on impulse.

Wise ways to stick to your budget

The bottom line for determining what you can afford for a new car is your available cash — a question of savings — and, if you finance, how much debt you can afford.

You should already have a household budget that tells you how much of your income is available for a car loan. If not, figure your auto allowance by subtracting your monthly expenses from your monthly income. Your car payment can come from what's left over after regular expenses and obligations like rent or mortgage, utilities, and groceries.

Next, find out how much the car you'd like to buy will actually cost. Include all car-related expenses like fuel, insurance, maintenance, tags, and taxes.

If you have a computer, you can go online for help in figuring out your car budget. Intellichoice at *www.intellichoice.com* has a page of calculators, one of which figures "What car can I afford?"

A simple rule of thumb is the "20 percent rule." It says you should spend no more than 20 percent of your monthly take-home income on automobile expenses. By setting a limit like this, you won't be tempted to buy more than you can afford. It also will help you be a more cost-conscious car owner.

Beware of devious ways dealers attempt to make cars more affordable.

- Low-cost leases. You may have lower payments, but when the lease ends, you own nothing.

- Loans that will outlive the car.

- Financing that ends with you owing more on the car than the car is worth.

Finally, what you can afford depends on your skill at negotiating the purchase. The lower your final price, the more money in your pocket. So stay on the target you've come up with, and negotiate for the price you want.

Search slowly for better savings

Don't wait until your old clunker dies to start your new car search. If you know you'll be in the market soon, it makes sense to gather information about prices, performance, safety features, and reliability on cars you're interested in.

Putting yourself in a pressure situation could cost you. Dealers will drive a harder bargain if they sense your eagerness to buy. An unhurried approach makes salesmen hungrier for a sale and more willing to deal.

So take your time, shop around, and make a wise decision — before you even have to.

Opt for the options you need

You probably know which accessories are important to you in a car. But when you get to the dealership, you may discover some you never knew existed. Such options can greatly inflate the price of your car. Don't let dealers rip you off this way. By avoiding the options scam, you'll save plenty the next time you buy a new car.

The list of available options may seem overwhelming. You can choose air bags, air-conditioning, antilock brakes, antitheft packages, colors and finishes, cruise control, power features (locks, windows, doors, mirrors, seats), roof racks, sound systems, wheels, and window tinting to name a few.

The main thing is to consider your needs and decide which options are most useful to you. If you plan to eventually resell the car, you also may want to consider those that help your resale value.

Some options come as standard equipment on certain vehicles, and others come bundled together in packages. Option packages are often used as sales promotions and can save you money. But watch out for things like window etching and extended warranties that may be slipped in by a dealer as though they're not options at all. These are often their money makers.

To check out vehicle options, browse through publications like *Road & Track, Car and Driver, Motor Trend* or their Web sites for reviews. Manufacturers' Web sites also offer information on factory options and how much they cost. Try *www.automobiles.honda.com*, *www.gmbuypower.com*, *www.fordvehicles.com*, *www.toyota.com*, and *www.daimlerchrysler.com* to see what they offer.

> There's more to the cost of auto ownership than meets the eye — certainly more than the initial purchase price. Other things to consider:
>
> - Fuel
> - Oil
> - Maintenance
> - Repairs
> - Tires
> - Insurance
> - Depreciation
> - Financing
> - Taxes and fees
>
> Edmunds.com has a service that allows you to figure out what your new car will cost over the span of five years. Visit *www.edmunds.com*, click Tips & Advice, then True Cost to Own.

Once you decide on your options, add them up to see how much they will add to the basic cost of the car. You will then be prepared when you approach the dealership, and you'll have a better chance of driving away with the options you want.

Tips for timing it right

Timing is everything when it comes to getting a great deal. Knowing when to buy can save you a bundle. It helps to make your move when salesmen are weary, distracted, and under pressure, say industry insiders. Here are the secrets to striking dealerships for great deals.

- Wait until the end of the month. Dealers face unmet quotas, so they're willing to sell at a discount. Manufacturers get in on it, too, offering low rates and rebates.

- Shop late in the day. Salesmen may be tired and ready to go home. Assure them that you want that car, but drag it out. Your salesman's eagerness to leave may prompt him to make you a great deal.

- Keep an eye on the business section of your paper. When sales are sluggish, manufacturers and dealers alike are ripe for picking your car at a bargain.

- January, April, and May are slow months for auto sales. Showrooms are deserted. Sales are slow. It's a great time to buy. Or, if you don't need a model hot off the assembly line, wait until the end of the year. New models arrive in the fall. Dealers are eager to swing deals on last year's models.

- The Christmas holidays are also a great time to shop if you can find the time. Dealers want to reduce inventory, so they'll be willing to sell you this year's stock at invoice — or less.

A rainy weekend, a holiday, an hour before closing — these put you in the driver's seat when it comes to car shopping. Use them to your advantage, and you'll come out ahead.

Get a deal on the lot

You drive by the dealership every day on your way to work. One car has caught your eye. It's been on the lot for weeks. It's not the color you'd hoped for — but if the price is right, it may be time to make an offer.

The longer that car sits on the lot, the more expensive it is for the dealer. It may have some options you don't need or want. Ask if he'll remove them and reduce the price. Or, better still, see if he'll throw them in as a bonus for the favor you've done him by helping him get rid of that slow-moving inventory.

How to handle a long test drive

Car makers have found that a day-long test drive is pretty effective at clouding customers' good judgment. If you decide to take the dealer up on a 24-hour test drive, treat it like serious business. Don't let the pleasure of driving a new car make you forget to seriously critique the car and negotiate for a bargain.

Here are some suggestions for how to spend the day.

- Dedicate some time to driving with no distractions. Concentrate on the car — not the kids, radio, or cell phone.

- Critique the car in light of how you'll use it — carrying babies in car seats, hauling soccer teams and groceries, or simply commuting.

- Check the view. How is the rear and side vision? How is the view at night? Any blind spots?

- How does it handle — turning radius, driveway maneuverability, garage fit, highway-speed stability, acceleration for entering the highway?

- Are controls visible and within reach? Check instruments and accessories — day and night dash visibility, radio, A/C, mirror adjustment, seat and steering wheel adjustment.

- Do doors open and close effortlessly? How easy is it to access passenger and engine compartments, trunk, roof rack? Hear any rattles or squeaks?

When it's over, and you return the car, simply say "thank you." Then leave, go home, and think about it. The marketing ploy behind the 24-hour test drive is to get you to fall in love with the car and buy it without negotiating price. That would be an expensive mistake.

Smart strategy for avoiding lemons

A car under warranty that breaks down several times within a certain amount of time is, by law, a "lemon." To avoid the frustration and expense of owning such a vehicle, get smart and learn as much as you can before you buy.

You can go online to find an official list of cars notorious for their defects. Get a heads up on these cars at:

- National Highway and Traffic Safety Administration at *www-odi.nhtsa.dot.gov*. Click on Defect Investigations.

- Center for Auto Safety at *www.autosafety.org*. Click on Lemon Laws and Auto Defects.

- Carfax at *www.carfax.com*. Click on Lemon Check.

According to a recent survey, Kia was the most likely lemon candidate with an average of more than five defects per vehicle. Volkswagen was next with close to four, and Mercedes-Benz had slightly more than three per vehicle. But any car can turn out to be a lemon.

Once you realize you've got one, find out what you're entitled to — a refund, a cash settlement, or a replacement. Car companies usually offer to replace your lemon with a new car or give you the cash value of the car.

There are several federal lemon laws, and each state also has its own. State lemon laws vary, so check with the sites listed above to discover what your state's law says. If you have a problem understanding the law, you can get some help at *www.defect.com*. Click on Lemon Links.

Master the art of haggling

W. Somerset Maugham once wrote, "He preferred to be over-charged than to haggle." Don't let that statement describe you when you're car shopping.

Haggling is the art of chipping away at high prices until you reach a bargain. Once you've haggled your way to a great new-car deal, you'll drive away feeling pleased and refreshed — not drained and beaten.

Your goal is to keep your cool and remain objective. The remedy for getting emotional is to do your homework, know your stuff, and have the facts ready when the pressure is on during negotiations.

- Be prepared. Before you enter the showroom, know which car you want, its invoice price, the amount you're willing to pay, and what your trade-in is worth. Armed with these non-negotiables, you'll remain steady throughout the battle of wits at the dealership.

- Have a strategy. Dicker over one thing at a time — say, the purchase price. Stick with it until you have it in writing. Don't allow anyone to sidetrack you with talk about your trade-in, the financing, extended warranties, or anything else. Talking about too many things at once gets confusing.

- Enlist support. If you need moral support, take someone along — someone you know is levelheaded and will come to your rescue when a sales clerk fluent in Dealer-ese starts to confuse you.

- Find a stand-in. If haggling isn't your cup of tea, remove yourself from the fray. Free online services can arrange for dealers in your area to negotiate among themselves for your business. Check out InvoiceDealers.com, Cars.com, and Autoweb.com.

You have the key bargaining chip — one a dealer can't use against you. As good at haggling as you may be, the time may come for you to simply walk away. That alone is a huge advantage. Don't hesitate to use it if you have to.

Watch for rebate savings

Cash rebates are a great way to save big on new cars — especially cars that haven't been hot sellers. Even those rebates offered to dealers by manufacturers figure in to your negotiations. Those rebates lower the actual dealer cost.

Keep an eye out for rebates in newspaper and television ads. If you have computer access, you can quickly check those currently available in your area. Try these sites:

- AutoSite's New Cars at *www.autosite.com*

- CarPrice's Rebates & Incentives at *www.carprice.com*

- Edmunds' New Cars at *www.edmunds.com*

- Intellichoice's Dollars & Sense at *www.intellichoice.com*

Beware the small print in service contracts

You may be tempted to get a service contract on your new car after hearing it will cover all your repairs and provide towing and transportation while your car is in the shop.

But consider it carefully. The manufacturer's warranty will cover almost everything on your car for several years. And your car insurance may already provide for towing and substitute transportation.

As far as taking care of "all" your vehicle repairs, that term takes on new meaning when you read the small print in the contract. You'll find plenty of limitations.

Keep these two rules in mind when considering any optional service contract.

- You are not obligated to purchase it. And if you think you might, you don't need to do it on the day you buy the car. Every car has its competitors. So do service contracts. Your automobile insurance company may provide an extended warranty, and it's probably cheaper than the one offered by the dealership.

- You are obligated to know what the service contract says, fine print and all. If you expect it to cover a repair, you'd better understand what the limits, deductibles, and exclusions are. A simple technicality may negate the insurer's responsibility to make the repair. And what if you break down at the other end of the country? Will you have to be towed home to take advantage of the warranty?

A third point to consider is the source of this service contract. Who is backing it? The car manufacturer? The dealership? A third-party insurer? How is that third-party insurer rated? Will you be able to find it when your car is on the blink?

If you buy a service contract through the dealer, make sure you get written confirmation that the dealer paid the service contract company and that you're "on file" with that company.

When it comes to service contracts, the last thing you want is a surprise.

Add value to your trade-in

Don't get ripped off when trading in your car. Doing it right can get you the discount you deserve on your new purchase.

A hard — but important — lesson

Angela was enjoying the drive home from college in her new compact car. Suddenly, she saw a piece of tire tread ahead in her lane. Because of traffic, she couldn't avoid running over it. She heard it glance off the floorboard. A little farther down the road she pulled over to check for damage. There, beneath the engine, she saw a dangling wire.

The next morning she took it to the dealer where she'd bought the car and the extended warranty. It wasn't long before the service manager approached her with news that the oxygen sensor had been damaged and the repair would cost a little over $500. "Boy," Angela thought, "am I happy I bought that extra service plan." Between college and the new car payment, she was in no position to pay for costly repairs.

Then came the words, "Sorry, ma'am. That part isn't covered by this warranty. It says down here in the fine print ...."

Angela now says she's learned her lesson — the hard way. "From now on, I'm reading the whole contract, fine print and all, before I sign anything. No more expensive surprises for me."

For starters, know your car — mileage, optional equipment, repair history, the works. Show the dealer its service record. And top it off with a vehicle history report you can obtain from Web sites like *www.autocheck.com* or *www.carfax.com*. It's only $19.99 and gives a third-party perspective on the history of your vehicle — accident and flood damage, emissions inspections, and more.

Next, visit the Edmunds Web site at *www.edmunds.com*, click on Used Cars, look for Trade-In, and find two important figures — the suggested "private party" selling price of your car and the industry standard trade-in price. It's obvious you'll get more by selling the car yourself. But if you still want to trade it in, these pointers will help you get top dollar.

If you do not have access to a computer, Edmunds also has books available at most bookstores and libraries.

- Avoid talking about the trade-in until you've settled on the price of the new car.

- See if your trade-in will reduce the sales tax on your new car.

- Make sure your engine oil is clean and topped-off. Clean oil is a sure-fire sign that the motor has been cared for.

- Clean your car inside and out. And fix everything that needs fixing. Each flaw eats away at a car's value. That clean, well-maintained look enhances your car's "curb appeal" and assures a higher trade-in value.

■ Used cars

How to get a better deal

Buying a used car is not much different than buying a new one. The main thing to remember is to prepare before you start negotiating. Knowing the value of the car you're interested in gives you the upper hand and makes it possible to get a better deal.

You can easily research car values by looking through print guides such as Edmunds or the N.A.D.A. Official Used Car Guide. They publish their statistics monthly. But if you want numbers that are even more recent, check out their Web sites. Sites like *www.nadaguides.org*, *www.edmunds.com*, and Kelley Blue Book's site, *www.kbb.com*, feature prices that are sometimes updated every day.

Corporate 'leftovers' a bargain

Car dealers aren't the only companies who sell used cars. You can get good deals on used vehicles from banks, rental car agencies, airport limousine services, and corporations getting rid of their company cars.

Rental cars can be a good purchase because rental companies perform regular maintenance. The cars are usually only a year or two old, which means the rental company has already taken most of the car's depreciation. Most rental cars still have valid factory warranties, which you won't find at some places.

Banks and lenders auction off cars they have repossessed because the previous owner could not pay their loan. Just like any used car, you should have it checked out before you bid. But you might get a bargain since the bank just wants to pay off what's left of the loan.

Enjoy 'giveaway' prices at an auction

Have you checked with the police department in your search for a used car? From time to time, law enforcement has to thin its inventory of surplus, seized, and impounded vehicles by

It pays to buy a used car

New cars usually lose a quarter to half their value over the first two years, and then depreciation slows down. Since the average car tends to last nine years, the smartest strategy is to buy a car that is one or two years old. That way you don't suffer the depreciation, and you save 20 to 30 percent over the cost of a new car.

You can find out how much a car will depreciate by using the Depreciation Calculator in the Calculators sections at CarPrice.com. Most likely, you'll find a used car is the better value.

holding auctions. They're announced in newspapers and posted at town halls and post offices, but you can also check with your local police department.

These auctions give you the opportunity to buy cars — even luxury models — at "giveaway" prices. At first glance, an auction may look like the world's biggest car lot, but be careful. You need to pick and choose carefully, and here's why:

- Some of these vehicles were abandoned and impounded. They may only be good for parts and salvage.

- Some were seized from criminals. They may have an "exotic" allure. But, like their previous owners, they're often loaded with problems of their own. These cars may have been damaged in the search for drugs or weapons. You may have to replace a gas tank or make other repairs to make them roadworthy. Auctioneers usually let you know in advance about these kinds of problems.

- Department vehicles being rotated out of service may have had a rough life. But you can be sure they've been well maintained.

Once you've found a vehicle that looks interesting, check the Kelley Blue Book for its trade-in value. If you have a computer, go to the Web site at *www.kbb.com* for a free appraisal. That's the amount you'll use as a guide in your bidding.

Then go for a sneak preview. Ask to see the car's title, start it up, and check the transmission. Find its Vehicle Identification Number (VIN), and do a vehicle history search at *www.carfax.com* or *www.autocheck.com*.

Do all this before the auction, and when the time comes for you to bid, you'll be in the driver's seat.

Bid for online bargains

You can find lots of good deals on used cars through online auctions. Just remember to relax. The key to online auctions is patience. If you give yourself plenty of time to shop around for the best bargain, you'll save thousands of dollars on your next car.

First of all, do the same research you would for any used car. Request the service records, and have a vehicle history report done on the car's Vehicle Identification Number (VIN) at *www.carfax.com*. Ask the seller to have a mechanic check the car out for any problems, and have the mechanic do a test drive as well. In the meantime, do a test drive of the exact same model yourself.

Find out what the car is worth by looking in Edmunds, Kelley Blue Book, and NADA.com for the retail and wholesale value. Retail is what the car would normally sell for, and wholesale is the trade-in amount a dealer would give for the car if it were in top condition.

For an online auction, any number at or below the wholesale price is a good deal. Remember to include travel and delivery costs in the equation since you'll have to either pick up the car or have it shipped after you buy it. Decide what you're willing to pay for the car, subtract the costs of travel and delivery, and then only bid up to that number.

Do not, under any circumstances, get caught in a bidding war. You may pay too much without thinking. Bid up to your determined price, and then walk away. Play it cool, and you'll get a great deal.

Save with a private seller

Cars automatically cost less when you buy them from a private seller instead of a dealer. Here's why.

- Private owners tend to ask 20 percent less for the same car than dealers do. Dealers price their cars higher because they've got overhead, and their livelihood depends on the profit they make.

- Buying from a private owner cuts out the middleman and allows you to negotiate with someone who is not a professional salesperson.

- Private owners usually enjoy talking about their cars, so you can find out more about the vehicle's true history.

- Some states don't require you to pay sales tax on a car if you buy it from a private owner rather than a dealer.

Make sure you're considering a decent automobile by asking the owner these important questions.

- "Why are you selling your car?" The car may have mechanical problems, so ask if you can have a mechanic check the car. If they don't let you, steer clear of this vehicle.

- "What is the car's mileage?" The average is 12,000 to 15,000 miles per year. An older car with lower mileage is still a good catch.

- "What needs to be worked on?" It's a good sign if the owner answers honestly and lets you know what minor repairs the car needs.

- "May I see the car's service records?" If they don't have the service records, move on to another car.

- "When were the brakes last done?" and "When were the oil and filter last changed?" These answers will tell you how well the owner has taken care of the car.

Come out ahead in the classifieds

You can find good deals on used cars by looking through the classified ads in your local newspaper. *Auto Trader* magazine is a helpful publication that features used car ads complete with pictures for you to browse.

You can also look online for classifieds at Kelley Blue Book's site, *www.kbb.com,* and at Auto Trader Online, *www.traderonline.com.* But be careful as you look into these deals. Not everyone is completely honest when they write their ads. Do your best to verify as much as you can.

Look for vehicles that have been owned by only one person. Concentrate on the ones with low mileage. If the ad doesn't mention mileage, it's probably too high. Do all the research you would do with any used car, such as looking through maintenance records, checking the car's history by its VIN, and having a mechanic check it before you make a decision.

One trick you may run into is the "dealer in disguise." Sometimes dealers will pose as private owners and place a classified ad for a used car. They pull this stunt because buyers are usually nicer to private parties, and some will only buy from private owners. Plus, owner classified ads are cheaper than the ones for dealers.

You'll get a better deal from a private owner, so make sure you're speaking with one. Ask the seller if he or she is a private party or not. If they answer confidently, they probably are. But if they hesitate, you could be on the phone with a sneaky dealer.

Sidestep common auto scam

Be a proactive used-car shopper, and protect yourself from scamsters who peddle their flood-damaged goods. These scoundrels "freshen up" damaged cars and resell them at bargain prices to naive and unsuspecting buyers. While flood damage to cars may not be easy to see, it can be every bit as harmful as that caused by wrecks.

Begin your investigation by asking for the title. If it's stamped "salvage," the car has already been totalled, perhaps by flooding. The title also tells where the car is from. If its most recent "home" is a state where flooding has been a problem, take note. Flood-damaged vehicles are routinely shipped to your area and sold as though nothing is wrong with them.

Next, scrutinize it for telltale signs of flooding. Watermarks will usually remain hidden from view. Open the hood and scan the engine compartment. Look at the radiator. Check the air filter for signs of water-borne debris. Does the engine oil look milky or discolored? It could be from water.

Check the trunk. Does it smell musty? Is the jack or tire iron rusted? Look under carpeting for signs of moisture. Do you see evidence of new, poorly fitted, or mismatched carpet or upholstery? Use a mirror to peer under seats where the metal parts can rust.

Flash some cash and save

Show the seller you're serious by letting them know you've got cash on hand. You may save money by making a cash offer even if it's less than what they're asking. Don't talk price too early in the negotiations. But if it comes down to getting a seller to agree on a lower price, flashing cash may clinch the deal. Whether you arrange your financing ahead of time or just withdraw from savings, having cash in hand is more than just a great negotiating tool. It will also keep you from going over budget since you'll be safe from expensive loan offers.

Check for mud or rust in hard-to-clean parts of the car. Be sure to check every electrical switch — locks, windows, lights, lighter, radio, horn, heater fan — and try each of them several times.

If you're still serious about the car, find the vehicle identification number (VIN), and use it to order a vehicle history report from *www.carfax.com* or *www.autocheck.com*. It will reveal the car's hidden past, including flooding.

Smart way to find a safe car

Hire a mechanic to inspect a used car before you even consider handing over your money. He will check for problems and possibly even give the car a test drive. Make an appointment with your mechanic ahead of time so he can work it into his schedule. The whole process should take about an hour.

The service may cost $50 to $100, but any amount the mechanic charges is worth it. It could save you thousands of dollars if the car turns out to be faulty. And if you hire a mechanic you work with frequently, he may even perform the service for free.

Some mechanics may go to the point of sale for the inspection, but most need you to bring the car to their garage. Take the car's owner with you. He probably won't want to let you disappear with his car for an hour while you have it checked.

If the seller refuses to let a mechanic look at the car, there's probably something wrong with it. You're better off moving on to the next option.

Get a free inspection

If you're a member of the Automobile Association of America (AAA), you don't need to pay a mechanic to check out a used car. AAA offers a free maintenance inspection to all its members. Just take the car you're interested in to one of their approved auto repair facilities, and they'll inspect the car for problems that usually lead to roadside breakdowns. Then they'll tell you in writing about any maintenance or repairs the car needs. The service is valued at $24.95, and you get it for nothing. You can't beat that price.

■ Maintenance

Keep your car in tip-top shape

The best way to protect your car's value is through regular maintenance. You can save a ton of money by replacing worn-out parts before they break and require a major repair. Check out these figures for estimated auto repair costs in 2006 from the Sam's Club Auto Service Plan:

- alternator $442

- engine $3,317

- starter $453

- transmission $2,245

- water pump $502

Obviously, you don't want to neglect those important parts. But even simple things, like changing the oil or fan belt, are critical to the overall health of your car. Besides saving money, here are the benefits of regular preventive maintenance.

- Improved performance. This means more pep, better handling, and improved fuel economy.

- Dependability. A well-maintained vehicle is more likely to start right up and less likely to stall or leave you stranded.

- Better safety. A little neglect over a long period of time makes your car an accident waiting to happen.

- More pleasurable driving. When your car doesn't make funny noises or do strange things, it makes for a better, more relaxing ride.

- Environmental protection. Poorly maintained automobiles are notorious polluters.

- Simpler schedule. Hit-and-miss servicing is easy to forget. Put your maintenance visits on the calendar. By planning ahead, you can budget accordingly.

- Higher resale value. A regularly serviced car holds its value better as the years go by. '

- Owner pride. Your car is one of the accessories you "wear." Keeping it up makes a positive statement about you.

Beat auto repair rip-offs

Develop a relationship with a good repair shop — one that knows your car — and you will be ahead of the game when it comes to maintenance. Learn which shops in your area have the best reputation. Good credentials are important for both shop and mechanic.

A shop that's affiliated with a reputable parts distribution and repair network (like NAPA) has an edge when it comes to getting quality replacement parts when you need them. Mechanic certification (like ASE) tells you that those working on your car are the best available.

Heed these four ways to keep any mechanic honest when he works on your car.

- Let him figure out the problem. Explain what you hear or see, and make sure your description is included in the work order. Keep it simple. Say, "It won't crank," not "I think it needs a new battery." This keeps spendthrift mechanics from automatically installing a new battery, even if the battery is not the problem.

- Know what you're entitled to. The U.S. Attorney General's Office says you should expect written estimates on repairs over $100 if you deal with the repair shop face-to-face. And the repair shop must have your permission for repairs more than 10 percent over the authorized estimate.

- Get all guarantees and warranties in writing, both for parts and labor. Take notes on your conversations with the mechanic. A good place to record the details of your agreement is on the work order itself. Make sure you understand what is written there. This will help you avoid expensive misunderstandings.

- Tell the mechanic you want all parts that have been replaced. If a part, like an alternator, can be exchanged and rebuilt, ask to see the receipt for the swap. Don't pay for a new part if all they did was clean and reinstall the old one.

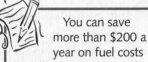

You can save more than $200 a year on fuel costs by following some simple rules.

- ✓ Keep engine tuned.
- ✓ Replace air filter regularly.
- ✓ Use recommended grade of motor oil and gasoline.
- ✓ Keep tires inflated to the recommended pressure.
- ✓ Avoid jackrabbit starts or sudden stops.
- ✓ Keep it under 60 on the highway.
- ✓ Avoid buying gas at highway stations.
- ✓ Shut the car off instead of idling.

■ Rental cars

Drive away with the best deal

Renting a car should be cheaper than buying one. Remember these tips the next time you rent, and you'll be able to spend all that extra money on vacation souvenirs.

- Book early. If you make the reservation for a rental car at least 7 to 14 days in advance, you are more likely to get a lower rate. Since rental car companies don't charge cancellation fees, book a car as soon as you can. If you have to make a booking at the last minute, opt for smaller rental companies. Their rates are usually lower, and most of their business comes from last-minute bookings.

- Avoid the prepaid gas option — the one that lets you return the car without filling up the tank. Rental companies don't refund you for the gas you didn't use. Also, most of the time the prepaid rates for gas are higher than what you could find at the gas station. Just don't forget to refill your tank before you return the car. The charge for gas you didn't replace can be twice or three times the usual price.

- Compare the daily rate with the weekly rate. Often, the weekly rate is so low it's actually cheaper to keep the car a few more days. In some cases, the charge for a week will be less than a three-day rental.

- Join a frequent renter club if there's one company you use again and again. The membership is free, and you generally get 5 to 15 percent off each rental. Some clubs let you earn points toward a free rental. Other incentives include express lines, free upgrades, and frequent-flyer miles.

- Choose a smaller car if you're headed overseas. Small cars get better gas mileage. In foreign countries, gas prices are close to $4 a gallon.

Smart way to compare prices

Booking a rental car online can save you money. In 2004, over 44 million Americans made some or all of their travel reservations online. Of those people, 40 percent made rental car reservations over the Internet.

If they can go online to save money, so can you. Compare prices and find the best deals by looking at the different rates available on these travel sites:

- *www.travelocity.com*

- *www.orbitz.com*

- *www.bnm.com*

- *www.expedia.com*

- *www.qixo.com*

You can also check out Web sites for rental car companies like Avis and Hertz for promotional offers and last-minute deals. Often, they will advertise sales, coupons, or free upgrades on their site, but make sure you read the fine print in case there are any hidden fees.

While you're looking at the sites for all the major companies, you might take a look at the smaller ones, too. Their cars may be older or secondhand, but their prices will be much lower. Check out Rent-A-Wreck at *www.rentawreck.com*, DiscountCars.net at *www.discountcars.net*, and Car Rental Express at *www.carrentalexpress.com*.

When you go shopping online for rental car rates, be wary of a few things. Some travel sites have a lot of banners and pop-ups, so make sure not to confuse all those advertisements with actual rate listings. Another trick to look out for is really great rates that aren't actually available. If you've chosen a rate that seems too good to be true, double-check to see if it's still available when you check out.

Also, find out if the rate includes all taxes, fees, surcharges, and any booking fees that might not have been mentioned. When you have finally chosen a rate and decide to make your reservation, pay for the booking with your credit card. Charge cards usually have the most federal protection in cases of error or security breach, so you can make your reservation without worry.

Avoid airport terminals and save

You can save at least 25 percent by making your reservation at an off-airport location, even if you rent from one of the major providers. Rental companies at airports usually charge "airport location fees" and security taxes, so it pays to take a cab or a shuttle to another location. Most of the time, you can return the car to an airport location without being charged extra.

Group members receive discounts

You can receive a discount at most car rental companies if you're a member of an organization, like AARP. In fact, some car rental companies give discounts for having a specific type of credit card.

The important thing is to be assertive and ask. Most companies won't automatically tell you about their discounts, so rattle off all the organizations you belong to and see if you qualify. Being a member of one of the following groups may also help you get a car rental discount. You will need to show proof of membership.

- motor clubs

- teachers' organizations

- government employees

- military

- vacation clubs

Get more mileage from free upgrade

You may want to think twice when the car rental company offers you a free upgrade. When you upgrade from a four-cylinder compact to a six-cylinder intermediate, you spend more money on gas. Four-cylinder cars give you more miles per gallon than six-cylinder cars.

Your extra cost will depend on how many miles you rack up, whether you're driving in the city or on the highway, and the price of gas, which varies around the country. These three variables can cause your gas expense to add up quickly.

Make and model	City	Highway
2005 4-cylinder automatic compact:		
Ford Focus	26	32
Chevrolet Cavalier	24	34
2005 6-cylinder automatic intermediate:		
Pontiac Grand Am	20	29
Mazda 6	20	27

If you want the comfort of an intermediate car but want to spend less on gas, ask the agent for a four-cylinder intermediate. They may be a little slower, but they're roughly equal in gas mileage to a compact.

Look to credit cards for insurance

Don't pay for insurance twice. Check with your credit card company first to see what kind of insurance coverage they offer when you're renting a car.

Diner's Club is the only card that offers primary coverage in the United States, but American Express, Visa, and MasterCard — at gold level or higher — typically provide secondary collision damage coverage.

Pass on the collision damage waiver, too. The $10 to $20 a day pays for a contract that is full of loopholes for the rental company to slip through and keep from honoring your policy in case of an accident.

New slant on renting a car

Owning a car is expensive. Once you do the math, your total cost of gas, insurance, and maintenance, plus your monthly car payment, could be $600 to $700 a month. That's okay if you use your car a lot, but what if you use it less than an hour a day, and two or three hours on the weekend? Then you may be spending more than you need.

Instead, check into joining a car-sharing program, like Flexcar at *www.flexcar.com* or ZipCar at *www.zipcar.com*. In some cases, the cost can be as low as $30 a month for part-time use of a car, including gas, premium insurance, maintenance, and 24-hour assistance.

Be aware that car-sharing programs often require an application fee. Also, you must reserve a car in advance, and they may be scarce at peak times. What's more, if you exceed the mileage or time limit, you can be charged hefty fees.

If you only need a car for the weekend, try Enterprise Rent-A-Car. They frequently offer special weekend rates starting at $9.99 a day.

Auto insurance

Repair your credit for better rates

Checking your credit report for errors at least once a year can do wonders for your insurance premiums. If your credit report has a mistake — and mistakes do happen — dispute the error.

Your credit score affects your insurance score, which then affects your insurance rates. Correcting mistakes in your credit report could bring down your insurance rates. Generally, an insurance score above 760 is considered good, and anything below 600 is bad.

If your credit score is over 700, look into companies like Allstate and Progressive who give better rates for good credit. If your score is lower, look into companies like State Farm and American Family Insurance who put more emphasis on other factors, like your driving record.

Handling an imperfect driving record

The easiest way to keep your auto insurance down is to have a perfect driving record, but for drivers with less-than-perfect histories, there are still ways to make the best of the situation.

If there is a flaw or two on your record, contact your local Department of Motor Vehicles to find out exactly how many points you have and when they expire. It may not be long before some of those points disappear, and your record improves. Wait until then to get insurance quotes.

Make sure there are no errors on your record, like a ticket you never got or a typo in your birth date. It costs a little to get a copy of your driving record, but it doesn't cost anything to correct it. You'll save a lot more in the long run by fixing any mistakes.

Do your homework to find a deal

The best way to find the lowest price on car insurance is to do your homework. Shop around before you sign up with any auto insurance carrier, and you'll be sure to save money. Rates vary from one carrier to another, so call each company to find out what they charge and give them the same details. Tell them how much coverage you're looking for, the amount of deductible you want, how frequently the car is driven, your age or the age of the driver, and the year, make, and model of the car.

If you're not sure exactly where to start, talk with the experts. Call your state insurance department and ask them for a list of auto insurance companies and the rates they charge. You can find contact information for the state insurance department by looking in the front of your phonebook or by doing an online search for their Web site.

Once you have the list, contact at least four of the companies with the lowest prices. Give them the same details mentioned before to find out what rates each of them charge for the same coverage. With that information in your hands, you can make an educated decision, and you'll feel good knowing you got the best deal in town.

Check out the following price quotes for a 2002 Ford Focus ZTW with 40,000 miles. The two drivers are married, currently have auto insurance, and don't have any traffic violations. The car, which is driven 10 miles to work, has an alarm system and is still being paid for.

Web site	Lowest quote for 6 months
www.insWeb.com	$456.00
www.geico.com	$469.10
www.progressive.com	$589.00
www.esurance.com	$737.00
www.electricinsurance.com	$951.00

Buy only what you need

You can save money by buying just the insurance coverage you need. Try raising your deductible for comprehensive and collision coverage. You can cut 15 to 20 percent off your insurance rate by increasing your deductible from $250 to $500 or $1,000.

You may be able to stop paying for comprehensive coverage altogether. If your car is paid off, switch to just liability insurance, and you could save hundreds of dollars a year. As a rule of thumb, comprehensive and collision coverage aren't worth the cost if the value of your car doesn't add up to 10 times the annual premium. If that's the case, all you need is liability coverage.

Don't pay twice for roadside help

The American Automobile Association (AAA) is an organization well-known for offering dependable roadside assistance, but why pay for an extra service when your own auto insurance probably offers it?

Most insurance companies offer roadside assistance programs for as little as $12 a year. That small fee usually entitles you to jump starts, lockouts, tire changes, towing, gas, and a toll-free phone number. AAA costs more because of additional benefits outside of roadside service, like travel discounts at hotels and restaurants, but if you don't travel a lot, it's a better idea to stick with your own insurer.

Fewer payments mean lower rates

Rather than finance your insurance payment into six monthly installments, pay your 6-month premium all at once. When you choose the extended plan and divide up your payments, the insurance company adds what they call an "installment payment service fee." It's a small fee they add to your payment each month for their processing expenses, but you don't get more coverage. Pay in full twice a year and those little monthly fees could add up to almost $100 in annual savings.

Combine insurance for a discount

Many great things come in pairs — peanut butter and jelly, Astaire and Rogers, auto and home insurance. Getting your auto insurance and your home insurance from the same carrier could earn you a big discount. You'll typically save 10 to 15 percent off your premiums.

Head off debt with GAP insurance

GAP insurance keeps you from paying for a car you no longer have. This Guaranteed Auto Protection insurance pays the amount you'll owe if your car gets totaled and you're left with a loan that is more than the total worth of your car.

So if you owe $20,000 for a car the insurance company says was only worth $16,000 when it was totaled, GAP insurance will cover the remaining $4,000. At prices ranging from $15 to

Pocket an extra $100 a month or more with money-saving auto insurance discounts you may be overlooking. Here are nine discounts, available from most insurance companies, that could save you a bundle:

✓ good driving record
✓ mature driver
✓ longtime customer
✓ defensive driving course
✓ carpooler or low-mileage driver
✓ anti-theft device or car satellite recovery system
✓ safety measures, like air bags and anti-lock brakes
✓ nonsmoker
✓ good student

$45 a year, it's a good value. Consider buying it if you're making a down payment of less than 20 percent.

More ways to save

There are even more ways to save money on auto insurance for the determined car owner. Driving less frequently or carpooling could earn you a discount, especially if you drive fewer than 5,000 or 6,000 miles a year. Parking your car in an enclosed garage instead of parking on the street could also get you a discount. Some companies even give discounts for being a police officer, a teacher, or a retiree. The discounts are there. You just have to ask.

So far the tips in this chapter have been helpful if you already have a car. If you're in the process of buying a car, keep this in mind — the type of car you drive affects how much you'll pay in insurance premiums. Choosing a car with a higher safety rating lowers your premiums.

To find out the insurance ratings of different cars, check out *Consumer Reports* annual car buying guides. The Insurance Institute for Highway Safety is another good place to look for statistics that could affect your premiums. Call 703-247-1500 or visit *www.carsafety.org* to contact them and find out the rating for your future car.

Baby goods

5 secrets of the best bargain hunters

From clothes to a playpen, you can get virtually everything you need for free or darn close to it.

- Stop by garage sales. You could snag fantastic deals, especially if you offer to take an entire bag or box of baby things off their hands.

- Create a network of people who know your needs. A quick phone call or e-mail is a great opportunity to let friends, neighbors, and family members know you're looking for baby bargains. Tell them specifically what you need, and ask them to keep an eye out for hand-me-downs and other good deals.

- Plan a swap meet. Churches, preschools, and community clubs are great places to meet and organize swaps with people who have baby items. Make it a swap party. You could even decide in advance what each person will bring, and link them up with someone who needs the same thing.

- Look for public bulletin boards in your grocery stores, pediatrician's office, church, and school. Here you may find parents trying to sell or give away their baby items. You can also post an ad of your own, asking specifically for the things you need. Be sure to ask the organization or company about their policy for posting "want" ads.

- Offer a trade with the people you know. Barter for their goods with something you know they need — a service like babysitting, cooking a meal, or even an item you own but no longer need. It's a great, cheap way to help each other out.

10 clever ways to save at yard sales

- Make a list of things you need to buy over the next several months, then stick to it. Items you don't really need will just clutter your house.

- Start early or go late. You'll find the best variety first thing in the morning, especially in furniture and appliances, but you'll snag the best deals at the end of the day when weary sellers are ready to bargain.

- Look for lifetime guarantees. No garage seller will guarantee their goods, but some companies will. Tupperware, Farberware, Chicago Cutlery, and Craftsman tools all carry lifetime guarantees backed by their manufacturers. So go ahead and buy the cracked Tupperware or rusted Craftsman wrench and call a dealer to exchange it.

- Ask for items you don't see. Need a baby stroller? Ask the seller if they have one. They may have forgotten to put it out, or another customer might tell you where you can find one.

- Think creatively. Buy items for their parts — cut rate clothes for their nice buttons, lamps for their shades, and so forth.

- Don't waste time at high-priced sales. You only want bargains. Some people are out to make money, not get rid of stuff, and they'll refuse to negotiate.

- Make sure it works. Ask the seller if you can plug in an item, or if they have batteries to test it. If they say no, don't buy it. It might be broken.

Great bargains abound at garage sales on almost everything under the sun. A few items top the list of most common finds.

✓ toys
✓ clothing
✓ furniture
✓ decorative items
✓ baby goods
✓ books
✓ kitchenware
✓ linens
✓ tools

- Check all clothes for stains, buttons, snaps, and working zippers. If you can't tell whether a stain will wash out or not, it's best not to buy.

- Always come prepared with coins and plenty of cash in small bills. Carry it in a pouch around your waste rather than a purse you might set down and forget.

- Ask for a lower price if you don't want to pay what a seller wants. The worst they can say is "no."

Safety checklist for used items

Classified ads, thrift stores, and yard sales can be the best places to pick up inexpensive baby gear and furniture. But for safety's sake, make sure the item passes these tests before you take it home.

- Is the construction still sound? Check for broken pieces, loose joints, and splinters.

- Do all the parts work properly? You don't want a stroller to collapse with your child in it, or the car seat to come loose in an auto accident.

- Is it clean? In other words, would you let your child chew on it? Some items can be easily cleaned, others not. If not, don't buy it.

- Could a child hurt herself with it? The U.S. Consumer Product Safety Commission (CPSC) warns some seemingly innocent items could kill children. A crib should have a firm, tight-fitting mattress and slats no more than 2 3/8 inches apart so a baby's head cannot squeeze through them.

- Has it been recalled? Find out by calling the CPSC toll-free at 800-638-2772 or visiting their Web site at *www.CPSC.gov*.

Superstores not so super

Giant specialty retailers, like Babies "R" Us, Toys "R" Us, even PetSmart and others, are neither discount stores nor outlets. They are large, specialized department stores. In general, they don't offer cut-rate merchandise. Instead, they offer a better variety than you'll find at most other stores, but with bare-bones service. It's a trade-off — more choices, less service, and few discounts.

Shop smart at membership clubs

You could save 26 percent on groceries and get rock-bottom deals on many other items at warehouse clubs, such as Costco, Sam's Club, and BJ's. These stores keep their costs low by selling in bulk, running a no-frills store, hiring less staff, and not advertising as heavily as their competitors. They pass the savings along to you. Often, they sell appliances, office supplies, even electronics in addition to groceries.

Unfortunately, they have disadvantages, too.

- Most membership clubs do not accept coupons, offer weekly specials, or sell generic brands. You may do better doubling coupons, checking grocery ads, or buying generic from your local grocer.

- They sell in bulk, which can yield great buys, but 5 lbs. of butter at 30 percent off is no bargain if it goes bad before you use it.

- They may not tell you the unit price, such as the cost of shampoo per ounce, like grocery stores do. That makes it hard to comparison shop. Check unit prices at other stores before you go to a warehouse club, then bring a calculator and do your own math.

- Their low prices can tempt you to buy things you don't need. Shop with a list and stick to it, and only carry cash to limit your spending.

- They offer lots of different products, but little brand variety. For instance, you might find 10 brands of spaghetti sauce at a grocery store and only two at a warehouse club. Decide if you want better prices or more choices.

- They rotate their stock, so the brand you like may not be there next time you go.

- Some only accept one kind of credit card but offer their own as an alternative — at exorbitant interest rates. Sign up for one, and they may also sell your personal information.

- They charge an annual membership fee, usually between $25 and $40 dollars. Some give guests one-day passes, as often as you want, to shop there, but tack on a 5-percent surcharge at the register. Still, if you spend less than $500 to $800 dollars a year there, you are better off getting a guest pass than buying a membership.

Some clubs offer free trial memberships, up to 60 days. Call and ask about this policy then test the place out before you join.

Banking

■ Banking services

Escape the ATM surcharge trap

Don't get nickel and dimed to death by automated teller machine (ATM) fees. Use these tips to help avoid them.

- Use your own bank's ATMs whenever possible.

- Find out if your bank belongs to a selective surcharge network. If so, you can use an ATM from any bank in the network without being charged a fee.

- Ask for cash back when you use your debit card for a purchase.

- If you're shopping for a bank, consider major banks with far-flung ATM networks or online banks.

- Plan ahead so you never have to make an "emergency trip" to a fee-charging ATM.

Discover direct deposit discounts

Banks may surprise you with discounted or free checking if you agree to "direct deposit" service. Under direct deposit, your employer deposits your paycheck directly into your bank account instead of giving it to you first. That means, you won't have to visit the bank to deposit a check — and your paycheck can't get lost or stolen.

Ask your employer if direct deposit is available. Then ask your bank what benefits you can expect if you agree to direct deposit. You may be pleasantly surprised.

Fend off bounced-check fees

A bounced check can trigger multiple penalty fees from your bank as well as additional fees from the business receiving the rubber check.

The best way to avoid such fees is to manage your account so you don't overdraw any checks. But if you think you need overdraft protection, your bank may allow you to cushion checks with money from your savings account, credit card, or a line of credit. Even if you must pay fees or interest, they may still cost less than one bounced check.

One warning — some banks automatically enroll customers in their own overdraft protection plans, which have unreasonably high interest rates. You should check with your bank, and opt out in writing if you find that's the case.

Cut yourself a check deal

You may get a much better price on checks if you buy from a third-party check seller. Order a catalog or visit the Web sites of vendors like these.

- *www.walmartchecks.com*

Source	Cost of single-style checks	Per check
www.checkworks.com	$7.95 for 200 checks (free shipping)	4 cents
www.walmartchecks.com	$5.96 for 240 checks + $1.70 for shipping	3 cents
www.checksunlimited.com	$21.90 for 400 checks + $4.50 shipping if not first order	7 cents
www.checksinthemail.com	$7.99 for 200 checks, not including shipping	4 cents + shipping
Major bank #1	$8 for 50 checks but first pack is free	16 cents
Major bank #2	$14.95 for 150 checks	10 cents

- *www.checksunlimited.com* or 800-204-2244 for a catalog

- *www.checkworks.com*

- *www.4checks.com*

- *www.checksinthemail.com* or 866-639-2432 for a catalog

- *www.deluxe-check-order.com*

Compare the prices these sellers charge with what you pay now. If you'd like to buy from these or any other third-party check sellers, you should take a few precautions.

- Ask about the security measures included on the checks, or look it up on the Web site.

- Find out how your personal information and privacy are protected.

- Check with your local or state Better Business Bureau, consumer protection agency, and State Attorney General's office to learn whether complaints have ever been filed against this seller.

Online bill paying pays off

Online bill paying could be a clever way to save — especially if you can do it for free. While the cost of mailing bills may not seem like much, it adds up quickly. And if you've ever had bills buried under paperwork or get delayed in the mail, you know how expensive late fees can be.

But online bill paying allows you to pre-arrange payments each month — perhaps up to a year in advance for fixed-rate bills. What's more, some bill-paying services even offer to send you reminders so deadlines won't slip by.

Shield checks from identity theft

Checks sitting unguarded in your mailbox put you at risk for identity theft. Keep your checks — and yourself — protected.

If you order checks from your bank, arrange to pick them up from a nearby branch. Otherwise, ask the bank or check seller to send your checks by certified mail. Also, never print your social security number on your checks.

For even more protection, install a lock on your mailbox to keep thieves away from checks and other financial or personal information.

Before you commit to a bill-paying service, ask questions like these to check whether the service is a good deal for you.

- Does the bank provide a way for you to authorize an amount and date for a bill's payment?

- Can the bill be paid and delivered even if the company is not available online?

- What features are included in online bill paying?

- What is the cost of online bill paying, and are there any requirements you must meet to use the service?

- How does the bank protect the privacy and security of personal and financial information?

- How long does a payment take to reach the biller?

Learn more good questions to ask, and read sound advice on both online banking and bill paying from the Federal Deposit Insurance Corporation. Visit *www.fdic.gov* and click the Consumers link. Under Consumer Resources, click Safe Internet Banking.

You can also write or call the FDIC for information at the address below.

Contact: Federal Deposit Insurance Corp.
             550 17th Street, N.W.
             Washington, D.C. 20429
             877-275-3342

Spend zero on financial software

Imagine having the money-managing power of Intuit's *Quicken* or Microsoft *Money* without paying for the software. You might — if you ask about free online services available from your bank or broker.

Compare the features of financial software with online services to see if online tools offer everything you need. For example, if you plan to spend hours tracking every penny for budgeting, *Quicken* or *Money* may still suit you.

But if you want to pay bills online or review all your bank, investing, and credit accounts in one place, free online services work just as well — without costing you anything extra.

■ Credit

Reap benefits of a high credit score

A credit score is a number between 300 and 850 that serves as a snapshot of your credit report at any given time. A low credit score could cost you up to $240 extra per month on a $100,000 mortgage, according to one estimate. That's more than $2,800 per year — even with rock-bottom interest rates.

Improving a low score can benefit you because a variety of people use it to help make decisions.

- Insurers may charge you a lower premium on car or homeowner's insurance. People with poor scores may pay extra and may be denied coverage or renewal.

- Lenders may charge you lower interest rates, fewer fees, or smaller fees — and grant you higher credit limits.

- Private mortgage insurance (PMI) may cost less.

- Landlords may request your credit score to help judge whether you'll pay rent regularly and on time. A high score could mean your rent application is less likely to get turned down. Deposits and fees might be lower, too.

- Your credit score may play a role in whether you're chosen for a job — particularly if the job requires you to be responsible for money.

- Utility companies — including cell phone service providers — may consider your credit score when they decide whether to offer you their services.

To help improve your credit score, find out what it is, and make sure mistakes on your credit report aren't keeping it artificially low. Your score will cost you, but you can purchase it while getting your credit report for free. If you find mistakes in your credit report, correct them.

Use these tips to help work toward a score of 720 or higher. Every little increase can help.

- Collections and late payments sink your score, yet that score improves as you build a history of paying bills on time. If you've missed payments, get current and keep current.

- Pay off large balances on credit cards. Keep those balances low.

- Don't open unnecessary new credit cards just to boost available credit.

- Handle your cards with extreme care. Keep the balances as low as possible, and meet every monthly payment deadline.

Pay zero for your credit report

Checking your credit report at least once a year can pay off —
especially if you catch mistakes that affect your credit rating.
And now you won't have to pay for the report itself, thanks to
a change in the Fair Credit Reporting Act. After Sept. 1, 2005,
you can get a free credit report every year from each of the
three major credit bureaus.

Even if the program is not yet available in your area, you can
get a free credit report if you're denied credit, insurance, or a
job because of information in your credit report. But you
must request the report within 60 days of receiving notice of
the denial.

To get your free credit report, visit *www.annualcreditreport.com*,
or call toll-free 877-322-8228. You can also write to the following address.

Contact: Annual Credit Report Request Service
             P.O. Box 105281
             Atlanta, GA 30348-5281

Be ready to provide your name, address, and social security
number. You may also be asked for other information. Then
you can choose to get just one credit report or all three — one
from each bureau. If you like, you can get one now and return
to check one or two of the other reports later in the year.

Perhaps the only bad news about this program is that your
credit score does not come with your free credit report.
However, you can choose to purchase your score when you
request a free report.

If you find a mistake in your report, contact the credit bureau
responsible for the report, and ask how to get the report corrected. Here's how you can reach these organizations.

- Equifax at *www.equifax.com* or the phone number at the bottom of your Equifax credit report

- Experian at *www.experian.com* or the number at the bottom of your Experian credit report

- Trans Union at *www.transunion.com* or 800-916-8800

And here is a bonus tip. To help prevent identity theft, ignore those ads, e-mails, and telemarketing calls that promise a free credit report. After all, they could just be scammers hunting for a way to steal your identity. Don't take the chance.

9 ways to erase credit card debt

You might save thousands of dollars in interest just by controlling credit card debt. Get started with these nine ways to erase your credit card debt fast.

- Find out how much total credit card debt you owe. Then figure out how long it will take to pay it all off — with the interest charges included.

- Transfer your high-interest-rate balances to one card with a low interest rate. Or pay off your higher-interest-rate credit cards first.

- Track your spending. You may be surprised at where your money is going. Prepare a budget that slashes unnecessary spending, and stick to it. Use the savings to pay off debt.

- Don't just pay the minimum every month. If you owe $1,000 on a card with a 17-percent interest rate, it may take 12 years and cost over $900 in interest by the time you pay it off.

- Never use credit card cash advances to make payments on other accounts.

- Stop using credit cards, and don't open any new charge accounts.

- Always make payments on time.

- Get a second job to help pay off your debts.

- Try a credit counselor if you want outside help. Contact the National Foundation for Credit Counseling (NFCC) at 800-388-2227, or visit *www.nfcc.org*. The NFCC can provide credit education and counseling and help you get better terms with your lenders.

Ban pre-approved credit junk mail

"You're pre-approved for thousands with our platinum card," proclaims that tantalizing offer from your mailbox. But that offer can pile up interest charges, build debt, and raise your risk of identity theft. Don't be tempted, especially if you're debt prone. Instead, help yourself save money by opting out.

Opting out means you ask the credit card bureaus to strip your name from their marketing mailing lists — the source of most pre-approved credit offers. Tell the bureaus to block those enticing envelopes for just two years or for life.

To opt out by phone, call toll-free 888-567-8688. You'll be asked for personal information, including your name, telephone number, and social security number. Don't worry — these details remain confidential and are only used to process your request. Just remember, you may have to fill out and return a consent form if you want the offers to stop permanently.

The offers won't stop coming right away, so what can you do while you wait? Don't risk a rip-off that could ruin your good credit rating. Before you throw that "junk" mail away, shred all pre-approved credit offers right down to confetti size. A whole offer in your trash can help thieves steal your identity, but confetti just leaves them frustrated.

Protect your score from card-hopping

Opening a new zero-interest card account every few months may seem like a money-saving idea, but it could sink your credit score. A number of factors go into calculating your credit score. How often you've applied for credit recently is one of them, and so is the percentage of available credit you've used.

Each new card may knock your credit score down a little more. However, if you have a long credit history, the drops may be less steep. The dip in your score may last just six months — unless the new card brings new trouble with it.

- Watch out for high balance transfer fees, low introductory rates that skyrocket after a few months, and any other fees that will make a switch more expensive than keeping the old card. These could boost your debt instead of slashing it.

- Be careful about transferring a hefty balance to a zero-interest or lower-interest-rate card. If the transferred balance is more than half your new card's credit limit, that transfer may trigger a credit score drop. Pay that debt down to below 50 percent of the limit, and your credit score should recover.

- Avoid card-switching or opening new cards if you plan to apply for a car or home loan in the next 12 months.

While switching to zero-rate cards has helped some consumers pay down their balances, card-hopping can still be a risky strategy, and it's not right for everyone.

Instead of card-switching, look into other solutions, such as Bankrate's Pay-down Advisor. Visit *www.bankrate.com* and click Credit Cards. Scroll down and click the link, Pay off balances quickly under Pay off your debt. Answer the questions to find various solutions you can try.

Close credit cards with caution

Closing several credit card accounts won't improve your credit score and could bring it down. Here's why.

One factor credit scoring considers is how much of your total credit you use. To calculate that, credit scorers divide the total balance on your credit cards by the total credit limit available on those accounts. The result is a fraction — the lower, the better. Canceling cards can raise that number, which is bad for your credit score.

Calculate which credit card to cancel

Belinda has five credit cards. Two are idle, so she decides to cancel one. But before she does, she checks whether cutting a card might cut her credit score as well.

Belinda's current total balance is $1,500, and her total credit limit is $12,000. She is currently using 12.5 percent (1,500\12,000) of her available credit, which is well below the 20-percent recommended limit. But that number could change drastically if she cancels the wrong card.

Belinda's appliance store credit card has a zero balance and a $5,000 limit. If she cancels that card, her limit totals will shrink from $12,000 to $7,000. But a $1,500 balance divided by $7,000 would be around 21 percent. Because that's more than the credit scorers' 20-percent safety limit, Belinda's credit score could drop.

On the other hand, Belinda's department store card has a zero balance and $1,000 limit. If she cancels that card, her total limit will slide from $12,000 to $11,000. Credit scorers will divide $1,500 by $11,000 to get a result between 13 and 14 percent — well below the 20 percent that triggers a credit score drop. Belinda will play it smart and cancel this card instead.

If you still want to cancel your unused cards, only cancel those with a zero balance. And if you plan to buy a house or car soon, don't close them until after you qualify for a loan.

Build your credit history wisely

Budgeting your money so you don't depend on credit cards is the responsible way to live. But when you do use credit cards, a wise strategy can help you build or restore a good credit score. Keep a good credit rating with these tips.

- Avoid frequently opening new credit card accounts.

- Open a new account only when essential, and be sure to read all the fine print before you do — especially information about fees, penalties, interest rates, billing periods, and grace periods.

- Pay on time.

- If you have been denied cards due to a poor credit score or no credit history, consider a secured card. It may help build a good enough credit history to qualify for an unsecured card after a year or two. Try for a low interest rate if you expect to carry a balance. Otherwise, seek a card with no annual fee.

- Thirty percent of your credit score depends on how much of your total credit limit you use. Charge no more than 20 percent of your total available credit so your score won't sink.

If you've made the mistake of opening too many accounts, order your credit report from all three credit bureaus. Find out which credit cards you have, check for mistakes, and get errors corrected.

Next, pick which cards to keep. Favor older cards because lenders prefer a long history of faithful bill paying. Keep at least one low-rate card. Also, determine how much balance you'll have each month. Then, select cards so that your total credit limit is five times that number, if possible.

When you choose which cards to pitch, pay off the balances, and then call to close them.

Find a money-saving card

Get help finding a credit card that will save you money by using a free tool on the Web. Visit *www.cardweb.com* for a credit glossary, news about the credit card industry, useful articles, and a page that helps you find better credit card rates.

On the Web site, click on the Find a Card link. Either choose the type of card you want — such as low rate, rewards, or no annual fee — or fill out a quick questionnaire for a list of only the cards that match what you want.

Just remember to use your credit card with care, and avoid running up debts that could take years to pay off.

Uncover the right rewards card

A credit card that delivers rewards can be a good deal. Just make sure you study the fine print in the offer or card agreement, and decide if the benefit is worth it. Web sites like these can help.

- *www.creditcards.com*

- *www.e-wizdom.com*

- *www.creditcardscenter.com*

According to *The Wall Street Journal*, cash reward cards give back around 1 percent. That means you have to charge a lot to earn any substantial savings. And you also have to spend quite a bit to earn enough frequent flier miles to take that Caribbean vacation you've been dreaming about.

But if you do use one credit card for your purchases, a rewards card might be a smart move. Just remember, if you don't pay off your balance every month, you may get stuck paying more in interest than you earn in rewards.

Watch for costly card tricks

Credit card companies try all sorts of legal tricks to get your money. Fight back each month by scouring your credit card statement for surprises like these.

- Check the due date for your next payment. Card-holders have been blindsided by late fees and other charges because they didn't notice the changed — and earlier — date.

- Monitor the interest rate. Even a fixed-rate card can change its rate as long as you're given notice.

- Watch out for low introductory interest rates that sky-rocket a few months later.

- A practice called universal default allows credit card companies to change terms without notice — leaving penalty rates and fees free to rise. Creditors can also monitor your credit report and raise your interest rate if they see late payments on your other accounts. If your account is subject to universal default, switching to another card may be worthwhile.

Also, monitor how your finance rates are calculated. Some methods can be costly. The adjusted balance method subtracts this month's payments from your previous balance — only charging interest on what is carried over. If no extra twists sneak in, this can be cheap.

	Adjusted balance method	Average balance without purchases	Average balance with purchases	Previous balance method
APR	18%	18%	18%	18%
Monthly APR	1.5%	1.5%	1.5%	1.5%
Previous Balance	$5,000	$5,000	$5,000	$5,000
Payment, day 14	$3,000	$3,000	$3,000	$3,000
Updated balance	$2,000	$2,000	$2,000	$5,000 (no update)
Charge, day 17	$1,000	$1,000	$1,000	$1,000
Finance charge balance	$2,000	$3,400*	$3,833**	$5,000
Finance charge	$30	$51	$57.50	$75

*(5,000 x 14 days)+(2000 x 16 days) = 102,000, and 102,000 ÷ 30 days = $3,400

**(5,000 x 14 days)+(2,000 x 3 days)+(3,000 x13 days) = 114,990 ÷ 30 days = $3,833

The average daily balance method may either exclude or include new purchases. If it excludes them, it will add up all your balances from each day of the billing cycle and divide that total by the number of days in the cycle. "Including new purchases" works the same way but raises your balance every time you use the card — costing you more.

The previous balance method charges the finance rate only on the balance you had at the start of the billing cycle.

Two-cycle average daily balance methods are the most expensive. Where other methods might use the balances from one month, two-cycle methods impose charges for balances from the last two billing cycles.

Beware of fee-heavy card upgrades

That credit card upgrade from your mailbox may sound like a new and different card — and it could be one you don't want. According to *The Wall Street Journal*, changes in your credit contract terms can legally be called upgrades, even if they mean higher costs for you. For example, upgrades to rewards cards may carry a higher annual fee.

If you get a card upgrade, read the fine print carefully to determine whether you come out ahead. While you may discover advantages, watch for features you don't want and for new or changed penalties and fees. If you'd rather keep your old card, contact the card issuer to ask how to refuse the upgrade and keep your old card in service.

ID theft insurance not a bargain

Identity theft insurance doesn't necessarily cover the charges a thief runs up on your credit card or money stripped from your accounts. Instead, you may pay up to $180 per year just for the cost of repairing your credit after the theft. You're better off skipping this insurance and checking your credit report regularly instead.

Ax useless card protection

Even if you're offered credit card loss insurance for just $7 a month, don't take the bait. This insurance promises to pay the charges if someone steals your card and runs up a bill. But federal law would prevent you from paying more than $50 of the stolen charges anyway. If you buy credit card loss protection, you'll spend $84 per year. Don't waste your money.

Save on unnecessary insurance

For most of us, credit life insurance is just plain bad policy. Credit life insurance may claim to pay off your credit card debt if you die, or cover your payments if you become disabled or unemployed. But this insurance is notorious for overpricing, so consider buying term life insurance or expanding your life insurance coverage instead.

However, if you can't qualify for regular life insurance coverage — term or otherwise — this coverage could be appropriate. If that's the case, be sure to read the fine print before you buy.

Watch out for new credit scams

The latest credit card scams may seem so genuine that you may not know you've been shammed until too late. Learn what you need to know to stop a scammer cold.

You may get a call from a con artist claiming to be the credit card issuer, your bank, or the police. The scammer may say your card has suspicious activity. He may even ask you specific questions about a purchase you never made and promise to remedy the problem.

But the scam comes when he asks for your PIN number, card expiration date, billing address, or part of the account number. The swindler already has most of the credit card information needed to steal your identity. He tries to get the rest from you.

The second new scam is the "gold and platinum card" racket. Some card offers may promise to improve your credit rating or help you get unsecured major credit or retailer cards. Not only do these cards limit you to purchases from a few select catalogs, they also do nothing to boost your rating or qualify you for unsecured cards. Watch out for these additional signs of gold and platinum card fraud.

- You only hear about one fee. But once you've committed to pay it, you're told you must pay even more fees to use the card.

- You must call a 900 or 976 number for more information — and pay the steep charges.

- You're required to make a cash deposit for each item before you can put the balance on your charge card.

Protect yourself from any credit scams with these tips.

- Investigate credit card offers before you apply. Check with your local Better Business Bureau, consumer protection agency, or state Attorney General's office for complaints against the credit card marketer.

- If a merchant promises to improve your credit rating, call the credit bureaus to see if the merchant is a member. Only members can send information about you to the bureaus.

- Keep an eye on your card during any transaction. Also, hold your card so no one can see and memorize your card number.

- Void incorrect receipts, and never sign a blank one.

- Save receipts to compare with billing statements. Open the statements immediately and check for questionable charges or wrong amounts. Report dubious charges to the card issuer right away.

Negotiate for a better rate

You may get a lower interest rate on your credit card just by asking. If you're a long-standing customer with a good credit score, try bargaining with your current credit card company. You might be successful at getting a better rate.

You'll have even more bargaining power if you get another credit card offer with a lower rate. If it's a genuinely good deal, use it to persuade your current credit card issuer to reconsider. Say you'll switch unless they match the new card's rate. If the answer is no, switch cards and enjoy your savings.

■ Loans and mortgages

Save through loan consolidation

Simplify your life by simplifying your loans. If you have several loans, you may be able to consolidate them at a low rate, saving thousands of dollars in interest.

Student loans in particular are easy to lump into one consolidation loan. If you have a child or grandchild who is graduating, he probably has more than one loan, each with its own interest rate. By combining all the loans, he can lock in one good interest rate and make one reduced monthly payment.

And because the lump sum is stretched out over a term of 10 to 30 years, the monthly payment is smaller and more manageable. The downside is you can only consolidate once, and a longer term means more interest charges in the long run.

If you choose to consolidate your loans, see if you qualify for any discounts. Some lenders offer incentives for good customers. Ask each of your lenders what kinds of discounts are available before you decide which one should consolidate your loans.

Be smart about home equity

Need money for home improvements? Got a kid in college who needs tuition? Maybe you need start-up cash for a new business. You may want to consider a home equity line of credit (HELOC).

Although you borrow money against the equity in your house, it works like a credit account. Rather than take out one lump sum, you have access to the money as you need it. You don't pay interest until you actually withdraw money, and even then, the interest is tax deductible.

HELOCs have interest rates averaging about 4.5 percent, which is low when compared to 10-year fixed loans with rates around 7.25 percent. But you may have starter fees, annual fees, and other costs like minimum-withdrawal fees, inactivity fees, and early-termination fees. So check the loan terms carefully. You don't want to take all the money you saved with a low interest rate and spend it on other costs.

Although it's best to save for any large purchase, a HELOC may be a good move if you don't know exactly how much money you'll need or when you're going to need it. It also makes a good safety net in case there's an emergency or a period of unemployment when you need cash right away.

But don't forget it's a loan against your house, and you could jeopardize your home if you can't pay it back. Stay away from a HELOC if you have a spending problem or want to use the money to pay off an enormous credit card bill. You would just replace one large debt with another.

If you take out a line of credit, plan on paying it off within a few years. The interest rate on a HELOC is adjustable, so the sooner you pay it off, the less chance your rate will go up.

A HELOC can save you money if you use it wisely. But if you think having cash at your fingertips would tempt you to over-spend, then be smart and find another source of cash.

Experts can save time and money

A mortgage broker can be a big help when you need a loan but don't know where to start. These experts can look through loan offers and find the one that's best for you.

According to the National Association of Mortgage Brokers, more than two thirds of homebuyers choose to get a mortgage through a broker. They save you time, and depending on their fees, can save you money. Broker fees usually range from 1 to 1.5 percent of the mortgage.

Some dishonest brokers may overcharge you with fees of eight to 10 points. Follow these tips to be sure you're working with someone who has your best interests at heart.

- Get referrals from friends and co-workers to help in making the right choice.

- Request a good-faith estimate of the broker's fees at the start.

- Get a written description of the loan program the broker offers so you can check out the rates, fees, and points.

- Ask the broker if he is affiliated with the lender to make sure he has no conflict of interest.

Negotiate for lower points

Nothing is written in stone when it comes to the cost of a mortgage. With some research in hand, you can use your negotiating skills to bring down lender's rates, points, or even fees.

The key is to arm yourself with information. Check the newspaper for current mortgage rates and points. Look online at Web sites like HSH Associates at *www.hsh.com* and LendingTree.com to compare rates from different lenders.

Be careful of lenders who advertise rock-bottom rates and points. They may compensate by charging outrageous fees. Let lenders know you're shopping around so they will compete for your business by lowering their points. One point equals 1 percent of the amount of the loan. So if you convince them to take off even half a point, you can save hundreds or thousands of dollars.

If you need to choose between paying lower points or a lower interest rate, keep these things in mind.

- Choose the lower interest rate if you plan to keep the mortgage for a long time.

- Go with lower points if you plan to sell the house in a few years, since you won't get the long-term benefit of a lower rate.

The same goes for fees. The longer you plan to keep your loan, the more fees you may want to pay upfront.

Remember to deduct any points you pay on your tax return. If you bought a house and split the points with the sellers, or

Know interest rate vs. APR

The interest rate on a loan is not the same as its annual percentage rate (APR). The interest rate is only the percentage of interest you pay on the loan. APR is the interest plus all the other costs, including points and fees. It is calculated by dividing the total cost of the loan by the number of years in the term. Use APR to compare loan packages when you look for a mortgage. Lenders are legally required to tell you the APR of their loan, so be suspicious if someone refuses to give you that information.

even if the sellers paid for all the points, you still get to deduct the full amount.

Compare online for best price

You already know you can save money by shopping around for the best mortgage rates. Now you just have to make sense of all the numbers you found. Put those figures into an online calculator to organize your information. You can find calculator programs at Web sites especially designed to help you compare loans.

LendingTree.com is a great place to start. You can submit an application and get rates from four competing lenders. Then compare the rates by plugging them into one of its financial calculators. For example, one will tell you if a 15-year loan or a 30-year loan would save you more money based on the mortgage amount and interest rates.

Interest.com has calculators that tell you what your monthly payments will be from the interest rate, the term, and the loan amount. You can also find out how much you can afford to borrow, how much you'd save by making additional mortgage payments, and how much you can deduct on your taxes.

FindLowerMortgageRates.com also has useful programs like a calculator that tells you how much money you should put down on your new home.

Other good Web sites to try are:

- *www.compareinterestrates.com*

- *www.bankrate.com*

- *www.loanweb.com*

Buy your home with a HELOC

You can use a home equity line of credit (HELOC) to actually buy a home. A HELOC is an adjustable-rate loan that works as a credit line rather than a mortgage. Usually, you get a HELOC with the equity you build up on a home. Now you can make a down payment on your home and use a HELOC to pay for the rest.

The interest rates for HELOCs are around 4 percent, which can save you a lot of money in interest charges. Since the rate is variable, it can go up or down. But it's still better than the traditional 30-year fixed-rate mortgage with rates closer to 6, 7, or 8 percent. With a HELOC you can borrow extra cash without having to take out another loan, and all the interest you pay is tax deductible.

HELOCs usually have much shorter terms than traditional loans. Rather than being stretched out over 30 years, a HELOC will have a term of 10 or 20 years. You may want to consider a HELOC if you plan to pay off your home in a short time.

If you like having stable monthly payments, though, you should try something different. The rates for HELOCs change with the market, so the payments will, too.

Pay off loan in half the time

Save tens of thousands of dollars by choosing a 15-year mortgage instead of a 30-year term. Your monthly payment will be higher, but cutting the time of the loan in half cuts off years of interest charges. Plus, interest rates are lower most of the time for loans with shorter terms.

Say your annual percentage rate is 7 percent, and you choose a 15-year fixed-rate mortgage over a 30-year mortgage. For every $100,000 you borrow from the bank, you'll save $75,000 in interest.

	30-year	15-year
Monthly payment	$1,100.65	$1,433.48
Total payments	$396,233	$258,026
Total interest	$246,233	$108,026
Money saved	$138,207	

Principal = $150,000 at 8.00%

	30-year	15-year
Monthly payment	$1,834.41	$2,389.13
Total payments	$660,388	$430,043
Total interest	$410,388	$180,043
Money saved	$230,345	

Principal = $250,000 at 8.00%

It may be tempting to stretch your loan out over 30 years. After all, who doesn't want to keep their monthly mortgage payment to a minimum? Sometimes, though, you have to spend money to save money.

Get a free discount

You can get an easy discount by having your loan payments automatically deducted from your checking or savings account. Most lenders will lower your APR by 0.25 percent or 0.50 percent just for making automatic payments.

Lenders like automatic deductions because it gives them less paperwork to do. At the same time, it's good for borrowers in a couple of ways. Not only do you get the lower APR, you don't have to worry about whether your check will arrive on time. And it's one less check you have to write.

A little prepayment goes a long way

Make an extra monthly payment on your mortgage every year, and you'll save thousands of dollars in interest. Just add a little to your check each month. Over the course of the year, it will add up to an entire extra payment.

For example, suppose you have 25 years left on a fixed-rate 30-year mortgage of $200,000 at 7-percent interest. If you add just $150 to your $1,300 monthly payment, you'll finish paying your mortgage more than five years early. Plus, you'll save almost $55,000 in interest over the course of the loan.

To find out how much you can save, visit *www.myfico.com*, and click on Credit Education. In the Calculators section, the Mortgage Payoff Calculator will figure exactly how much time and money you'll save by prepaying.

Split payment for huge savings

Another way to pay less interest is to split your monthly mortgage payment in half, and pay that amount every two weeks. By making biweekly payments instead of monthly payments, you'll make an extra mortgage payment by the end of the year.

For example, if your monthly payment is $2,000, and you pay that amount 12 times a year, that's $24,000. On the other hand, if you pay $1,000 every two weeks, or 26 times a year, you've paid $26,000 at the end of the year. That's a difference of $2,000 — an entire mortgage payment.

Check first to see if your lender charges a pre-payment fee. And don't get involved in a "biweekly prepayment program," where the lender charges you an annual management fee or an even bigger set-up fee with monthly service charges. It's not worth it.

Pick the right time to refinance

Refinancing your home can save you thousands, but only if the time is right. Before you decide to refinance, ask yourself a few questions.

- How much will I save each month?

- How much will it cost to refinance, and will I live here long enough to make it worthwhile?

- Will the new term be the same or shorter than the term is now?

Experts say if you can drop your interest rate by at least one percentage point — preferably two — and plan to stay in the house at least 18 months, refinancing may be a good idea.

The refinancing will cost roughly $2,000, so figure out how long it will take before you break even and start saving. If you move out of the house before that time, it will actually cost you more to refinance.

Try using the Mortgage Refinance Breakeven Calculator at *www.myfico.com*. It's a handy tool when you're dealing with a lot of numbers. Click on Credit Education, and look in the Calculators section to find the Mortgage Refinance Calculator. Run your figures through the calculator to find out when you would start saving if you refinanced.

Save steps and money

Refinancing your mortgage can cut your interest charges, but what about cutting the cost of refinancing? If you've refinanced once or twice before, you can knock at least $400 off the closing costs using what is called "streamlined refinancing."

Streamlined refinancing means you skip some of the steps you had to take last time you refinanced. If it's been two years or less since you refinanced, look into saving in these areas:

- Use the same attorney and lender. You will pay less in fees because they have already done the background work, and you will avoid state mortgage taxes.

- Ask your lender to use the appraisal plan from the last closing, and cut $250 off your closing costs.

- Use the plot plan from last time, and save another $150.

- Update your title insurance policy instead of writing a new one, and save from $400 to $1,000.

If you have a loan from the Federal Housing Administration (FHA) and you've kept up with payments, you can take advantage of its streamlined refinancing package.

No face-to-face meeting is required, you pay no underwriting fees, and you don't need an appraisal. You don't even have to undergo a credit check or income verification. This refinancing is available strictly to lower your monthly payments. It is ideal if your credit situation has improved since you first took out the loan.

Stay ahead of the market

One out of every three people buying a house today will borrow money with an adjustable-rate mortgage (ARM). Interest rates for an ARM are usually lower than fixed-rate mortgages — at first. But there is no guarantee market rates won't rise suddenly, and your mortgage payment will rise with them.

If the economy shows signs of inflation, go ahead and convert that ARM to a fixed rate before your monthly mortgage payments jump. It could save you money and save your house.

Smart way to slash your car payment

Refinancing isn't just for homeowners anymore. You might never have thought about it, but refinancing your auto loan could slash your monthly payment.

You should consider refinancing if interest rates have gone down since you bought the car. It's also a smart option if your credit rating has gone up because you'll be eligible for a lower rate.

Applying online can get you through the process in just 10 minutes. Visit a site like *www.eloan.com* that offers auto refinancing options. Also try *www.capitaloneautofinance.com,* where you can look at available rates and calculate what your new monthly payment might be.

To compare the rates of lenders in your area, visit *www.bankrate.com.* They will give you contact information and tell you whether each lender charges a fee.

Usually lenders do not charge fees to refinance your car loan, but you will have to pay to have your title transferred at the local Department of Motor Vehicles. The state charges anywhere from $5 to $65 to transfer the lien. That's little to pay, though, to save thousands of dollars over the life of your loan.

The table on the next page shows what you can save on a 36-month $20,000 loan by refinancing from a rate of 10.25 percent.

Pass on expensive loan insurance

Insurance is for people, not for loans. Just say "no" to anyone who offers you Credit Disability Insurance.

APR	Monthly payment	Total payments	Total savings
10.25%	$648	$23,317	$0
8.25%	$629	$22,645	$672
6.25%	$611	$21,985	$1,332
4.25%	$593	$21,337	$1,980

An Individual Credit Disability Insurance policy covers your monthly loan payment if you ever become disabled and can't make the payment yourself. Typically, the policy pays the minimum amount due up to 36 months.

With costs near $21 for every $1,000 of coverage, these policies are not worth the expense. If you already have some type of disability insurance, make sure it covers loan payments along with the rest of your expenses.

Lay off the unemployment insurance

Involuntary unemployment insurance is similar to credit disability insurance. It covers the minimum amount of your credit account payments for six to 12 months after you lose your job.

Coverage usually costs 70 cents for every $100 on the credit balance. But the policy only covers the minimum payment due, so interest adds up. You will probably wind up owing more money than you did when you had a job.

If you want peace of mind, your best bet is to put enough money for three to six months of living expenses into an emergency savings account.

Books

Read fine print on book club offers

Book clubs are like getting books by subscription. You just agree to purchase a few books during the membership period. If you want the selected title or an alternative selection, it'll be sent to your door at your request.

If you're a regular book buyer, clubs can be a convenient option to going to bookstores, and they may offer savings to boot.

Among the best-known clubs are Book of the Month Club, Doubleday Book Club, and The Literary Guild. A newcomer, but currently the most popular of them all, is Oprah's Book Club.

If you're interested in clubs for readers with special interests, visit Web sites like F+W Publications at *www.fwpublications.com/bookclubs.asp*. It features over 20 clubs ranging from gardening to science fiction.

But don't dive in with your eyes closed. These clubs also offer their share of headaches. Most arise because folks fail to look beyond those exciting introductory offers to what they're really committing themselves to. Common irritations arise from shockingly high shipping fees and the arrival of unwanted books.

Learn the ropes and get the facts before you jump for one of those "6 books for 99 cents" deals. And consider options to the clubs that require less commitment, like discount book services with mail order or online catalogs.

Members get bigger discounts

You love books. You're an avid book buyer, and you like giving them as gifts. Yet, serious book buying can be expensive.

A number of bookstores and their online counterparts offer membership clubs as a way for you to enjoy extra savings. Yes — you'll have to buy the discount card, but devoted book buyers may find the savings offset the membership price.

- Barnes & Noble's $25 annual membership fee cuts an extra 10 percent from purchases made at all Barnes & Noble, B. Dalton, Bookstar, Bookstop, Doubleday, Ink Newsstand, and Charlesbank stores, as well as online purchases at *www.bn.com*.

- For a $10 annual membership fee, Books-A-Million offers a discount card that can be used at any of its retail stores and for online purchases at *www.booksamillion.com*.

Great way to find unusual books

The Internet is the place to go for any book you could possibly want. Take advantage of the Web's exciting book-finding technology. You'll find retail and discount prices on new, used, rare, and out-of-print books — even scratch and dents. Here are a few sites to get you started.

- Abebooks.com at *www.abebooks.com*

- AddALL at *www.addall.com*

- AllBooks4Less.com at *www.allbooks4less.com*

- Amazon at *www.amazon.com*

- BookCloseouts.com at *www.bookcloseouts.com*

- BookFinder.com at *www.bookfinder.com*

- Christianbook.com at *www.christianbook.com*

- HamiltonBook.com at *www.hamiltonbook.com*

If you want to borrow, lend, and swap books for free, check out The Book Cart at *www.thebookcart.com*. You can borrow and lend paperbacks through the mail for the cost of postage and handling.

Before you buy a book, you should do two things — compare book prices and shipping and handling fees. The one thing that can undercut great online prices is high shipping and handling. Watch for promotions and special deals for reduced or free shipping.

Clever idea for collectors

Finding a rare book is what book lovers dream about. But shopping without a guide can end up costing you a fortune. Save a bundle on first editions and rare, signed, or out-of-print volumes by shopping with a

"Four books for 99 cents!" Sounds like a fantastic deal, but what comes next may take the wind out of your sails. Here's what to check before joining a book club.

✓ how long membership lasts
✓ how many books you have to buy during your membership
✓ how much the books are routinely discounted after the introductory offer
✓ how much shipping and handling will cost
✓ how you'll be notified about the next featured book — a flyer that allows you to decline the offer or the arrival of the book itself
✓ how soon you have to return a book if you decide you don't want it

trained eye. Several valuable guides can give you just the help you need.

- *Official Price Guide to Collecting Books* by Marie Tedford and Pat Goudey

- *Book Finds: How to Find, Buy, and Sell Used and Rare Books* by Ian C. Ellis

- *Pocket Guide to the Identification of First Editions* by Bill McBride

If you purchase books through a dealer, check their credentials. Organizations like Antiquarian Booksellers' Association of America at *www.abaa.org* protect consumers by monitoring their members for honesty and integrity.

Introduce yourself to Web reading

Avid readers have always enjoyed browsing bookstores and libraries for good books. Now it's time to browse digital libraries on the Internet. Think of them as huge libraries with an infinite variety of books. The best ones don't charge subscription fees or accept advertising.

Try visiting some of the old standby sites like Bartleby.com at *www.bartleby.com*, Project Gutenberg at *www.gutenberg.org*, or The Online Books Page at *http://digital.library.upenn.edu*. Another possibility is online Bible reading programs on sites like Crosswalk.com at *http://bible.crosswalk.com*.

Or use your favorite search engine and enter "books online." You can even add a qualifier if you're looking for a specific topic.

Lots of time in front of a computer can lend itself to eyestrain. Make sure your monitor is large and clear enough to let you read in comfort.

China

Smart way to spend less

Think you can't find fine china at outlet stores? Think again. Mikasa, Lenox, Noritake, Fitz & Floyd, and Royal Doulton are just a few famous brand names with outlet stores around the country.

You can save anywhere from 10 to 80 percent off retail by shopping at these factory outlets. What's more, you can buy a lot more than china at an outlet center. Make the most of your trip by:

- checking every piece of china for chips, cracks, and other defects.

- asking about the return policy, especially if you're buying it for someone else.

- making a list of must-have items, along with a budget.

- wearing a fanny pack instead of carrying a handbag to free you up for handling china.

Get VIP vouchers for favorite stores

If you are an outlet store warrior, you'll love *www.OutletBound.com*. This Web site lets you search for outlet stores and centers across the nation by brand name, category, or location.

You can even sign up for a "Shop Like a Pro" VIP voucher worth hundreds of dollars at participating outlet centers. Just fill out a short questionnaire online to receive your voucher. You will have to give Outlet Bound some personal information, such as your name, where you live, your e-mail address, and how often you visit outlet centers.

Shop from the comfort of home

Many of your favorite china makers offer special deals and discounts directly from their Web sites. You could save anywhere from 15 to 74 percent on select patterns and pieces, all while shopping from home.

So skip the middleman. Just type the name of a china manufacturer, like Mikasa, into the address line of your Web browser, then check their home page for mentions of clearance items or special deals. Or click on your favorite pattern and look for discounts off the retail price.

Start with these famous sellers, guaranteed to offer online savings.

- Lenox *www.lenox.com*

- Mikasa *www.mikasa.com*

- Royal Doulton *www.RoyalDoulton.com*

- Villeroy & Boch *www.Villeroy-Boch.com*

Clothing

The best place to hunt for a deal

Save as much as 80 percent, no matter where you shop. Get great quality, as well as low, low prices when you visit DealHunting.com. This incredible Web site offers bargains from hundreds of well-known stores in over 30 categories.

After you select a store or a category, you're immediately taken to a list of items on sale. Sometimes you're given a coupon code to enter. At other times, the site will simply let you know what's on sale. Shop at stores like Ann Taylor, Brooks Brothers, Sears, Gap, or JCPenney.

And if you're interested in other items, such as toys, electronics, cosmetics, or even gifts, this site can help you out there, too. Visit them at *www.dealhunting.com*.

Advantages of thrift store shopping

A thrift store is a great place to go for rock-bottom prices on clothes and accessories. Thrift stores are nonprofit organizations that offer previously owned items at bargain prices. They get their inventory through private donations, as well as manufacturers and retail stores.

The Salvation Army and Goodwill are both popular thrift stores, though there are others, like TVI/Value Village and Buffalo Exchange, which operate for profit. According to *Secondhand Chic* by Christa Weil, these for-profit thrift stores usually have a nicer atmosphere and are organized more like retail stores.

Weil also mentions a few pros and cons that come with thrift store shopping. The best part, of course, is the unbeatably low prices. You're not going to find cheaper clothes anywhere than you will in a thrift store.

Other advantages include their wide selection of styles and the variety of products available. They have everything from hats to shoes. You can even find brand new clothes in these shops since some retail stores now donate their unsold inventory. As a bonus, you get to support a charitable cause just by going on a shopping trip.

You should also be aware of the challenges of shopping at thrift stores. It will probably take you longer to look through all the

Resale shops the latest rage

Did you know that in the United States alone, there are more than 20,000 resale shops? On top of that, the number of resale shops in the country grows by 5 percent every year.

According to the National Association of Resale and Thrift Shops (NARTS), the resale industry is growing because people appreciate buying clothing and furniture for a quarter of the original price.

Experts say you can buy a designer suit for one-tenth of its retail price and completely furnish a room for under $1,000 by shopping at resale, thrift, and consignment stores.

merchandise simply because the clothes aren't usually organized into sizes or styles.

You may also run into a problem when you decide to try something on and realize there aren't any fitting rooms. Most bargain hunters, however, are happy to put forth a little effort for the savings they find.

Save a bundle on classy clothes

At consignment shops, you can buy classy clothes at below wholesale prices. Consignment shops sell higher quality clothing than thrift stores, carry a greater selection than garage sales, and offer deep discounts over retail. They're even better than outlet stores, especially for specialty items like formal wear and business suits. At consignment prices, you can save a bundle and look great, too.

Here are a few of the fastest-growing markets for consignment shops:

✓ furniture
✓ clothing for men, teens, and plus-sizes
✓ sporting goods
✓ music
✓ computer products
✓ toys
✓ home decor

You'll find the nicest items near the register or in the window. Some shops charge more than others or generally carry pricier merchandise. Shop around till you find one that fits your taste and your budget. Then visit it every couple of weeks to get first dibs on the latest deals. Become a regular and befriend the manager and employees. They may be more willing to haggle with you, help you find what you need, or hold certain items.

Check your yellow pages under "consignment," "secondhand," or "clothing, used" to find stores near you. Or visit the National Association of Resale and Thrift Shops (NARTS) on the Internet at *www.narts.org*. Here you can search for resale, consignment, or thrift stores by state, zip code, area code, type of merchandise you want to buy, or any combination of these.

Good advice for outlet shoppers

Outlet malls may seem like bargain heaven at first, but keep an eye out for full-priced merchandise in disguise. Some outlet stores sell their products at full price. Find out how much the clothes would cost at a retail store before you buy them so you know exactly how much you're saving.

Another trick to look for is "cut-ups." Rather than selling discounted retail clothing, the outlet sells last year's leftover fabric that's been cut to look like new styles. It's not the same product you would get at a retail store, but if you don't mind, then go ahead and take advantage of the lower price.

> An outlet store sells clothing directly from a manufacturer at lower prices than a retail store. It's owned by the manufacturer and only sells that manufacturer's products. An outlet mall is a collection of outlet stores in one shopping area.

Watch out for liquidators posing as outlets. Rather than selling the same clothes at reduced prices, liquidators sell discontinued or slightly damaged merchandise from several different companies. It's basically the stuff the manufacturer couldn't sell because no one wanted it. Make sure you're buying a quality product before you get swept away by the price tag.

Smart catalog shopping

Look through a favorite catalog and rip out the page of any item you're interested in. After that, pull out the order form and throw away the rest of the catalog. Wait a day or maybe even a week, then look over your torn out pages again. If you still want an item, you'll know this isn't an impulse purchase, and you can spend the money in good conscience. In addition, since you're only looking at a few pages, you won't be tempted to buy other items in the catalog.

How to talk the price down

Price tags aren't set in stone. It takes a little courage, but you can bring down the price of secondhand clothes just by haggling a little with the salesperson. They're more flexible than you'd expect. You may need to get over any fears of seeming pushy or cheap, but once you get going, you'll save money left and right. Here are a few tips to remember:

- Ask for a discount if there's a flaw, like a stain or tear on the garment, no matter how small. If the product is even slightly defective, you deserve a reduction in price. Salespeople want you to leave happy and come again, so they'll usually give you the discount if you ask.

- Use your buying power. Request a bulk rate if you buy a lot of pieces at once, or if you buy something expensive, ask them to throw in a free gift. Say you might consider purchasing this really nice gown if they add the handbag to the package. You could walk away with a bunch of free stuff.

- Be friendly with the salespeople. You'll be relieved to find out bargaining doesn't have to involve yelling and angry comments. Develop a good working relationship with the people at the secondhand store so they realize you're not trying to be difficult — you're just trying to get a good deal.

Get discounts with store credit cards

You can save a lot of money with department store credit cards if you use them wisely. Department stores give you additional discounts on purchases when you use their store credit card. Some stores also invite you to private sales where the store is only open to employees and cardholders for a short time. Just remember to pay off your balance every month, and never use the card to buy anything outside of your monthly budget. Department store cards have huge interest rates.

Keep an eye on seasonal discounts

Schedule your big shopping trips so they coincide with big sales. Wait until mid-summer to buy warm weather clothes and bathing suits at Fourth of July sales. If you're really patient, get your beachwear at the Labor Day sales in September when it's on clearance. The same goes for winter clothing. Retail stores stock up on winter clothes before Christmas and then mark them down by 50 percent through January. By March, you can get a winter coat for a fraction of what you would have paid the season before.

2 ways to curb impulse buying

You can stay on budget by avoiding impulse buying. Studies have shown that impulse buys make up 27 to 62 percent of all purchases made in department stores.

Save money by making a list and only buying what's on the list. If you see something else you like, wait until you get home and add it to the list for next time so you'll have time to think before you buy the item.

If you don't have a list but do have a spending limit, bring only the amount of money you're willing to spend in cash and leave your checkbook and credit cards at home. That way, you can't go over budget.

Never pay full price for shoes

You need new shoes. Don't worry. There are good deals all over the place. You just have to find them. Follow the sales and make use of coupons, and you'll never have to pay full price again.

Always look for quality before you look at price. Quality shoes may cost a little more, but they'll last longer, which means you won't have to keep buying new shoes. When your shoes wear out, have them repaired. It's cheaper to replace the sole or the heel of a well-made shoe that's comfortable and fits you well than to toss it out and buy a new pair.

Be kind to your feet and buy the proper shoes for different activities. Have enough pairs in your closet so you can switch them every day. Wearing the same pair of shoes day in and day out isn't good for your feet — or your shoes.

If you know the style and size of shoe you want, you can save money by buying brand name shoes online. The following companies offer sale prices over the Internet. Just be sure to check the shipping and handling charges so you don't spend more online than you would have originally.

- Eastland *www.eastlandshoe.com*

- Florsheim *www.florsheim.com*

- Nike *www.nike.com*

Identifying quality clothing

Quality clothes look better, fit better, and last longer. Buying cheap clothes and replacing them when they fall apart can be expensive. Spending a little more money on clothes you can wear again and again will save you money in the long run.

Shop for clothes that are well-made. When you see a piece you like, inspect it for quality workmanship before you buy it. There are lots of clues that tell you whether a garment is made well. Check the hem and seams to make sure they're well stitched, and look for telltale signs like holes and snags. Any

Make your clothes last longer

Take good care of your clothes so you won't have to spend money replacing them. Here are a few tips to get you started:

- Buy good-quality clothes.
- Fold, rather than hang, delicate fabrics and knits so they don't stretch.
- Invest in quality wooden or plastic hangers. No wire hangers!
- Don't store clothes in plastic dry cleaning bags.
- Hang slacks from the waist on hangers with clips.

- Sort laundry loads by color type — light or dark — and wash them in the recommended temperature to preserve colors.
- Take care of stains immediately. Blot them. Don't rub. Then have them treated within 24 to 48 hours.
- Dry clean clothes once toward the end of every season unless, of course, they're soiled or stained. Clothes may shrink if they're dry cleaned too much.

patterns, like plaids or stripes, should match across seams, lapels, and between pieces, like a suit jacket and pants.

If the item has a zipper, the teeth of the zipper shouldn't touch your skin. Pockets should be even and have clean stitching wherever they connect with the garment. Quality buttons made of brass, horn, or pearl are a sign of a quality garment, so keep that in mind as well.

Remember to look inside, too. The interior of the garment should look as good as the outside, with the seams cleanly finished rather than rough and frayed. Jackets, pants, and skirts should have a lining on the inside if they're made of a winter fabric, like wool. Otherwise, you'll be uncomfortable when you wear them.

The most important thing to look for in clothes is the fabric. Learn to pick out quality fabrics by going to a department store or fabric store. Get to know how cotton, wool, silk, and cashmere feel and how they're different so you can identify them when you shop. Every fabric has its advantages and disadvantages.

Cottons and linens are cooler because they breathe better, but they've been known to develop holes after a while. Silk drapes beautifully, but it requires high maintenance. Look at the care label on the garment to see what it's made of and what kind of care it needs. The more you know about the garment, the more confident you can be that it's a worthwhile purchase.

A new detergent may save you money. Tide Coldwater gets clothes just as clean in cold water as most detergents do in warm water. Washing your clothes in cold water saves a lot of energy, which saves you money on your utility bills. According to the Alliance to Save Energy, using cold water to do your laundry can save you up to $63 a year.

Update old clothes to latest styles

Chances are a small change to an out-of-style outfit hanging in your closet could make it fashionable again. If you're handy with a needle and thread, you can update your wardrobe with a few minor alterations. In fact, even paying for an alteration can be cheaper than buying new clothes. Think about putting in or removing shoulder pads or changing buttons and other trim. Something as simple as raising or lowering a hemline can make those clothes stylish again.

When to call in the pros

Dry cleaning can give your clothes a longer life. They won't shrink or bleed as much when they're dry-cleaned, and dry cleaning can get rid of oily stains that don't come out in the wash. Also, have your clothes dry-cleaned if you think they might lose their shape or their colors in the washing machine.

Not all clothes with the "Dry Clean Only" care label have to be dry-cleaned. You can wash some garments in cold water by hand with a gentle cleanser. Then lay them out flat on towels to dry so they don't lose their shape.

Collectibles

Uncover coin collecting secrets

Is that old penny really worth $100? Find out using free information about coin collecting. The United States Mint — the ultimate coin authority — offers free information for both avid and amateur coin collectors on its Web site, *www.usmint.gov*. Click on Consumer Awareness for valuable tips on how to tell real collectible U.S. coins from fakes. Or click on About Us and go to the Collector's Corner for free advice on finding, buying, and caring for your coins.

Free newsletters from coin traders and collecting societies provide price lists and insider's advice. Coin dealer Ellesmere Numismatics puts out *The Winning Edge* newsletter, a widely circulated price list guide for rare U.S. coins. Best of all, it's free for the first six months. Just call 800-426-3343 or subscribe online at *www.ellesmerecoin.com*.

Sign up now, and they will also send you two free booklets on coin collecting, *638 Coins with a Fundamental Reason to Rise in Value* and *The Nine Most Common Mistakes Made by Rare Coin Investors*.

Your local library is also a helpful resource for valuing your coins. Put a price on your money with these books.

- *A Guide Book of United States Coins* by R. S. Yeoman (updated yearly)

- *The Standard Catalog of World Coins* from Krause Publications

Best bet for antique bargains

Flea markets are like giant indoor yard sales with vendors hocking the usual toys, tools, and clothing. But they're also treasure troves of art, antique furniture and jewelry, and other collectible wares.

By shopping these bazaars, you can decorate like royalty — without spending a fortune. Make the most of flea market finds with this advice from *Secrets to Affordable Antiques*.

Learn to spot hot collectibles

The more you know about collectible items, the less likely you are to be swindled by a "fake" and the more likely you are to buy and sell at the right price.

Educate yourself on the collectibles you love, starting with these resources.

- Your local library or bookstore will have books explaining what makes furniture, glass, and other items valuable, as well as a few pricing guides for serious collectors.

- Visit the official Web sites for brand name collectibles. For Barbie, try *www.barbiecollector.com*, or for Hummel figurines, go to *www.mihum el.com*. For other items, type the name of your collectible in the Internet address line and see where the Web takes you.

- Join clubs and organizations specializing in the items you treasure, like the American Political Items Collectors online at *www.apic.us*.

- Look for monogrammed flatware. Most people prefer plain pieces, leaving you super deals on real initialed silver.

- Buy antique furniture in single pieces. Sets cost more money. Even George and Martha Washington did not own matching bedroom furniture.

- Pay for the art, not for the name. Buy unsigned paintings for the best value, or pictures by little-known artists.

- Hang pictures with tears or damaged frames above the stairs, over a bookcase, or elsewhere high on the wall. It's hard to see flaws from a few feet away.

- Touch up scarred frames with matching acrylic paint.

- Try the same technique with chipped, cracked vases, china, and ceramics. Display them high on shelves and turn the damaged sides to the wall.

- Repair tears in canvas or paper with a little masking tape across the picture's back and hang it high.

- Don't shop for collectibles in the town where they were made. Pottery, furniture, and other antiques are always more expensive in their hometowns.

Quick tips for flea market shopping

Not every flea market item is a steal, but savvy collectors know how to sniff out the best deals. This guide can help you walk away happy, too.

- Arrive early for the largest selection. The best deals disappear early.

- If you need a particular item, find out how much it sells for in retail stores before you hit the flea market.

- Inspect items carefully for chips, missing pieces, or tears before you buy. Generally you can't return a flea market find.

- Before you spring for that antique table and chairs, make sure you have a way to get them home. Most dealers don't deliver.

- Find a stall you especially like? Get the vendor's card and ask how often she sells there, when she gets in new pieces, and where else she exhibits. You may want to visit her again.

- Walk away from an item you aren't sure about buying. If it still calls to you from two aisles away, go back for it. Better yet, if business is slow for that seller, wait until the day's end when he will be happy to make a deal.

- Shop around at several vendors before you buy. Dealers occasionally buy from the same wholesale sources, so some may offer the same goods at different prices.

Insider's guide to online auctions

Internet auctions work a lot like regular auctions — Yahoo, eBay, Amazon.com and other virtual auction houses act as proxies between buyers and sellers, awarding goods to the highest bidders.

- You can buy anything under the sun at mega auction sites, but don't sell the small ones short. Large auction sites, like eBay, don't guarantee an item's authenticity, but some specialized Internet auction sites do. You may also have more luck finding what you want.

- Read every site's Terms of Service agreement and Privacy Policy so you understand the rules sellers and buyers play by. For example, all sales are final at some, while others let you return goods. Some let you withdraw your bid, others don't. Know the terms before you shop.

- Set a ceiling on how much you are willing to pay for an item, and stick to it. Don't get caught up in the bidding frenzy and spend more than you had planned.

- Check the piece's going price at stores and recent auctions before you bid on it to avoid overpaying.

- Read all the specific information the seller gives about an object. Look for details about its condition and whether any pieces are missing. You can complain to the auction company and, in some cases, return the item if the seller misled you.

Win online auctions with ease

Online auctions, like eBay, let you choose from a huge selection of items and, generally, pay less for them than you would anywhere else. Some people even make a living buying goods at Internet auctions and reselling them retail.

Competition can be stiff, so be prepared to fight for what you want — at least until it costs more than you can spend. Try these bid-winning tips from *eBay the Smart Way*.

- Refresh the Web page often during the final minutes of an auction so you can see the latest bid. Go to the auction page for the item you want to buy, and click the Refresh button on your Internet browser.

- Bid the Bay Way. Choose how much you're willing to pay for something, then ask eBay to bid for you, up to that amount. You can even set the increment, how much eBay raises your bid each time, by 50 cents, $1, $5, and so on. Each time someone bids higher than you, eBay will raise your bid above theirs by the increment you set, up to your maximum, saving you both time and money.

- Use the 10-cents difference trick. eBay forces you to raise your bid by at least a certain dollar amount each time, usually a round number, like $1 or $5. Increase yours by that amount plus 10 cents to get a jump on your competition and raise your odds of winning the auction.

- Become a Sniper. Sniper software lets you swoop in and bid at the last minute, with the idea that if you raise the bid say 15 or 30 seconds before the auction closes, you will win because no one else will have time to counter. You can buy Snipe software on eBay or subscribe to a Web service that will Snipe for you.

No strategy guarantees you a win, but auctions are supposed to be fun, right? Win or lose, always enjoy the game.

Protect yourself while bidding online

The Federal Trade Commission (FTC) hears lots of complaints about online auctions every year. Most involve sellers who fail to ship items, ship them late, or falsely advertise their wares, while some deal with fake electronic payment services and con men posing as legitimate dealers.

You don't have to be a victim. Follow this advice from the FTC.

- Read the auction site's Terms of Service agreement to see if they offer money-back guarantees, free insurance, complaint handling, and other protections for buyers.

- Get more info. E-mail or call the seller and ask if the item comes with any warranties or service agreements, what types of payment they accept, who pays for shipping and how much it will cost, and what their return policy is. Don't bid until you get answers.

- Check out the seller. Many sites have feedback ratings where people who bought items from a seller rate their service. Use these as guidelines, but don't depend on them exclusively. Get a seller's phone number, and call it to make sure it works before you send them money.

- Pay with a credit card if possible. It protects you the most from fraudulent dealers and incorrect transactions. If the seller does not accept credit cards, consider paying through a reputable payment or escrow service, like PayPal.

- Protect your identity. Thoroughly research the seller and payment or escrow service, if you are using one, before you give out your bank account, credit card, or Social Security number. Call the Better Business Bureau and state attorney general both where you live and where the seller and payment service are located and ask if they have complaints filed against them.

Should you have problems with a purchase, try to work it out directly with the seller, payment service, or auction Web site. If you can't get satisfaction, file a complaint with your state's attorney general, consumer protection agency, and Better Business Bureau, and call the Federal Trade Commission toll-free at 877-382-4357.

Sell online without a computer

You no longer need a computer to sell items on eBay. Now, a company called AuctionDrop will do it for you, and even pack and ship it to the buyer.

Call them toll-free at 866-376-7486 or fill out a form online at *www.auctiondrop.com*. Then drop off your item at one of the company's 3,700 drop-off locations. AuctionDrop photographs your item, puts it on eBay, and ships it to the buyer. They tell you when it sells, collect their commission, and send a check to you for the rest.

It's always a good idea to read the fine print before jumping in. Every auction house charges a commission, but you'll pay a premium for this service. AuctionDrop keeps 38 percent of the first $200 dollars you make from the sale, 30 percent of the next $300, and 20 percent of anything over $500, plus a small commission they pay to eBay. In some cases, they may charge a flat fee. You would pay a much smaller commission — and keep more of your own money — if you sell your goods yourself on eBay.

Check this chart to see how much you would really earn selling through AuctionDrop versus on your own at eBay, and decide if the cost is worth the convenience.

If your item sells for	Using AuctionDrop, you earn	Selling it yourself on eBay, you earn
$250	$147.50	$242.50
$500	$319.63	$485.63
$1,000	$705.88	$971.88

Computers

■ Hardware

'Downgrading' saves you money

You wouldn't buy the latest, greatest food processor to make a peanut butter and jelly sandwich. Similarly, you don't need to buy a state-of-the-art computer if you're only going to use it for basic functions, like word processing, surfing the Internet, and sending e-mail.

Luckily, many stores or manufacturers let you configure your own system. It's a good way to save money on some areas and improve your computer in others. You can opt for a slower processor, smaller hard drive, and less memory than the top-of-the-line models. As long as the computer meets your needs, it's OK to downgrade.

Escape the name-brand trap

Instead of buying a high-priced computer from one of the top brand names, consider clones. You can save lots of money without giving up quality. Think of clones, or white box PCs, as generic versions of name-brand models. They're basically the same, without the fancy label.

Often, you can configure your own system, choosing from a wide selection of components. This is probably best for when you want an unusual configuration with specific parts.

While clones can cost considerably less, they do come with some concerns and drawbacks. For instance, they may not come with as much software or technical support as the major brands. Having to buy an operating system and software could offset any savings on the machine. Make sure you'll be able to return the system if there are problems.

Look for white box PCs in local computer shops. This makes it convenient when you need repairs or upgrades. You can also go through online dealers. Either way, check out the company first. You don't want a fly-by-night outfit that can go out of business at any time.

Save up to 80 percent off retail

You've heard the expression "good as new." Buy a refurbished computer, and you'll get one that may be even better. Not only do you get a quality computer with as much power as you need, you can also save a lot of money.

Refurbished computers come in all shapes and sizes. While the computer might have been returned because of a slight defect, often it's something much less serious. Maybe it had a cosmetic blemish or perhaps the previous owner simply opened the box before deciding he didn't want it. Demonstration models and overstocked items may also be considered refurbished. No matter what the problem, the computer has been fixed and cleaned up for resale.

When buying refurbished items, you need to take some precautions. Make sure you still get a warranty and access to technical support in case something goes wrong. Also make sure you know what's included — you don't want to find out later that your computer doesn't come with a monitor or an operating system.

Dell Inspiron 1150 Notebook	New	Refurbished
Processor speed	2.80GHz	2.80GHz
Operating system	Windows XP	Windows XP
Memory	256 MB	256 MB
Hard drive	60 GB	60 GB
CD/DVD drive	24X	24X
Cost	$1,127	$730

You also want to buy from trusted sources. Your best bet is to buy directly from manufacturers, like Dell, that stand behind their refurbished merchandise. Go to *www.dell.com* to buy from its factory outlet. You can also buy refurbished Dell computers from *www.dfsdirectsales.com*. Other sites that offer refurbished computers include *www.refurbdepot.com, www.cdw.com,* and *www.outletcomputer.com.*

Keep in mind that with refurbished machines you can't configure your own system like you can when you shop for a new computer. But, if you shop around, you should be able to find a computer that suits your needs.

Easy way to dig up rebates

There's nothing better than getting money back after you buy something pricey, like a computer. Go to your favorite search engine, like Google, and enter the brand name of the computer you're eyeing and the word "rebate." You'll get links to Web sites that offer rebate information you can print or download.

Uncover hidden printer expenses

When is the cheapest printer not really the cheapest printer? More often than you think. Here are some of the hidden costs to watch out for when shopping for a printer.

- Ink or toner. This is where the printer companies get you. They can sell the printer dirt cheap, but make their money back — and more — by charging a lot for this essential item. Consider these expenses when comparing printer costs. Some laser printers, like those made by Samsung, come with a toner-saver button. This feature increases toner capacity 40 percent by using the minimum amount of toner to print each page.

- Paper. The price of plain paper will be the same no matter what printer you buy. But don't forget about photo paper, transparencies, and other special paper that might vary from printer to printer.

- Repairs and service. A cheap printer might require more repairs, which can offset any savings you pocketed. Also keep in mind any regular maintenance you'll need to do, such as replacing an imaging drum in a laser printer.

You'll also want to take into account resolution and speed. A cheap printer isn't much of a bargain if it produces blurry pages or takes too long to do its job.

Reduce printing costs with refill kits

Paper may come from trees, but printer cartridges sure don't grow on them. Luckily, there's a money-saving alternative to buying cartridge after expensive cartridge. Refill your cartridge — and your wallet — with an ink refill kit.

The idea behind ink refill kits is simple. Instead of tossing your empty cartridge, you recycle it. Just refill it with some new ink, and it's as good as new. You should be able to refill the same

Printer cartridge	Black	Color
New brand-name cartridge	$29.99	$32.99
Compatible cartridge	$12.95	$18.95
Ink refill kit	$9.95	$14.95

cartridge at least 3 to 5 times, and maybe even as many as 8 to 10 times. It depends on the condition of the cartridge and printhead. Make sure to refill your empty cartridge right away. Otherwise, the remaining ink may dry and clog the nozzle.

Follow all refilling instructions carefully. One big drawback of refilling your printer cartridges yourself is the potential for messiness. One product, called Inke Inkjet Auto Refill System, makes the refilling process easier and less messy because you never come in direct contact with the ink. Just put the cartridge in one slot and a tank of ink in the other and push a button. Inke only works with certain print cartridges. For more information, go to *www.inkeinkjet.com*.

Not all refill kits are created equal. Watch out for shoddy knock-offs. In general, refill kits work better for text and basic graphics than for photos. But it's possible to find high-quality refill ink.

Because certain manufacturers rig their cartridges so they can't be refilled, you might have to buy compatible cartridges. Often, the same companies that sell refill kits also sell these bargain cartridges. Make sure you know the exact model of your printer. You'll need this information to buy the right ink or compatible cartridges.

Some online sources for ink refill kits include *www.atlanticinkjet.com*, *www.inkusa.com*, and *www.inkjetcartridge.com*. Atlantic Inkjet promises savings of up to 75 percent on their compatible inkjet cartridges, while InkjetCartridge.com features a free support line you can call if you're having trouble using its ink refill kit.

Find the link to cheap ink

Save up to 80 percent on printer cartridges by shopping online. Many Web sites sell replacement cartridges, which work just as well as the brand names but at a fraction of the cost. Make sure you know your printer model so you can find a compatible cartridge.

Check out the savings at sites like *www.123inkjets.com*, *www.abcco.net*, *www.inksell.com*, *www.pacificink.com*, and *www.printpal.com*. Comparison shop, making sure to factor in shipping and handling. Some companies even offer free shipping. You'll never pay top dollar again. Many merchants make buying from them a no-risk offer — satisfaction guaranteed or your money back.

Extend the life of your cartridge

If you do a lot of printing, you use a lot of ink and that costs a lot of money. But now there's a way to control how much ink you use. By extending the life of each cartridge, you can save hundreds of dollars in ink costs over the life of your printer.

Just buy InkSaver software. It works with all inkjet printers and all types of ink, including refill kits. You can adjust InkSaver for a maximum savings of 75 percent. A handy feature called Ink Savings Estimator even lets you know how much money you save at various settings. Best of all, although you use less ink, your resolution doesn't suffer. You can buy InkSaver for $34.99 at *www.inksaver.com*, where you can also download a free 15-day trial.

■ Software

Sample software with shareware

Even if you get a great deal on a computer, you still need software to make it do anything. And that can get expensive. That's where shareware comes in.

Shareware is software you download and try for free. If you like it, you pay a fee to keep it. Freeware is similar to shareware, except there's never a fee. Either way, you pay less than you would for packaged software from major vendors.

You can find shareware for virtually anything, from antivirus software to organizational tools to games. It's a great way to sample software and save money. However, you need to keep some things in mind when dealing with shareware — or anything else you download from the Internet.

Beware of unwanted extras. Software can come with hidden surprises, like spyware and adware. With adware, you get bombarded with ads when you open an application. It's the price you pay for cheap or free software. Spyware is even more sinister. It tracks which Web sites you visit on the Internet and reports back to advertisers, who can then target you more efficiently.

Viruses can do even more damage. While some just display words or an image on your screen, others can change, delete, or damage files in your computer. Some might even keep your computer from working at all. Like spyware and adware, viruses can sneak into your system when you download something from the Internet.

To protect yourself, do your homework. Read several reviews of products before downloading them, and download only from reputable sites. Also, read the entire software agreement to uncover any mention of spyware or adware. Of course, you'll also want the latest antivirus software guarding your computer.

Download only programs you really need. Check if your computer comes with an application to do what you're trying to do before resorting to shareware. And make sure you can easily uninstall the program if you don't want it.

Remember, shareware means not having to share your wealth with big software companies. Just make sure the software you download isn't "sharing" an unwanted surprise with you.

Sign up for cheap computer classes

Knowledge is power — especially when it comes to computers. It's amazing what you can do with today's technology. It's also amazing how inexpensive it can be to learn about it. Here are some places to check for low-cost computer classes.

- Libraries may offer free computer training. They also provide free use of online computers so you can practice your skills. Call your local library and see what it offers.

- Computer stores, like Apple Store, sometimes provide free classes or workshops. You can also pay for classes for more in-depth learning.

- Internet cafes, places where you pay to use the Internet, may also feature free or low-cost computer classes.

- Colleges and universities usually have continuing education departments that offer low-cost computer classes for beginners. If you're a senior citizen, you might be able to enroll in computer classes in the regular curriculum at reduced rates or even for free.

- Learning centers provide a great environment for getting up to speed. SeniorNet, which has over 200 centers in the United States, Europe, and Japan, teaches folks over 50 basic and advanced computer skills. Small classes, small fees, and hands-on training make this program a success. Go to *www.seniornet.org* or call 415-495-4990 to find a learning center near you.

Check local senior centers and recreation departments, as well as YMCA and YWCA programs.

- A tutor gives you valuable one-on-one instruction. Hire a computer-savvy person to help you learn at your own pace. College students, friends, neighbors, even your own grandchildren might make good tutors. You can probably negotiate a fair price.

- Online tutorials let you use your computer to learn more about computers. To begin, you just need to know how to get on the Internet. Choose from a wide range of topics and ability levels. Go step-by-step, at your own pace, from the comfort of your own home. Web sites such as *www.seniornet.org* or *www.thirdage.com* offer free tutorials.

Pros and cons of printing photos

You can often save money by doing things yourself rather than paying others to do them for you. But when it comes to printing your own digital photos at home instead of paying to have prints made, the savings is questionable. You might save money ... but you might not.

The cost of printing your own digital pictures can add up quickly. For starters, a digital camera capable of taking film-quality photos will cost at least $900.

You'll probably also need to buy software, like Adobe Photoshop, that lets you edit, touch up, and otherwise tweak your pictures before printing them.

And, of course, you'll need a good photo printer, which can cost anywhere from $150 to well over $500. Along with the printer, you'll need a constant supply of color ink and photo paper.

On the other hand, if you opt to pay for prints, you need to pay a processing fee, usually about 29 cents per print, plus shipping. Of course, you'll still need the digital camera.

If you prefer traditional film photos, you can save a lot of money on the camera, but you'll need to buy rolls of film and pay to get them developed.

For most casual photographers, an elaborate home printing setup is probably not worth the hassle and expense. It's easier — and likely cheaper — just to get prints made of your digital photos. Or even stick to film for now.

Share your photos with an online album

Many of the same companies that make prints of digital photos, such as Ofoto, Shutterfly, and Snapfish, also give you the option to create online photo albums. This allows you to share your pictures for free with family and friends.

Keith Rokoske, a Web application developer from North Carolina, takes advantage of this high-tech idea to save money.

"I've used online photo albums quite a bit. It's an excellent, quick, and low-effort way to allow friends and family anywhere in the world to view your latest photographs," Keith says.

"It seems like I post them every time we take a vacation or some major event occurs — a big snowstorm, class reunion, etc. Because I spend so much time on the computer, digital photography has essentially replaced ordering prints."

Give an online photo album service a try. It's a big change from the old days and a big improvement on your finances.

"The amount of money, and time, that I save by using an online album service is remarkable," Keith says. "Instead of creating a limited amount of photos that I'd then have to mail to individuals, I can post as many photos as I'd like and distribute them to everyone I want to see them. My 96-year-old grandmother has even looked at some of my online photo albums!"

But, if you do a lot of printing, an expensive home setup might be worth it in the long run. You won't be spending money on film, developing or processing charges, or shipping. As an added bonus, you'll get your pictures instantly.

Go online for quality, low-cost prints

Thanks to digital technology, now it's easier than ever to snap photographs, instantly view them, and e-mail them to friends and family.

But chances are you still want hard copies of your photos. There's nothing like flipping through family photo albums or rummaging through boxes of old pictures to bring back memories.

With online digital printing services, you can get quality prints for peanuts. Just get your pictures to the service's Web site, either by uploading them with special software, e-mailing them, or simply dragging and dropping the pictures from your desktop. Then place your order.

Here's a quick look at four online digital printing services. Prices are for 4x6 prints with standard United States Postal Service shipping.

- Shutterfly, *www.shutterfly.com*, offers prints for 29 cents. Shipping costs $1.79 for 1 to 10 prints and up to $14.99 for 251 to 300 prints. You can save more with a prepaid print plan. Get 100 prints for $24 (24 cents each), 200 prints for $44 (22 cents each), or 500 prints for $99 (just 20 cents each). As a bonus, you get 15 free prints when you join.

- Ofoto, *www.ofoto.com*, is owned by Kodak and charges 25 cents per print. Shipping ranges from $1.49 for 1 to 10 prints to $14.99 for 250 to 299 prints.

- Snapfish, *www.snapfish.com*, features prints for just 19 cents. Shipping starts at 99 cents for 1 to 5 prints. Add 49 cents for each additional 10 prints. Prepaid plans let you save even more. Buy 150 prints for $27 (18 cents each), 300 prints for $51 (17 cents each), or 600 prints for $90 (15 cents each). Create an account and you'll get 20 free prints.

- XPPhoto, *www.xpphoto.com*, charges only 17 cents per print. Expect to pay $1.49 in shipping for 1 to 20 prints, up to $8.99 for 318 or more prints.

■ Internet services

Pay less for Internet service

In Hollywood, big stars command big salaries. In the world of Internet service providers, the same logic applies. Big names, like AOL, MSN, and Earthlink, cost up to $23.90 a month for dial-up service.

But just as you can find plenty of good movies without big stars, you can get quality Internet access without paying steep monthly fees. Cheaper options include Juno or NetZero for $9.95 a month or Mailaka for $6.95.

Good places to look for cheap national or local Internet service providers include *www.thelist.com*, *www.all-free-isp.com*, and *www.findanisp.com*.

Some companies may still offer free Internet service — but these arrangements may not be true bargains. Be prepared to be bombarded with ads and to sacrifice speed, reliability, live customer service, and privacy.

Bundle services for big savings

Christmas isn't the only time you find a pleasant surprise in a package. When you combine your Internet, cable, and phone services, you can save 30 percent or more.

Internet services	Dial-up	DSL	Cable
Monthly charge	$9.95 - $26.00	$49.00	$49.00
Second phone line	$20 per month	NA	NA
Total	$29.95 - $46.00	$49.00	$49.00

It makes paying bills easier, too, since you just send one check to one company. Big cable companies, like Comcast and Cablevision, offer these deals.

Check your Yellow Pages for cable providers and ask about any available packages. You can also go to the National Cable & Telecommunications Association's Web site at *www.ncta.com* for links to your state's providers.

Compare prices and make sure you'll get good use out of all the services. It also helps to know if your home has existing wiring and which kind because this can affect installation fees.

Ring In savings with online caller ID

Tired of missing telephone calls while you surf the Internet with your dial-up connection? Instead of paying more for cable, DSL, or even a second phone line, consider an Internet answering machine.

For just under $4 a month, you can get a service like CallWave or BuzMe. These services notify you of incoming calls, record voice messages, and even let you take calls without losing your Internet connection. Both services offer free 30-day trials. Go to *www.callwave.com* or *www.buzme.com* for more information.

Enjoy e-mail for free

With e-mail, keeping in touch with friends and family has never been easier. Or cheaper. In fact, you should never pay for e-mail. There are too many freebies out there. Here are a few of the many free e-mail services available.

- Hotmail, Microsoft's free e-mail program, is the most popular. Sign up at *www.hotmail.com*.

- Yahoo! also provides a popular and easy-to-use free e-mail program at *http://mail.yahoo.com*.

- Gmail, Google's e-mail program, features an innovative way of sorting your mail and great search capabilities. Check it out at *www.gmail.com*.

- Hushmail, as its name implies, offers the most privacy because it uses encryption. Go to *www.hushmail.com* for more information.

- Mail2World, a relatively new service, has storage and features to match the big boys. Learn more at *www.mail2world.com*.

Dental care

Volunteer for free dental work

Participate in dental clinical trials, and you could not only get free dental care, you might even get paid for your time. The government sponsors many dental trials through the National Institute of Dental and Craniofacial Research (NIDCR). Often, they look for people with specific dental problems to participate in their studies.

If you qualify, they may treat your condition for free or at a very low cost. Sometimes, they even reimburse you for expenses, like travel, child care, meals, and lodging.

You can visit the NIDCR Web site at *www.nidcr.nih.gov* and click on NIDCR Studies Seeking Patients to see which trials need volunteers, or call them at 301-496-4261 and ask what research studies you qualify for. You can also write to them for information (see the next page for the address). Just be sure to include your contact information.

Private companies, like Thomson CenterWatch, also conduct dental clinical trials, and they may pay you to participate. Visit *www.centerwatch.com* and click on Trial Listings, then Dental/Maxillofacial Surgery for a list of studies looking for volunteers. Or you can call CenterWatch at 617-856-5900.

Contact: National Institute of Dental and
            Craniofacial Research
            Office of Communication and Health Education
            45 Center Drive
            Building 45, Room 4AS-19
            Bethesda, MD 20892

Free fillings, dentures, and cleanings

Medicare only covers dental care under rare circumstances, and it never covers routine care, like cleanings. Neither does Medicaid, unless your state specifically offers dental coverage under their program.

Thankfully, you have another option. You can get free and discounted dental work through a remarkable government program dentists hate. The Bureau of Primary Health Care, a branch of the U.S. Department of Health and Human Services, works with health centers around the country to offer quality health care to low-income people on a sliding fee scale. The cost is based on your income, which means anyone can afford it. You will receive care even if you can't pay.

Participating health centers provide a number of services, including cleanings, fluoride treatments, fillings, bridges, extractions, dentures, and other dental care, all performed by licensed dentists and hygienists.

Contact your local health department. You can find their phone number in the blue pages of your telephone book. Tell them you are interested in low-income health services and mention the kind of service you need. They can refer you to a nearby health center and get you started on the paperwork. You can also look up participating health centers near you on the Internet at *www.ask.hrsa.gov/pc*.

Dental schools offer reduced rates

Letting a dental student drill your tooth may not sound pleasant, but it could save you loads of money. Dental schools frequently offer low-cost services to people willing to let students do the work. Don't worry — a trained and licensed dentist closely supervises the students.

Check the yellow pages for your state's dental association. They can direct you to dental schools and clinics offering dental care at reduced rates. You can also get a list of dental schools on the Internet. Go to the National Institute of Dental and Craniofacial Research's Web page at *www.nidcr.nih.gov* and click on Finding Dental Care.

Treat yourself to a free dinner out

Don't waste time waiting for coupons to arrive in the newspaper. Get the deals you want now — online. Many Web sites offer coupons galore. Just choose your favorites.

Here's how it works. Popular restaurants, like Shoneys and Red Lobster, occasionally offer free meals and gift cards for a limited time. To find these deals, visit sites like *www.aplusfreestuff.com/food.shtml* or *www.mychoicerewards.com/info.*

A word of caution — you may have to share some personal information and participate in a marketing promotion or survey to get your freebies. Be sure to read their privacy policy and terms-and-conditions pages before submitting any personal information.

Be an early bird to get a meal deal

Schedule a late lunch or an early dinner, and save with early-bird specials. Since business slows between peak hours, restaurant owners want to make it worth your while to dine with them during off-peak hours. Some even offer special

early-bird menus. These deals are a boon to folks whose sched-
ules allow them to eat whenever they please.

The hours and discounts vary, so call ahead. It won't be long
before you've learned every early-bird schedule in your area. And
don't miss early-bird discounts when you're traveling or vacation-
ing — times when you really want to stretch every dollar.

Easy way to uncover special deals

Some discounts are only for the bold and inquisitive. Say you're
a member of AAA or AARP — or you're employed by a major
company or a small company. You're not sure there are discounts for any of these special groups, but it can't hurt to ask.
Whether its company policy or
merely the whim of the manager,
you may find yourself eligible for
a variety of meal deals.

If you can't call in advance, ask
the hostess or manager about
available discounts when you
arrive.

The best bargain in town

Whether you're looking for a
good meal close to home or while
traveling, a hospital cafeteria is a
great place to eat. Not only do
they serve good food, they're
inexpensive and convenient.

Bland, you say? What about tasty
dishes ranging from ham and
Swiss cheese omelets for $2.35 to
bowls of chili for $1.25? The only
place you'll beat that is at home.

7 ways to pay less
for a good meal:

✓ Eat during off-peak
hours and enjoy
early-bird specials.
✓ Order soup, salad,
or an appetizer
instead of an entrée.
✓ Be on the lookout
for coupons.
✓ Check out hospital
cafeterias.
✓ Snag restaurant pro-
motions on the Web.
✓ Get paid for being a
restaurant critic.
✓ Ask if you are enti-
tled to a special
discount as a mem-
ber of a certain
organization.

And hospitals are consistently one of the easiest "restaurants" to find, thanks to their signs along every highway and thoroughfare. Still can't find one? Ask at the visitor's center or your hotel's concierge.

Where to look for restaurant coupons

The effort restaurants use to get coupons in your hands testifies to how much they want your business. And they're pretty creative about it, too. Here are a few sources you should consider.

- Coupon cards and booklets are favorite fund-raisers for schools, churches, youth groups, and clubs. They include a year's worth of substantial savings on good eating.

- Lots of restaurants offer discounts to customers who present a church bulletin or a good report card at the time of purchase.

- Local newspapers and advertising circulars that come in the mail are packed with coupons for weekly specials.

- Phone books often come loaded with discount coupons.

- The back of your grocery receipt is rarely blank anymore. Look there for restaurant coupons.

- Find Web addresses for your favorite restaurants. Then check them for printable coupons and other special offerings.

- A Web search for "restaurant coupons" will yield page after page of results. Some are truly freebies. Others offer discount coupons for a small charge. Be sure to read the fine print.

- Check calendars. Yes, calendars. Many people make a regular habit of enjoying monthly specials thanks to the detachable coupons on the calendars they receive from advertisers.

Why you should skip the entrée

A common refrain among restaurant patrons goes something like, "This entrée is enough to feed my whole family!"

The problem is more than portion size. It's also one of cost. Entrées are expensive. You don't want to pay for more than you can eat. But there is a solution.

The next time you dine out, skip the menu's entrée pages and start browsing the appetizers, salads, and soups section. For a fraction of the price of a single entrée, you can enjoy a delicious meal.

Earn money when you eat out

Dine out for less than the price of a home-cooked meal ... and even free in some restaurants. Mystery dining takes the mystery out of getting 100 percent free restaurant meals. Mystery dining is a widely practiced, part-time job for folks like you who have an eye for detail, the ability to accurately remember and report about their dining experiences, and a love for eating out.

The restaurant industry is looking for qualified mystery diners to eat at all kinds of dining establishments. Restaurant chains employ research companies or mystery-shopping companies. They, in turn, hire you as a subcontractor to check out the quality of food, the service, and the tidiness of particular restaurants. People do this every single day!

Most of the time, you keep your status as a mystery diner a secret. You rate the professionalism of host, server, and management. You assess your meal — Did you get what you ordered? Was it prepared like you wanted? You check the time of service — How long was it before your order was taken? How long did it take to get your drink, appetizer, and entree?

Occasionally, you may get to make yourself known and reward a server for her good work. Did she offer you today's special or a piece of their delicious pie for dessert? Then surprise her with a gift certificate given to you to use as a reward.

The opportunities for mystery dining are abundant. Most major restaurant chains want their establishments visited at least monthly, sometimes weekly. And fast food chains may have their locations checked three times a day.

You can do it as often as you like, and you'll always be thoroughly prepared for your assignment. If you think mystery dining sounds like a great way to earn a free meal, visit *www.justshop.org* or *www.ncpmscenter.org* for information on how to safely and intelligently enter the field.

Electronics

How to tell a real deal from a rip-off

Just because the electronics store has a "Sale" sign in its window doesn't mean you'll get a good deal. Instead of merely taking the store's word for it, learn how to avoid sales rip-offs.

There's a simple way to tell if that sale item is really a bargain. You don't even have to leave the house. Just go on the Internet and do some comparison shopping.

Several sites, like BizRate or Pricegrabber, let you compare prices from a variety of merchants. You can scroll down a list or view a side-by-side comparison of specifications, ratings, and prices for two or more products. They even tell you if the item is in stock and how much extra you'll pay for shipping and tax. It makes it easy to find the best price and tell a great deal from a sales rip-off.

Good comparison shopping sites include *www.bizrate.com*, *www.pricegrabber.com*, *http://shopper.cnet.com*, *www.nextag.com*, and *www.shopping.com*, a combination of the DealTime shopping search engine and Epinions' ratings and reviews.

To compare prices in your area, check out *www.salescircular.com* or *www.shoplocal.com*. Enter your state or ZIP code and get the lowdown on all the local sales, including how long they'll last. Whether you're searching for specific brands and models or just browsing for TVs, DVD players, stereos, or other electronics equipment, make the Internet your first stop. Remember, comparison shopping means savings beyond compare.

Bring ad to avoid confusion

You spotted an advertisement in the newspaper or received a circular announcing low prices in the mail. The electronics store has done a great job promoting its latest sale — except among its own employees who look at you as if you have two heads when you mention it. Next time, bring the ad with you. That way, the store is legally obligated to honor the offer.

Take advantage of price guarantees

Make stores put their money where their mouth is. If a store claims it will match the lowest price you can find, or even lower it by 10 percent, take advantage of the offer. Stores hope these lowest price guarantees simply guarantee that you won't shop around. But, if you do your homework, they can actually guarantee you a great deal.

You'll have to do some thorough comparison shopping to find the best available price. Use several online comparison shopping sites. Just make sure you're comparing the same make and model number. Otherwise, the lowest price guarantee doesn't apply.

Watch out for inflated discounts

Wow! That sounds like a great deal ... but is it? Beware of the inflated discount, a trick advertisers use to transform minor markdowns into major bargains.

Common with things like hotel rooms and senior discounts, the inflated discount can apply to any goods and services, including electronics.

Don't automatically rejoice when you see "50 percent off!" Instead, ask yourself "50 percent off what?" If the listed starting price is higher than the normal selling price, the discount is misleading. It may not even be a discount at all.

The Federal Trade Commission has strict guidelines about these deceptive advertising practices. But it doesn't hurt to keep your eyes open for suspicious ads and to have a good idea of an item's actual original price before the "discount."

Save a fortune every time you shop for electronic equipment. Remember these four ways to get TVs, VCRs, stereos, camcorders, cameras, and more at the cheapest possible price.

✓ Comparison shop.
✓ Use online coupons.
✓ Take advantage of lowest price guarantees.
✓ Buy discontinued, returned, or floor models.

Consider buying floor models

Who says your new stereo or DVD player has to come in a box? Ask your local retailer if it sells floor models. You can save a bundle if you don't mind a little wear and tear. Just make sure you get a demonstration so you know it works. Chances are a lot of people have been handling it.

Buy discontinued or returned items to snag similar discounts. Ask about a warranty, the store's return policy for such items, and if you can get a manual. You might have to forego packing material, but that's a small price to pay for a great bargain.

Wait for lower prices and fewer bugs

Patience is a virtue. It's also a money saver. If you rush out to buy the latest, greatest, state-of-the-art electronics as soon as they hit the market, you'll pay through the nose.

Simply wait a while, perhaps six months or a year. Not only will the price come down, the gadget in question will also work better because the manufacturer will have had time to work out any bugs.

Strategies for catalog shoppers

According to the Direct Marketing Association, 58 percent of Americans shop from catalogs and 27 percent of catalog shoppers buy electronics. That's because it's more convenient and often cheaper than shopping at a store. But you should keep some things in mind before you fill out that order form.

Stick to well-known names, whether you're buying directly from the manufacturer or ordering from a catalog company, like Crutchfield, that carries several brands.

Check the company's return policy, and keep a record of your order. Never send cash. Send a check or money order or pay with a credit card.

Post office auctions deliver savings

Neither rain, nor sleet, nor snow, nor hail shall keep you from finding a good bargain. Fortunately, the United States Postal Service makes it easy for you to "stamp" out high prices for electronics.

Just attend a mail recovery auction, where the post office sells lost or unclaimed items or those on which an insurance claim has already been paid. You can often find stereo equipment, televisions, radios, and VCRs at these special sales.

The two main locations for mail recovery auctions are Atlanta and St. Paul, Minn. But keep your eyes open for local and district sales as well. These can be regular auctions or sealed-bid auctions. Contact your local postal facility for more information.

Each lot, or group of similar items to be auctioned together, has a minimum acceptable bid — but it can go for a much higher amount. Cash, credit cards, and money orders are accepted at all post office auctions.

You'll get a chance to inspect each lot up for bid before the auction starts. Make sure the items you're interested in are in good shape. You might want to bring a knowledgeable friend with you if you're not an electronics wiz.

Remember, just as with any auction, set a maximum price you're willing to spend for each item and stick to it. It's too easy to get caught up in the excitement of an auction and overpay. And that's no bargain at all.

7 ways to shop safely online

You can't beat the convenience of shopping on the Internet. Unlike a regular store, it's always open. And where else can you find a whole world of choices right at your fingertips?

But, for all its benefits, online shopping does have a dark side. Beware of unscrupulous Web sites, identity thieves, and other tricks and traps.

According to the Federal Trade Commission (FTC), you should follow these tips to make your online shopping experience a safe one.

- Use a secure browser that encrypts, or scrambles, your purchase information.

- Shop only with companies you know and trust. Beware of shady fly-by-night companies. Research a company before buying from it.

- Keep passwords private. Don't use anything obvious, like your date of birth or phone number.

- Pay with a credit card. That way, your transaction is protected under the Fair Credit Billing Act.

- Keep a record of your transaction.

- Guard your personal information. Know who is collecting information and why. Give out as little as possible.

- Examine each site's privacy policy. Make sure they won't use your personal information in ways you object to.

Even if you take these precautions, there's no guarantee you'll get a good deal online. You still need to use smart shopping techniques.

Don't automatically buy from the first site you visit. Comparison shop. Make sure you factor in the shipping costs and check the site's refund and return policies before ordering. And don't get caught up in online auctions where you can overspend just to "win."

Remember, the Internet can be a great tool for great savings — but only if you use it wisely.

Slash prices with online coupons

You clip coupons before going to the grocery store, so why not take the same approach when shopping for electronics? Using the Internet, you can find rebates, discounts, and promotional coupon codes that help you save when you shop online.

Several Web sites — such as *www.couponmountain.com*, *www.couponcraze.com*, and *www.couponsurfer.com* — are dedicated to finding these deals. You can also do your own searching. Go to your favorite search engine, like Google, and type in the brand or product you're looking for and the word "coupon" or "rebate." For example, "Sony stereo AND coupon." You'll be amazed how many money-saving options you'll uncover.

How a pawnshop works

Think of a pawnshop, and you probably picture shabby characters making shady deals in a seedy part of town. But pawnshops actually provide super — and completely legal — savings on electronics.

In fact, televisions, stereos, VCRs, and other home electronics rank among the most common items for sale in pawnshops. While you might not find the latest and greatest models, you're sure to find quality goods at great prices.

Here's how it works. People who need cash use personal items, such as a TV or stereo, as collateral for a small loan. Either they repay the loan, with interest, in a certain amount of time or forfeit the item, in which case the pawnbroker sells it. They can also sell used merchandise outright.

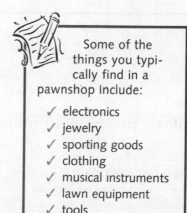

Some of the things you typically find in a pawnshop include:

✓ electronics
✓ jewelry
✓ sporting goods
✓ clothing
✓ musical instruments
✓ lawn equipment
✓ tools

While pawnshops may seem shady, they actually operate under some pretty strict rules. For instance, each day a pawnshop owner must provide the police with a list of every item pawned, including a description and serial number. That way, they can check if any of the items have been reported stolen.

Pawnbrokers also make sure the merchandise works, because they don't want to be stuck with shoddy goods. People pawning items must present a photo ID and are often fingerprinted, while pawnshop owners and employees must undergo background checks by police.

It all adds up to a low-risk, low-cost shopping experience. So don't think of it as seedy — think of it as savvy.

Entertainment

9 ways to get cheap tickets

Why pay full price for your entertainment? You'll enjoy yourself even more when you find a way to pay less.

If you're 50 or older, start looking for senior discounts. These deals come in handy for almost any situation. Movies, museums, amusement parks, national parks, ski areas, the opera, theaters, and bowling alleys are just some of the places that might offer a break to older folks. Even if there is no advertised senior discount, it doesn't hurt to ask — you might get a deal anyway.

But you don't need to be a senior to take advantage of great discounts. Many movie theaters offer ticket booklets at discounted prices. Check with your local cinemas for details.

The Internet also gives you plenty of opportunities to save on tickets. If you enjoy live theater, check out *www.theatermania.com* for big discounts in your area. Or buy and sell tickets to concerts, plays, or sporting events at *www.stubhub.com*.

You can also try these tried-and-true strategies for low-cost entertainment.

- Volunteer to usher at a local theater or concert venue.

- Take in a matinee, or wait for your movie to come to a dollar theater.

- Be quick and call when your radio station offers ticket giveaways.

- Write to the Guest Relations departments of television networks to get free tickets to live tapings of TV shows.

- Buy coupon books with entertainment vouchers.

- Sign up on mailing lists of art organizations to find out about last-minute discounts.

- Check your membership benefits through AAA or any other clubs you might belong to.

- Subscribe early to the theater or symphony for deep discounts.

- Keep your eye open for free public events or festivals.

Sneak a peek for less

Practice makes perfect — and perfect prices. Instead of paying through the nose for professional opera or theater tickets, attend a dress rehearsal or preview performance.

It's just like the real thing, only cheaper. By this time, the actors know their lines and where to move onstage. The cast and crew have also worked out the technical aspects of the show. All they need is an audience. That's where you come in.

Call local theaters and ask about pricing for these special performances. You might also see them advertised in your local newspaper.

Go back to school for great deals

Living near a college means putting up with rowdy students. But it also means great opportunities for low-cost entertainment.

You can attend guest lectures, concerts, and student plays or recitals for reasonable prices — or even for free. If the college has a strong music or drama program, these performances can rival professional productions.

Call nearby colleges for information on discounted tickets. Often, matinees and weeknight performances are cheaper. Ask if the school offers senior discounts.

Get in free on special days

Some venues, like museums and zoos, feature "free days" when admission is free. It's a great way to admire fine art or learn about exotic animals at absolutely no cost.

Often, these special days are advertised on the venue's Web site. You can also look for ads in your local newspaper or even call nearby zoos and museums for information.

If you'll be visiting these cities, check out their free festivals.

- French Quarter Festival, New Orleans, April
- Main St. Fort Worth Arts Festival, April
- Atlanta Jazz Festival, May
- Northwest Folklife Festival, Seattle, May
- Shakespeare in the Park, New York City, June
- Museum Mile Festival, New York City, June
- Outdoor movie screenings, several cities, summers
- Berkeley Kite Festival, summer
- Bele Chere, Asheville, N.C., July
- Ethnic Enrichment Festival, Kansas City, Mo., August
- Chicago Jazz Festival, September

The best way to save on DVD rentals

You love watching movies from the comfort of your own couch. But you don't love going to the video store — or paying late fees when you don't return the movie on time.

Save time and money with online DVD rental services. For a small monthly fee, you can rent all the movies you can handle. And you'll never pay late fees or shipping charges.

It's easy. Just compile a list, or queue, of the movies you want to see. As they become available, the DVDs will be mailed to you. When you're done watching them, send them back in postage-paid envelopes. Then wait for your next round of movies to come in the mail. You can always edit your queue to reposition, add, or delete movies.

Here's a look at the three most popular DVD rental services.

- Netflix, the pioneer in DVD rentals by mail, charges a monthly rate of $17.99. You can have up to three movies at a time. Go to *www.netflix.com* to sign up for a free trial.

- Wal-Mart costs only $12.97 a month, but you only get to have two videos at a time. You can also sample the service with a free trial. Visit their site at *www.walmart.com* and click on DVD Rentals.

- Blockbuster, the latest to enter the field, charges $14.99 per month. You get three videos at a time — as well as two in-store DVD rentals a month. When you join, you pay just $9.99 for the first month. Go to *www.blockbuster.com*.

With over 35,000 titles, Netflix features the best selection, especially for hard-to-find films, but Wal-Mart is fine for mainstream hits. Blockbuster, with more than 30,000 available movies, also lets you rent games.

You can't find a more convenient way to rent movies. But, before you commit, think about how much use you'll get out of the service. If you think you'll watch only one or two movies a month, it's not worth it. You're better off making an occasional trip to the video store. But if you're a movie buff, it could be a wonderful deal.

Enjoy DVDs for free

Instead of paying lots of money to buy or rent DVDs, consider borrowing them from your local public library. In some areas, DVD rentals are free with a library card. In others, you may have to pay a small fee, usually $1 or $2. Ask your local library about its policies.

While the selection won't be as extensive as that of a video store or online service, you can still find worthwhile things to watch. Along with popular and classic films, you can check out educational, travel, and nonfiction videos.

And it gives you the perfect opportunity to find out which is better — the movie or the book.

Enjoy fitness freebies from FreeCycle

Freecycling is the perfect way to dispose of — or acquire — exercise equipment. This novel approach to recycling involves Web-based recycling communities in small towns and big cities across the country. Community members list items they want to give away on the Web and communicate with one another by e-mail.

Keep in mind it's not a money-making scheme. Everything has to be given away. It's a great convenience to givers and a great bargain for receivers. The variety of give-away items is unlimited, but exercise equipment is standard fare.

Deron Beal of Rise, Inc., a nonprofit organization that promotes recycling, launched the movement in 2003. There are now over 2,500 Freecycle communities with more than a million members. Membership is free. Information about freecycling is available at *www.freecycle.org*.

The best time to buy a bike

Many pedalers shop for a new ride when the weather warms up. But spring is not the best time to hunt for a bargain. Wait until fall when new models are hitting the showrooms. Like cars, last year's models go on sale to make room for the new models, often at discounts of 15 to 25 percent or more.

If you're looking for a quality, pre-owned bicycle, the season for bargain buys extends into the dead of winter. Find great buys posted on bike shop bulletin boards, in the classifieds, and on eBay.

Beware of the allure of cheap bikes. Bike enthusiasts agree that cheap, mass-market bikes ride poorly and have short life spans.

Uncover deals on used machines

It's a fact of life. The world is full of impulse buyers — people who buy on a whim. Nowhere is that more evident than in the area of exercise equipment.

After a year or so, the device they'd drooled over is collecting dust. Just looking at it reminds them of how quickly their commitment to actually use it disappeared. Now they just have to find a graceful way to get rid of it.

Here's your chance. These folks use several predictable avenues for disposing of their surplus goods. The classifieds. Yard sales. Thrift stores. Used sports equipment stores. If they're Internet savvy, eBay.

Try these alternatives to costly fitness equipment.

- Canned goods, milk jugs, and books instead of dumbbells.
- Socks filled with dried beans and tied shut for extra weight.
- Staircase or some stadium bleachers instead of stair-climbing machines.
- Bicycle raised on a stand as a substitute stationary bike.
- Walls, sturdy chairs, old neckties, books, and blankets to help you stretch.

Begin your search by knowing what you're looking for — type of equipment, brand names, and model numbers. Do some research so you'll recognize a good price when you see one. Pay careful attention to prices followed by OBO (or best offer).

Get wise to slick advertisers

Infomercials are glamorous and alluring. These program-length advertisements have the look of real talk shows or educational programs. Buyer, beware! You won't be able to verify their claims.

But what if you're intent on getting in shape and convinced a certain piece of equipment will help you reach your goals? Before you call in your order, do yourself a favor. Ask these questions.

- Can this or a similar product be purchased for less at a nearby fitness store, through the classified ads, or at a yard sale?

The scoop on infomercials

This year marks the 20th anniversary of the infomercial. Consumers (mostly women) spend more than $1 billion buying everything from exercise equipment to pasta makers through infomercials. If you include the in-store sales that the commercials drive, the gross revenue rose to $154.1 billion in 2003. That number represents an 81-percent increase in a six-year period.

If you combine radio, TV, and Internet "infomercials," sales reached $256 billion. There are 339 networks trying to capture consumer attention today — in 1980 there were only 28.

In 1991, an infomercial had a one-in-seven chance of turning a profit. Today, only one in 69 can make that claim. But as long as you have successes like ProActiv Solution, a way to fight acne according to spokeswoman Vanessa Williams, it's likely people and networks will keep churning out the 28-minute TV ads. Last year, ProActiv Solution sold $600 million worth of skin products.

- What's the product really going to cost? When you've figured in the shipping and handling, sales tax, and setup fees, will it still be a bargain?

- How about those "money-back guarantees"? They're not so great if you have to pay return postage on a bulky exercise machine.

Keeping fitness club costs down

Your thoughts may turn to fitness clubs when the urge to get in shape strikes. Their ads are appealing, but membership can be expensive.

Here's a strategy for making the most of your money.

- Commit yourself to wellness. If you join a club, use it. A $450 annual membership works out to $2.88 per visit if you go three times a week, $8.65 if you go once a week, $18.75 if you only go twice a month.

- Don't test your resolve to stick with the program by buying a year-long membership. At first, pay month-by-month to test your determination and be sure the club you've joined meets your needs.

- Find out how much the fitness club is really going to cost. Are there hidden fees that will negate the savings you thought you were getting at those special introductory rates? Know what's included in membership and what's not.

- Be sure the club is convenient. If it's too far from home or work, you probably won't go regularly.

- Make sure it has the facilities, programs, and hours that will meet your needs. Don't just compare membership fees. Compared to a bare-bones, lock-and-key gym, a club with a well-trained, helpful staff and state-of-the-art facilities may be worth the extra dollars.

- Compare membership packages. Buy one that suits you. Look for discounts on plans for families and seniors.

- Shop outside the box. Some of the best deals in health and fitness are alternatives to the name-brand clubs — YMCAs, hospitals, schools, and churches. And see if your HMO or medical insurer offers discounted fitness club memberships or will pay a portion of the club dues.

Your hospital's best health buy

Today's hospitals are aggressively promoting health and wellness, offering exercise programs and state-of-the-art fitness centers.

Hospitals with their own health clubs usually require membership fees or pay-per-visit charges, but they're still a bargain compared to other health clubs. What's more, some hospitals let their volunteers use the fitness center for free.

The Newnan Hospital Health and Fitness Center in Georgia offers a variety of memberships and programs. Individuals under 62 can join for $35 a month, seniors for $25, and family plans start at $45. Classes include weight training, cardio workouts, stationary cycling, yoga, and Pilates. They even offer free classes for seniors that focus on joint mobility and balance.

Give your local hospital a call, and ask what they offer. Don't be surprised if you find a real fitness bargain.

Opportunities grow for instructors

Veteran teachers will tell you they've learned more as teachers than they did as pupils. The same is true for physical education.

If you're ready for a new challenge, why not share your expertise and lead a class. Give your local recreation center or YMCA a call to see what classes they have scheduled and what it takes to be an instructor.

The short-term investment of time and money to become certified could be more than repaid by perks, like free health club membership. You could even get paid for your service.

How to find the best class for you

Before you get pumped about a health club membership, find out if there are any fitness classes being held at your local recreational center or a private studio. Then compare the fees for the class to the fees you'd pay to attend the health club.

Keep in mind the style of teaching may differ between health clubs and studio classes. A health club instructor leading a kickboxing class will be more concerned with burning calories, while a martial arts instructor will focus more on the art itself. Determining which strategy is better is completely up to you.

Look at the following table to compare a health club membership with prices for similar classes offered at other venues. Just remember that monthly membership fees at a gym or health club include all of the classes.

	Yoga	Cycling/ spinning	Kickboxing
Health club or gym	$49 per month (class included in monthly fee)	$49 per month (class included in monthly fee)	$49 per month (class included in monthly fee)
Recreation Center	$40 per month	N/A	N/A
Private studio	$75 per month	$15 per month	$39 per month

Furniture

■ New furniture

How to spot top quality

Here's the best way to bring home quality-packed furnishings that are worth your hard-earned money.

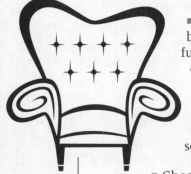

- ■ Look for back panels made of wood rather than cardboard or fiberboard.

- ■ Make sure the underside, the backside, and the interior of the furniture look every bit as well-constructed as the parts of the furniture that are easily seen.

- ■ Inspect the hinges on all doors. Make sure they're securely attached.

- ■ Check the doors and drawers. They should open and close freely and smoothly. When you shut a door, it should catch the latch easily and stay closed.

- ■ Check for dovetailing, a type of interlocking joint, at the fronts and backs of drawers.

- ■ The rod or track that guides a drawer is best when it's all wood, but metal can work well, too.

- Does the drawer have a stop to make sure it doesn't pull all the way out of the furniture? Wood stops are best and metal is satisfactory, but avoid plastic drawer stops.

- Look for drawers with smooth interior surfaces.

- Look for joints that fit snugly together and hardly flex at all when you pull, push, or lift the furniture.

- Table leaves should raise and lower without a hitch, and they should have locks that help hold them in place.

- New tables should never wobble.

- Suppose you need to slide the furniture out a few inches to vacuum behind it — or maybe you need to move the item to another room. Do the legs of the furniture have something on the bottom that will help protect your floors from scrapes or other damage?

- Most floors are not perfectly level. If the item has doors, ask the salesperson to show you the leveling devices at the base of the piece.

3 ways to spot good craftsmanship

You may have found a super value if bargain-priced wood furniture can pass this simple quality check.

- Find the furniture's joints — any place where one piece of wood connects to another. The two pieces of wood should fit tightly together. Push or lift or pull to see how strongly the joints are attached.

- Inspect the undersides of wood chairs. If you see screws or nails, they may have been added to reinforce a weak, poor-quality joint.

- Check for dovetailing on the backs of drawers. If you see an interlocking pattern where the sides of the drawer connect to the back panel, you're looking at the durability and quality construction of dovetailing.

Buy top-rated wood at cut rates

Get excellent quality in wood furniture without paying the high price of luxury wood, like mahogany. Just be sure to hunt for these prize characteristics found in the finest furniture woods.

- Strong enough and hard enough to defend against dents and scratches.

- Resists swelling or shrinking as humidity changes.

- Doesn't warp.

- Stains evenly.

Mahogany is known for these qualities, but you can also find them in teak, walnut, oak, and cherry. Even better, you can get excellent oak and cherry furniture at prices that are more inviting than mahogany's steep cost.

But you might save even more if you want furnishings without curves or carved trimmings. For straight-lined furniture styles, lower-priced maple and birch are nearly as good as the top varieties of wood.

On the other hand, if you simply must have the look of walnut, you may still have a chance to save. Walnut wood comes in two varieties. English walnut is a little easier to carve, but American walnut offers nearly as high quality for fewer dollars.

But be careful. Just because an item is labeled as "solid wood" doesn't mean you'll get the four characteristics of top furniture wood. The term "solid wood" can refer to almost any kind of wood you can think of — including three that may astound you.

Particleboard, Medium-Density Fiberboard (MDF), and High-Density Fiberboard (HDF) all count as "solid wood," but they score poorly on the qualities needed to make good furniture. After all, particleboard is just glue and pressure-treated wood chips or sawdust. MDF and HDF use wood fiber, so they're a little better than particleboard.

But even when these three products are covered with gorgeous veneers, they can't give you the advantages of quality wood. None of them last as long as wood. They're also hard to repair, heavier than quality wood, and very vulnerable to swelling and shrinking with humidity changes.

So don't settle for a vague description, like "solid wood." Ask for details about the wood used in making the furniture, so you'll know when you've found quality at last.

Shatter veneer myths and save

You might be surprised to learn that veneer isn't necessarily a sign of poor-quality furniture. In fact, you may find attractive quality furnishings at cut rates if you choose veneer furniture wisely.

Think of veneer as a thin slice of wood that overlays parts of wood furniture. For example, a mahogany veneer may be attached to the top of an oak dining table.

Perhaps the key to saving money with veneer furniture is making sure you get both quality veneer and quality furniture. Ask the salesperson questions like these.

- Is the furniture veneered?

- Is the veneer three ply, five ply, or seven ply?

- What kind of wood is underneath the veneer?

If the furniture is veneered, five-ply (five layers) or seven-ply veneer delivers more durability than three-ply. Good wood underneath the veneer can also be a sign of good furniture. Remember, if the base wood is good and the veneer is made of an expensive wood, like teak or cherry, you may get a low price on furniture that looks much more expensive.

But beware of veneers that hide poor quality. If the wood beneath that veneer is particleboard, High-Density Fiberboard (HDF), or Medium-Density Fiberboard (MDF), the furniture is almost surely second rate. To check whether particleboard or fiberboard may be lurking beneath a veneer, pull out drawers and adjustable shelves. You'll see exposed wood, fiberboard, or particleboard. If the item doesn't have drawers or shelves, check its underside or another usually hidden portion of the furniture.

Examine the rest of the furniture. By the time you're done, you'll probably know whether this is a shoddy veneer piece or a great value.

Inspect sofas and chairs like a pro

Spot signs of first-rate quality in upholstered furnishings with these tips.

- Ask what's in the seat cushions. At the least, each cushion should have a core wrapped in foam or batting — and that should be nestled inside a decorative cover. A cushion with an inner core or springs swathed in several layers of batting, foam, and fabric is even better.

- Avoid cushions that only have unwrapped foam under the outside fabric cover.

- Go for seat cushions with zippers.

- Sit on it — or lie down — and then get up and eye the furniture. If you can see an imprint of where you sat, the quality of the furniture is probably poor.

- Sit or lie down and then get up again. Was that easy? If you have to struggle to get up or out of any piece of furniture, you probably don't want it.

- Can you feel any springs or boards? You shouldn't feel anything but cushion when you lean against the backing, seats, or armrests.

- Check how the legs are attached. Look for legs that are glued to the rail — not just screwed or nailed in. If you find corner blocks, that's even better. If you're not sure what corner blocks are, ask the salesperson to show you.

- Back pillows are best filled with foam instead of down.

- The shape of the frame should match the shape of the furniture. Where the furniture curves, the frame should curve, too.

- Ask what wood the frame is made of and whether the lumber was kiln-dried. Hardwoods, like birch, are better than softwood or particleboard. Kiln-dried lumber means more quality and durability.

Become a leather expert

Find the leather furniture that meets your needs without straining your wallet. Use these hints to help choose leather wisely and to detect when you may not be getting the quality leather furniture you hoped for.

Read the labels and descriptions. Top grain means you've found superior quality leather taken from the outermost hide, but split grain is a weaker leather from the hide's interior.

Pick the kind of top grain that matches your lifestyle best so you get the perfect value. Aniline leather is delightfully soft because these top-grade hides only get a little processing — a soak in something called aniline dye. Aniline is the best-quality leather, but it's not the most resistant to scuffs and stains.

If you need durability, go cheaper. Semi-aniline leathers have a little coating or pigment added so they're slightly better protected from stains and fading. But you'll get the best stain resistance and scuff protection from cheapest and stiffest leather — pigmented leather.

Not all leather furniture is truly 100-percent leather. Know what you're getting so you don't overpay. After all, that luxurious-looking leather sofa may be mostly vinyl, except for the leather pillows and cushions.

Or perhaps leather covers all the furniture parts your body normally touches, but the back of the couch, the skirt base, and the outer section of the arms are all vinyl. Even if the sofa is all leather, you may find that only the cushions and pillows are top-grain leather. The rest is split-grain leather. Make sure the price you pay matches the amount — and quality — of leather you'll take home.

Dig for prize bargains at outlets

You can find buried treasure at factory outlets — at prices that may make you feel like a million bucks. Just be prepared to do a little searching to uncover that treasure.

Outlets may contain top quality new furniture or furniture that's imperfect, discontinued, overstocks, scratch-and-dents, or floor samples. Instead of frills, like in-house interior designers or glamorous displays, you'll find bargains of 50 percent off or better — and sometimes as high as 70 to 90 percent off. Just be sure to inspect the furniture carefully before you buy. Returns and refunds aren't usually allowed.

Guide to fabulous furniture deals

Don't pay retail for furniture! Instead, find out exactly how to lavish your home with top-quality furniture for up to 70 percent off. Your best bet is to visit America's furniture capital,

After pricing furniture in the Atlanta area, Stephen Worth and his wife went shopping in Hickory, N.C. "With one trip to Hickory, we got to see a wider selection, experience less traffic and travel time, and purchase all of our furniture — plus an impulse purchase," Stephen says. He estimates that he saved around $2,000 on six items — an average discount of about 50 percent off.

And, even better, those savings came after Stephen paid the costs of shipping an executive desk, large computer hutch, two media-style cabinets, and a chest-of-drawers. "The more items you get, the more your savings offset the shipping costs," he explains. "Buy in bulk at Hickory. Redecorate entire rooms."

Over a year after buying his furniture, Stephen is still happy with the results. He has enthusiastically encouraged his family and friends to buy furniture from Hickory and plans to make his future furniture purchases there as well.

North Carolina — where you can save 40 to 70 percent on every piece of furniture you buy.

Many furniture manufacturers are based near Hickory or High Point, so you can find a nearly endless selection of well-discounted, top-name brands in either city. And you can probably get the furniture shipped to your door. You might be worried that the costs of the trip and getting the furniture home would erase every last penny of savings. But if you buy a room's worth of furniture or more, chances are good that your total furniture savings can more than cover your trip and shipping costs. To be sure, run the numbers before you make the trip.

Planning ahead can help, too. In her book, *Shopping the North Carolina Furniture Outlets*, Ellen R. Shapiro recommends that you don't visit Hickory or High Point during the International Home Furnishings Market in April and October. You'll probably have better luck with your shopping if you pick another time.

Also, keep in mind that your new furniture might take weeks to arrive. If you have a deadline, time your trip accordingly. And don't forget you'll be far from the rooms and colors your new furniture needs to match. Take measurements and write down anything else you'll need to know. If you want to coordinate the furniture with the color of your curtains, wallpaper, carpet, or paint, take color samples with you.

If you really don't want to make the trip to North Carolina, you might be able to order from the discounters by phone. About 15 percent of the discounters aren't allowed by manufacturers to take phone orders, but you can place a phone order with the others. Before you do, find the furniture you want at a local store and get the exact model number of the furniture and the fabric. Retailers may make it difficult for you to get that information, but you might get lucky.

For more information on shopping the North Carolina discounters, contact the High Point and Hickory Convention and Visitors Bureaus.

- High Point Convention and Visitors Bureau at 800-720-5255 or visit their Web site at *www.highpoint.org*.

- Hickory Metro Convention and Visitors Bureau at 800-849-5093 or visit their Web site at *www.hickorymetro.com*.

Score even more Carolina discounts

Plan ahead and you might save on more than just furniture when you travel to North Carolina. You might also cut the cost of eating, driving, hotels, and entertainment while you're there.

Visit *www.highpoint.org* to find online discount coupons or take advantage of the Passport to Savings. This program recently included discounts like these.

- hotel bargains for familiar names like Howard Johnson and Courtyard by Marriott

- markdowns on High Point attractions and entertainment

- restaurant specials and deals

- savings on car rentals

- special discounts at selected furniture stores

Even without the Passport or online coupons, you may get part of your hotel bill paid. Some outlets and discounters will reimburse you for part — or all — of your hotel bill if you buy enough furniture. The minimum amount varies from one store to the next, so just ask whether this sweet deal is available.

> You negotiated 10 to 15 percent off the price and now the salesperson won't budge. That doesn't mean you can't get more for your money. Pack extra value into a furniture deal by negotiating for free extras like these.
>
> - delivery to your home
> - warranties
> - repairs
> - fabric protection

If you plan to shop at furniture malls or superstores, check their Web sites for hotels that offer furniture shopper's discounts. You can also call a store's receptionist or the furniture mall's main number for similar referrals.

Check with the furniture malls for other savings opportunities, too. For example, Catawba Furniture Mall in Hickory offers a Shop'n'Stay weekend four times a year. This may include a free lunch, transportation, a pack of information about the mall's offerings, and discount coupons. Visit *www.catawbafurniture.com* to learn more or check with other furniture malls to see if they have similar programs.

Save more at retail stores

Getting furniture discounts at a retail store may be tricky, but it's not impossible. If you need to safari into the retail furniture jungle, keep these tactics in mind.

Retailers price items extra high so they can mark them down to catch the attention of customers. That's why you should wait to buy an item until it's marked down at least 20 percent.

Plan to take your time with retail furniture shopping. Spending more time to find the right item can literally pay off by saving you extra money. For example, when you find the right item, be sure to check a similar item in another store. Then you'll know where the better price really is. However, if you get in a hurry to buy the item, you might try to skip comparison shopping — and could miss out on big savings.

Consider floor samples — the furniture the retailer puts on display in the showroom. After awhile, floor samples get sold, but usually at a deep discount. Watch for floor sample sales or clearance sales. Or just ask how floor samples and imperfect furniture are sold, just in case these sales are unadvertised. Check any floor sample over very carefully to inspect its quality and make sure it's in good enough condition to suit you. Also, take measurements to confirm that it matches the size you expect.

Some stores accept returns of used or damaged merchandise and try to resell them. These items are also deeply discounted but should be inspected and measured with extreme attention to detail. Do this legwork well and you might get a fine piece of furniture at a deeply discounted price.

Retail stores may not always have the right furniture at the right price for you. For what you need at the price you want, try alternatives like these.

- garage or yard sales
- used-furniture stores, including Goodwill
- consignment shops
- "big box" stores, such as Walmart and Costco
- flea markets
- classified ads
- estate sales
- unclaimed freight
- unfinished furniture stores
- antique stores

Prevent costly buying mistakes

When you go furniture shopping, take a notebook containing a sketched floor plan, preferably to scale, of the room you plan to furnish and exact measurements. This will keep you from making expensive mistakes, like buying too many pieces or buying pieces too large for the space. Include windows, doorways, closets, built-ins, and even electrical outlets. If you're furnishing an upstairs room, get the width of your staircase and any landings.

Fend off pricey add-on tricks

Guard against helpful salespeople who try to sell you warranties or other extras you don't need. For example, you'll probably be offered fabric protection on upholstered furniture. Don't pay for it. If you're worried the fabric isn't stain resistant, treat it with Scotchgard yourself.

Also, plan how you'll say no to salespeople who encourage you to buy matching accessories or furniture or try to tempt you to "move up" to a high-end version of the item you want. Save your money and only accept these kinds of extras if the final price has been settled and the upgrades are free.

The inside scoop on advertising

Sales are supposed to save you money, but some furniture ads might lead to more expenses if you're not careful. Protect yourself with advice from Leonard Bruce Lewin, author of *Shopping for Furniture: A Consumer's Guide.* Remember these cautions the next time you read a furniture ad.

- 10 percent off, or any other percentage, may not apply to every product the store carries.

- "Zero Interest until 2009" sounds great until you learn about all the restrictions that come with it. Read the fine print.

- Watch out for ads that give all kinds of details describing how wonderful the product is but never hint at the price.

- Be prepared for product claims that don't tell you everything you need to know. For example, an ad for incredible discounts on leather furniture may not say exactly how much of the furniture is genuine leather.

- Watch out for vague buzzwords and unclear phrases. Does "prices slashed" mean you can expect 80 percent off — or just 15 percent? Does "mahogany collection" describe furniture that's 100-percent mahogany or items with a thin mahogany veneer over cheaper wood?

- What you see in the pictures may or may not be the exact item on sale. You may also see extra furniture or features that aren't included. When it comes to furniture ads, pictures aren't worth a thousand words.

Beat zero-percent financing tactics

Zero-percent financing sounds like a fabulous chance to save, but trouble lurks in the details of this gimmick. Discover how to protect yourself so you don't lose money. You can start before you even visit a showroom.

- Check with the Better Business Bureau (BBB) for information about the company. Visit *www.bbb.org* to get contact information for the BBB nearest you.

- Check your credit score. Often you need flawless credit to qualify for the zero-percent offer, and you may also have to apply for a high-interest store account.

- Examine your income, expenses, and debts to determine whether you can make the monthly payments without straining your budget. If you can easily pay off the entire debt before the zero-interest period ends, this might be a bargain after all.

- Compare prices and merchandise quality. Learn how to recognize whether you're getting the best price.

Start asking questions as soon as you meet a salesperson or call ahead to ask questions. The zero-percent gimmick may be intended to lure you into the showroom for an impulse buy, so don't wait until you fall in love with an item. Waiting could mean you get "up sold" into a deal with a higher interest rate.

Instead, find out upfront whether you can qualify for the zero-percent offer and go after the offer's nitty-gritty details. Understand payment deadlines, late fees, penalties, and grace periods. Often, zero-percent financing ends after a short period. Unless you can pay off the money before that deadline, you might have to pay costly interest that's been piling up during the interest-free time.

Read the sales contract carefully. Make sure you understand and agree with everything before you sign.

Pay less and pick your own finish

With a little elbow grease, you can get discounted furniture with any finish you want. Just find a place that sells unfinished furniture and then do the finishing yourself, advises Kimberly Causey, author of *The Insider's Guide to Buying Home Furnishings*.

Unfinished furniture is usually well constructed and made of solid wood. However, it isn't top-of-the-line quality, so don't try to use it to decorate your formal living and dining rooms. On the other hand, if you want "working" furniture for the kitchen, den, or the kids' rooms — at a moderately discounted price — this may be a clever way to save on a custom finish.

Keep upholstery looking good longer

When choosing a sofa or other upholstered furniture, match the fabric to your lifestyle, recommends Leonard Bruce Lewin, author of *Shopping for Furniture: A Consumer's Guide*. A rarely used living room sofa won't require the same fabric as the family room sofa constantly used by three kids and a cat nicknamed Shredder.

Also, don't assume that a high price means more durable fabric, Lewin warns. A few expensive fabrics may wear well, but stick with cheaper, tougher materials for durability. Reserve expensive or fragile fabrics for seldom used items.

Most important — no matter which fabric you choose for upholstery, treat it with a soil and stain repellent. You'll always be glad you did.

Clever ways to update old furniture

Imagine how much money you'd save if you could give your old furniture a face-lift instead of replacing it. Before you spend hundreds on new furniture, consider the transforming tactics recommended by Kimberly Causey, author of *The Insider's Guide to Buying Home Furnishings*.

- Refinish an old dresser to give it a more fashionable color — or just to make it look new again.

- Change the drawer pulls, locks, hinges, or other hardware for a different look.

- Paint a favorite piece an interesting new color or use decorative painting techniques, like stenciling and faux finishes.

- Add new pillows.

- Rearrange the furniture in a room or move an item to a different room.

- Switch to the hottest new look in slipcovers.

Another option is having your furniture professionally reupholstered. If that doesn't fit your budget, take a class and learn to do it yourself. Or find a student or someone who is just starting in the business. You may get a deep discount if you're willing to give a testimonial or serve as a reference.

Get a good mattress for your money

Even if you only get six hours of sleep every night, you spend 42 hours a week in your bed. That's why it pays to be choosy when buying a mattress. Use these tips to help.

- Shop around. Compare prices, delivery fees, and the quality of the mattresses.

- Wear comfortable, slightly loose clothing so you can climb on and off the mattresses without effort. Wear shoes you can remove quickly. If you wear makeup that comes off easily, bring a small towel so you won't be afraid to rest your head on a pillow.

- Check the tag on a mattress to see whether you're buying a new mattress or one that's used. A tag that describes the mattress as "containing all new materials" probably means the mattress is new. A "used" tag may state that the mattress includes used materials.

- Even if you plan to buy a new mattress, ask if the store also sells used bedding. Then be sure to check the tag to verify whether it's new or used. If the mattress has no tag, move on to another mattress.

- Ask about the number of coils. The more a bed has, the better.

- The innerspring is the part of the mattress support that's filled with coils. It should be at least 9 inches thick. Ask about it.

- Never just sit on the edge of the mattress to test it. Recline with your whole body on the bed and try to imitate how you'd position yourself for sleep.

- A rock hard mattress may not be best for your back. If the mattress is a little softer, your hips and shoulders may sink into the mattress enough to keep your spine straight and comfortable.

- Buy the mattress with its box springs at the same time. They belong together.

- Get a mattress with a 10-year warranty.

- Before leaving the store, ask about the seller's refund and return policies until you're sure you understand how they work. Then get written copies of these policies.

Alternatives to inflated rent-to-own

A rent-to-own customer may spend as much as $2,400 in rental payments for an item that might cost as little as $200 in retail stores. While that's probably a worst-case scenario, rent-to-own is still more costly than it seems.

At first glance, rent to own sounds like a great way to have your cake and eat it, too. Even if you're unlucky enough to have poor credit or no credit history, you don't have to worry. The rent-to-own company may not run a credit check at all. And if they do, they still may not refuse you if you have an income, a place to live, and a personal reference or two.

You might even be able to pick how often you'll pay. And while you rent, you can use that stereo, television, furniture, or appliance as if you already own it. Even if you eventually can't make the payments, you probably won't get in trouble. The rent-to-own company may just take the item back with no fuss.

The problem with this enticing package is that you're still likely to shell out at least two times the price of the item before you can own it. That's almost like paying a 50-percent annual percentage rate.

Before you rent-to-own, consider other options, like a layaway plan or saving up for a used version of the item. A rent-to-own program might help you build a credit rating, but you'll pay through the nose to do it. On the other hand, if you avoid rent-to-own, you might accumulate enough savings to buy that big-ticket item twice over. Then you could pay cash for the item and buy other things, too.

■ Used furniture

First-class furniture at no-frills price

A rolled-up newspaper could be your ticket to fantastic bargains. What's more, you'll avoid salespeople, and you might even find items you can't get from stores. Just browse through the furniture classified ads in your Sunday paper.

According to James L. Paris, author of *Absolutely Amazing Ways to Save Money on Everything*, you could save up to 80 percent on furniture if you read the classified ads and keep these tips in mind.

- You can find all kinds of furniture and all kinds of furniture styles in these ads, but you'll have to call the seller, and perhaps visit him, in order to see whether you've found the item you want.

- You can find like-new furniture — items that have rarely seen use — if you're willing to work at it.

- Expect a wide range of prices. The person preparing to transfer across the country will sell top-of-the-line furniture at a much cheaper price than the casual seller. If you're prepared to bide your time, a future seller might offer the same item for far less.

Be sure to ask questions and inspect the furniture carefully before talking about price. After all, returns and refunds are almost surely out of the question.

Also, find a way to do your own furniture delivery if you can. Even if the seller offers to transport the furniture, you may be able to haggle for a better price if you can move it yourself.

Unusual auctions offer great deals

You don't always have to attend traditional auctions to find great pieces. Here are some places you might not think to look.

- Scan the newspaper or drive through business areas for hotel liquidation sales or auctions. If a hotel is closing or renovating, they'll often sell their furnishings and fixtures. Other businesses can offer specific types of items. For instance, defunct offices may auction off business furniture. Or daycare centers going out of business will need to get rid of a variety of baby goods.

- Get everything from grand pianos to woodworking tools to desks at a school district auction. Items considered unusable, unneeded, or out-of-date are offered to other schools first, then auctioned off to the public. Find out about them by scanning newspapers or looking up school districts' Web sites on the Internet.

- Visit local county government Web sites for information on annual auctions of furniture and equipment from county departments and agencies.

- Shipping and storage companies often auction off abandoned property. Contact freight lines or local businesses that offer self-storage units to rent.

- Theaters amass a huge amount of props, like furniture, clothing, and set dressing, which takes up valuable space. They'll often sell or auction off items to make a little money and a little room for the next production.

Simple tactics for flea market buffs

Get a great deal on used furniture by going to a flea market early in the morning. Try to be one of the first people there. You'll find quality furniture for low prices before the crowds arrive and snatch up all the bargains.

Professional dealers who own antique stores know to show up before the flea market actually opens so they can buy the nicest furniture at the cheapest prices. Take your cue from the pros and be there an hour before opening time. That's when vendors first make their furniture available to the public.

Vendors try to sell their wares in the parking lot before the market opens so they can skip the process of moving the heavy pieces of furniture to their sales booth. They also want to reach their sales quota early in the day, so the prices are steeply discounted at that time. Catch them before they move to the booth, and you may get the vendor to take off another 15 percent.

Many of the pieces you find are for sale because they have a flaw. Use the flaw to your advantage by pointing it out and lowering the price of the furniture. Buy it cheap now and fix it up later.

Remember to factor in other costs before you agree to a purchase. Consider what it will cost to rent a truck or a trailer, to fill up that truck with gas, and to buy the tools and supplies you'll need to fix up your find.

6 super tips for garage sale shopping

Your next piece of furniture could be waiting around the block. A garage sale can be a treasure chest of cheap, used furniture. You could get a quality piece for half its original price by following this advice.

- Keep an eye out for garage sales in your neighborhood and look through your local newspaper for upcoming sales. Early in the morning is a good time to go if you want a bargain. So is later that afternoon when other customers have all gone home.

- Be prepared before you leave for the sale. Dress in comfortable clothes with layers in case of unpredictable weather.

- Bring a tape measure to make sure furniture is the right size and a camera if you need pictures of the item. Rope and other packing supplies are also handy if you plan on moving a piece of furniture back to your house.

- Go ahead and offer roughly two-thirds less than their asking price. Sellers are prepared to haggle with you. Most likely, you'll wind up paying 20 percent less than they originally asked.

- Let the seller know you have cash in hand if you offer a lower price. If they realize you're serious about buying, they're more likely to meet your offer.

- Be confident when bargaining with a seller. Remember anything they don't sell has to be dragged out to the curb for the garbage man to pick up. They want to make a sale, and time is on your side, so let the bargaining begin.

Save big bucks on decorator pieces

Look like you live in a model home for a fraction of the cost. Buy the used furniture and accessories you see in model homes for a tenth of their original price.

Residential builders only need the furniture while they're selling property. Once they've sold out, they aren't concerned with making a profit off their used furniture. They just want to get rid of it so the asking price is low.

Tell a salesperson you're interested in the model's furniture so you can attend a public sale or auction. Once you're at the sale, you can choose from a variety of beds, chairs, entertainment centers, children's bedroom sets, artwork, vases, and much more.

Gifts

Beware of buying gift cards

If you're buying gift cards for your friends and family, you better read the fine print. That's because many of the gift cards sold by retailers have expiration dates, or dates after which monthly fees are charged to the card if it has not yet been used, reducing its original balance.

Gift cards "should come with a warning attached," according to Charles Schumer, D-N.Y. Survey results released from his office show that some companies deduct up to $2.50 per month if a card isn't used in a certain amount of time. These fees are often allowed to run up to 67 percent of the original worth of the card.

Now that the word is getting out about what merchants have been doing, some states are passing laws against gift card fees. And the merchants themselves are starting to change their policies for fear of driving their loyal customers away.

For instance, recently Starbucks and Circuit City changed their policies and stopped charging gift card fees. Walgreens and Chili's charge $2 per month after the card has not been used for 12 months.

So if you're buying gift cards, you better make sure you know what the policy of your merchant is so you can tell the receiver. Or maybe it's better to boycott those cards that charge fees altogether until retailers get the message that customers aren't going to stand for gift card fees of any kind.

Guide to incredible seasonal sales

Some goods go on sale like clockwork every year — linens in January, for instance, and new cars at the year's end.

Month	Sales
January	holiday cards, calendars, linens, appliances, and furniture
February	President's Day sales and clothing catalog closeouts from companies like L.L. Bean
March	winter clothes clearance and spring goods like gardening tools
May	travel deals, luggage, jewelry, gardening supplies, outdoor furniture, even mattresses
July	fantastic Fourth of July sales on tires, appliances, electronics, and furniture, along with swimwear and summer clothes specials
September	travel bargains, school and office supplies, new cars, and Labor Day blowout sales on warm-weather clothes and shoes, outdoor items, kitchenware, and tires
December	free calendars from businesses, candles, planners, holiday lights and decorations, and "after-Christmas sales"

Why buy high-priced roses from a fancy florist when you can get beautiful buds cheap, even free. Try these locations for fresh-cut flowers.

- local farmers' market
- wholesale flower market
- downtown street vendors
- wholesale clubs, such as Costco
- grocery stores with floral departments
- your own garden

Of course, if you buy them during a major holiday, they will cost more than usual, but these sellers will still give you the best deals.

Seasonal sales like these offer the best deals. Take full advantage of them by shopping for gifts year round and tucking them away in a box for holidays, birthdays, and other special occasions.

Pay less for flower deliveries

It doesn't pay to call an 800 number to wire flowers or order them through an Internet site. Here's why. Your local florist can make the same arrangement and deliver it for less.

In fact, when you place an order with one of these big companies, they simply order your flowers from a small florist near you who then delivers them.

The difference — you pay more, perhaps 25 percent more just for placing your order through a Web site or 800 number rather than directly with your local florist.

Next time a special occasion rolls around, cut out the middleman and go straight to the source. You'll support small businesses and save money, too.

Sniff out deals on fancy fragrances

Don't buy perfume from departments stores — shop online instead. Major department stores carry rich scents at even richer prices, but Internet sellers offer the same smells for less. You can even get fragrances online that you can't find in stores.

Start with these respected Web sites. Before you buy anything, compare prices at your department store with those you find online. Factor in shipping and handling charges for the Internet sellers, and see if they still offer a better deal.

- www.perfumania.com

- www.scentiments.com

- www.perfume.com

Give the gift of time

Sometimes the best gifts are those you make yourself and give from your heart, and if you have a large family, it may be the only gifts you can afford.

That's what Jim Garver discovered. He and his wife have six siblings between the two of them, and they learned early on to stretch their slim budget by handcrafting holiday gifts.

"One year I got free calendars from my insurance agent featuring Currier & Ives prints. I mounted the prints on plywood and used molding to build a frame around them, then gave one or two to each of my brothers and sisters," he explains. Not good with wood? Never fear. You could also put the prints in inexpensive dime-store frames.

His family got in on the act, too. "My brother and his wife found large blocks of wood — about 4 inches cubed — and used stencils to make giant alphabet blocks. Some sides had letters. Some had holly, candy canes, or things like that. There were enough of them so you could set them up on the mantle to say 'Merry Christmas' 'Happy Holidays,' or 'The Garvers.' We still have those, too."

Get creative with your own gift giving. Write down favorite family recipes for a loved one moving out on their own, or give a gift certificate for a favor you could do for them. It's free for you and a cherished memory for them.

Groceries

What to do before you shop

Before you head off to the supermarket, plan your meals for the week. Check your pantry or cupboard to see what you have and then check the supermarket ads to come up with some ideas. Crosscheck your meals with your calendar to see what nights you won't be home for dinner. When you take the time to plan, it's easier to save money.

4 things to take to the store

Once you have your meals planned and you know what you need, it's time to make a shopping list. Then you're ready to head to the supermarket. Besides your list, make sure you're armed with your supermarket's floor plan, a big fistful of coupons, and either cash, your checkbook, or a debit card. Stick to the items on your list. Don't let yourself be dazzled by anything that's not written down.

Easy way to buy less

The only thing a grocery store manager likes better than a hungry shopper is a store filled with hungry shoppers. If your stomach is empty when you shop, you'll most likely spend 10 to 15 percent more than you normally would. Remember the word HALT — hungry, angry, lonely, and tired. Try not to shop if you're feeling out of sorts.

Uncover great prices on produce

You're better off buying locally grown fruits and vegetables in season. Otherwise, you'll pay more at the register. The cost of transporting food from other areas increases the price. That's true whether they're shipping it from another part of the country or from South America. If you really want to save, buy extra fruits and vegetables in season, then blanch and freeze them to use another time.

Take advantage of senior discounts

Check with your favorite food store to find out if they offer senior discounts. Most supermarkets set aside one day a week for seniors to get a percentage off their total bill.

Look high and low for savings

There comes a time in almost all grocery shopping trips when you have to venture into the processed food jungle. To help you keep your budget intact, remember to look at products on the top shelves and the bottom shelves. Shelf space at eye level is the priciest. You will have to look up and down for the lesser-known, cheaper brands.

Buy generic and save 50 percent

Generic brands can save you 50 percent or more off name-brand prices. And you may be surprised how similar they are to the products you usually buy. Don't think twice about buying generic staples, like sugar, flour, salt, pepper, light bulbs, cleaning products, and paper goods. But you might want to do

Item	Brand name	Generic	Savings
17.3 oz. wheat bran cereal	Kellogg's $2.84	Wal-Mart $1.50	$1.34
20 oz. loaf white bread	Colonial $2.17	Publix $0.99	$1.18
5 lbs. sugar	Domino $2.69	Publix $1.69	$1.00
1 gallon 2-percent milk	Mayfield $4.35	Kroger $3.48	$0.87
2 lbs. 8 oz. peanut butter	Jif $3.74	Wal-Mart $2.98	$0.76
1 lb. stick margarine	Land o' Lakes $1.39	Kroger $0.75	$0.64
2 liters cola	Coke $1.59	Kroger $0.99	$0.60
16 oz. cheddar cheese	Kraft $3.54	Wal-Mart $3.14	$0.40
1 lb. frozen green beans	Birds Eye $1.33	Publix $0.99	$0.34

a taste test on canned goods and snack foods. Still, any generic items you buy will help reduce your grocery bill.

Action plan curbs impulse buying

Don't let creative displays, especially near the checkout, lure you into buying things you can't afford. Marketing experts know how to get you to spend more. Don't give them a chance. Most grocery stores are set up with the staples, like meat, bread, dairy, and produce, around the edges. If you just walk the perimeter, you'll avoid the temptations lurking in the aisles.

Why you should do-it-yourself

You don't have to peel and mash potatoes anymore. Just buy them ready made and heat in your microwave. Unfortunately, that package costs about $5 but only saved you 7 to 10 minutes of cutting and mashing.

If you earn $15 an hour, you make $5 for every 20 minutes of work. You just spent that $5, which took 20 minutes to earn, on something that only takes 10 minutes to make.

So remember, whether it's shredded, assembled, diced, pre-cooked, or packaged into single servings, it will cost you more. Think twice before spending money on something you can easily prepare yourself.

Unit pricing comes to the rescue

A unit is a quantity, such as ounces, servings, or pounds. Most grocery stores have the unit pricing on the label that shows the product's price. But there are items you may need to figure out yourself, so keep your calculator powered up.

For example, if a 16-ounce can of olives costs 88 cents, its unit price is 88 cents divided by 16 or 5.5 cents per ounce. Compare that to a larger 24-ounce can at $1.09. Its unit price is $1.09 divided by 24 or 4.5 cents per ounce. The larger can is the better value.

Bulk buying brings big savings

If you can afford to spend the extra money upfront, think about buying some of your grocery items in bulk. Foods like rice, cereal, pasta, pet food, sugar, flour, and even peanut butter may be your ticket to big savings.

But it's only a good deal if you use it all. Do the math to find out if it's really a bargain or just an illusion. Be smart so you don't throw your savings out with the trash.

Protect yourself from overcharges

A recent study revealed that supermarkets charged the wrong price on over 10 percent of their products. Make sure you're charged fairly for the items you buy. As you shop, make a detailed list of your items and put an asterisk beside any sale items. Watch the prices as the clerk scans your order. If you prefer, after you're done checking out, step to the side and compare your cash register receipt with your list. If you find an item that doesn't match, go to customer service for a refund. Some stores will let you have the item free of charge.

How to save money on breakfast

You can spend lots of money on milk, eggs, and packaged cold cereals. But you can slash your breakfast expenses significantly if you switch over to eating hot cereal in the morning.

Don't buy the little packages of instant oatmeal. They are expensive. And the one- or two-pound cylinders of oats in the stores can be a bit pricey, too.

You will want to check out co-ops and the like to see what kind of bulk deals you can find. You may be able to purchase about 25 pounds of oats for about $10. If you do purchase in large quantities, divide the oats into smaller portions and store them in airtight containers in cool places.

You can serve the oats as a hot breakfast or even make your own granola, which is significantly cheaper than what you can buy in stores. Consider keeping powdered milk in the house to make your recipes. It's cheaper and more convenient than keeping stocked up on fresh milk.

Slice 50 percent off your grocery bill

Coupons can help you slice up to 50 percent off your grocery bill, especially when you combine them with special sales, like double or triple coupon days and buy one, get one free offers.

Here are some clever tips to help you make the most of your coupons.

- Buy a coupon organizer to separate your coupons into categories.

- When you make your shopping list, put a "c" by the items you have coupons for.

- Ask at the customer service counter for a store directory. On shopping day, separate your coupons by aisle and product.

- Look for products with instant coupons on the outside of the packaging.

- Watch out for the fine print. Many coupons have restrictions, like size or style.

- Clean out expired coupons from your organizer.

- Ask someone in customer service when they'll be having double and triple coupon days.

- Combine sale items, coupons, rebates, online coupons, and double coupon days for extra savings.

Make your trip to the grocery store worthwhile with some big savings. Here are 12 shopping tips that will slash your weekly grocery bill.

- ✓ Plan weekly menus.
- ✓ Stick to your shopping list.
- ✓ Eat before shopping.
- ✓ Buy fruits and vegetables in season.
- ✓ Shop on senior discount days.
- ✓ Buy generic brands.
- ✓ Avoid impulse buying.
- ✓ Don't buy prepared foods.
- ✓ Look high and low.
- ✓ Use unit pricing.
- ✓ Buy in bulk.
- ✓ Watch for checkout errors.

■ Be dedicated. Clip, call, or go online often to reap the savings you want.

No-hassle way to collect coupons

You can save up to $1,000 or more on groceries each year. Just sign up with a coupon clearinghouse. For a small fee, you'll have unlimited access to all the coupons you want.

Pay for a coupon? That's unheard of. But if you buy the Sunday paper for coupons, the cost is about equal, and you don't have to clip them yourself. Plus, you have the coupons you want, not a bunch of coupons you'll never use. Each service is slightly different, so take a good look at them to find the best one for you.

Centsoff.com at *www.centsoff.com* charges a small, one-time sign-up fee and $7.50 for a set of 50 coupons. OnlineCoupons.com at *www.onlinecoupons.com* charges a $99 annual membership fee. You can get the annual fee waived with an access code when you click on a link to one of their sponsors. The sponsor gives you the access code if you accept a free trial of their product or service. OnlineCoupons.com charges 10 percent of the face value of the coupons you choose, plus a handling fee of 75 cents.

GroceryCoupons.com at *www.grocerycoupons.com* is similar to OnlineCoupons.com minus the annual fee. All three of the above services mail your coupons to you within a week of your purchase.

Here are some other coupon clearinghouses you might want to check out.

■ *www.valpak.com*

■ *www.dealsdujour.com*

■ *www.homebasics.com*

Secret to finding rebates galore

You can find dozens of money-saving rebate offers on one unique source. Visit RefundSweepers Online Savings at *www.refundsweepers.com* and check out the Rebates section with offers for many different types of products. Some offers even make the items you want absolutely free. Click on Free Items to browse through complimentary gifts ranging from coffee makers to ink cartridges.

Rebates generally require you to pay full price for an item, and then you send in documentation to receive a rebate by mail. Remember to keep copies of all paperwork when applying for a rebate. According to the Federal Trade Commission, those copies are important because they will be the only record you have of the transaction if anything goes wrong.

> If saving time is just as important to you as saving money, do your grocery shopping on Tuesdays. According to the Food Marketing Institute, only 9 percent of shoppers shop on Tuesday. Your next best days are Monday and Thursday at 12 percent. Friday and Sunday see 16 percent of all shoppers, while 22 percent shop on Saturday.

Enjoy brand-name products for less

Make friends with your computer to save money on many of your favorite brand-name products. Start by searching manufacturer's Web sites, which are sometimes listed on the product packaging, for coupon deals. Some companies, like Wyeth Consumer Healthcare, the maker of Advil and ChapStick, allow you to print coupons directly from their Web sites.

Other companies have information on their sites about items that are on sale. In addition, many manufacturers have toll-free phone numbers on their packaging, too. Call them and request the coupons you want. You'll be surprised how much you can save with a free phone call.

Get paid for your opinions

Marketing research companies are always looking for people to fill out surveys so they can learn more about public opinion.

One company, I-Say at *www.i-Say.com*, gives members the opportunity to fill out surveys in exchange for the chance to win cash awards and prizes. As a bonus, i-Say holds regular drawings where members can win up to $250.

To find even more survey opportunities, visit RefundSweepers at *www.refundsweepers.com*, and click on Surveys paying cash in the Freebies section.

You will have to share some personal information to participate in these surveys, so it's important to choose surveys from honest companies. For example, i-Say is a division of Ipsos Insight, a marketing research company and a member of the Council of American Survey Research Organizations (CASRO). CASRO is a trade association of survey research organizations that requires its member companies to follow a Code of Standards and Ethics for Survey Research.

Before you give out any personal information, check the CASRO membership directory at *www.casro.org* to make sure the company is a member.

Discover how to get paid to shop

Many grocery stores will actually pay you to shop at their store. If you have good written and oral communication skills and are good at noticing details, you may be a candidate for a job as a mystery shopper.

Over 750 companies hand out shopping assignments to mystery shoppers. A mystery shopper acts like a real shopper, while evaluating the services of supermarkets and other retail establishments. When you're finished shopping, you turn in a written report about all aspects of your shopping experience.

Depending on how many assignments you choose, you can shop full time or part time.

To get started, educate yourself about the mystery shopping industry to make sure it's right for you. *Mystery Shopping Made Simple* by Dr. Ilisha S. Newhouse is a good place to start. You can find a lot of information about mystery shopping on the Internet — but be careful. If a company wants you to pay a fee or buy a list of company names, don't fall for it. If it costs money, it's probably a scam.

To become a Certified Customer Service Evaluator, contact the National Center for Professional Mystery Shoppers & Merchandisers at *www.ncpmscenter.org*. They offer four different online programs ranging in price from $49 to $98. The one-and-a-half to two-week courses teach you everything from getting contracts to business writing techniques. All the programs lead to certification and include continuing education courses.

If you want to earn some money while you shop, give mystery shopping a try. Then feel free to shop 'til you drop.

Fetch lower prices for pet supplies

You can find everything for your pet at great discounts when you know where to look. Instead of buying from a veterinarian, try these five sources of dirt-cheap pet supplies.

- Visit the online clearance outlet at *www.drsfostersmith.com*. You can find pet supplies for up to 70 percent off, but don't stop there. Sniff around at other online stores, too. Try *www.petmarket.com*, *www.petsmart.com*, and *www.kvvet.com* — just for starters. Compare costs and check whether you'll have to pay shipping and handling.

- Try local stores of specialty retail chains, like PETsMART and Petco. They may offer you great prices without the cost of shipping and handling.

- Check out membership clubs, like Sam's and Costco. These clubs usually charge a membership fee, so figure your potential savings before you become a member. Don't be surprised if you still save money — even with the membership fee.

- You can request a wholesale catalog from most of the companies you find online, including UPCO at *www.upco.com*.

- Selection might be limited, but don't miss discount opportunities at big box stores, like Home Depot and Lowe's.

Health and beauty

Find super deals on supplements

Mail order catalogs and Web sites can help you get the best deals on herbs, minerals, vitamins, and other nutritional supplements. These sellers offer deep discounts over retail stores and carry a wider variety, too.

The Vitamin Shoppe is one of the most trusted names in the business. Browse their Web site at *www.vitaminshoppe.com* for great deals, or call them toll-free at 800-223-1216 to order a catalog. You could qualify for free shipping if you spend $75 or more.

Internet users will love the deals they discover online at Walgreens. Just go to *www.walgreenshealth.com* and click on Mail Service Pharmacy. Then, click on the link Order Non-Prescription Items. From here you can download an ad for the latest deals on personal care items, as well as herbs, vitamins, and other supplements. These deals change regularly, so check for updates. Specials abound with these other sellers, too.

- Get a free catalog from Swanson Health Products by calling 800-824-4491, or shop online at *www.swansonvitamins.com*.

- Order online from VitaCost at *www.vitacost.com*, or request their free catalog at 800-793-2601.

- Herbal Remedies gives you free shipping on orders over $75 at *www.herbalremedies.com*.

- Drugstore.com serves up specials on their Web site at *www.drugstore.com* and promises free shipping if you spend at least $49.

The bargains may be great, but take a few safety steps when ordering from a new dealer. Call your local Better Business Bureau (BBB) to learn more about a company before you buy from them. And always look for the BBB seal of approval when shopping online.

Why you must have an FSA

A Flexible Spending Account, or FSA, can lower your tax bill and pay for health care. This program lets you set aside part of your pretax income, then use it later to reimburse yourself for health care costs not covered by your insurance — copays and

A cheap way to 'clean up'

You should never buy toiletries at the grocery store or drugstore, says the Consumer Credit Counseling Service of Atlanta. You're throwing your money away if you purchase items like shampoo, bath soap, toothpaste, and shaving cream there. Instead, head to a large discount store, such as Sam's Club or Costco. These giants can save you anywhere from 20 to 50 percent on toiletries, as well as laundry detergent, cleaning supplies, and other household items. Or save big at your local dollar store where you'll often find name brands.

deductibles on doctor visits, prescriptions, hospital stays, glasses, and now some over-the-counter items.

Depending on how much you spend on health care each year, you could trim your tax bill by a few hundred dollars. The money you set aside in an FSA comes out of your paycheck before federal, Social Security, Medicare, and most state taxes. This lowers your gross income, which in turn lowers the taxes you owe. It can even drop you into a lower tax bracket.

Setting up an FSA is simple. Here's what you should do.

- Find out if your employer offers an FSA program.

- Decide how much money you expect to spend on health care during the next calendar year.

- Divide that amount by the number of paychecks you will receive. This tells you how much to take out of each paycheck and put in your spending account.

- Sign up for the FSA through your employer, and tell them how much to set aside from each paycheck.

- When you pay your copay on drugs or doctor visits, simply fill out a reimbursement form and send it off. You'll receive a check in the mail for that amount, which comes out of your FSA account.

In 2004, the Internal Revenue Service began allowing people to use FSAs for some, but not all, over-the-counter (OTC) items. According to the IRS, you can claim these and many other OTCs.

- aspirin
- anti-itch creams
- cough remedies
- cold medicines
- laxatives
- adhesive bandages
- hot/cold packs
- hearing aids
- glasses

Items like vitamins, herbal supplements, sunscreen, and skin creams used for general good health or cosmetic reasons may not be eligible. Your doctor must recommend a certain dosage for a specific medical condition to get reimbursed for these.

The one downside to an FSA is that, in most plans, you must spend all of the money you set aside by the year's end or you lose it. The best way to get around that — only set aside money for drugs, treatments, and doctor visits you know you will have over the next year.

Perk up your hearing for less

You no longer need to shell out big bucks for custom-made hearing aids. Now you can order ready-to-wear devices off the Internet for a fraction of the cost and have them shipped straight to your home. Prices vary widely, but they almost always cost less than custom hearing aids. The quality of sound varies, too, so you may have to try more than one to find the right "fit."

- Hearing Help Express sells several aids, including the EarMate-65, which comes with five different sizes of tips so you can choose the one that best fits your ear — and for only $299 each. Call them at 800-221-2099 or visit their Web site *www.hearinghelpexpress.com*.

- Crystal Ear also offers products starting at $299 apiece. They are available by phone at 800-374-5959 or online at *www.crystalear.com*.

- Some hunting products do double duty as hearing devices, muffling loud noises like gun shots while enhancing soft sounds. They aren't officially hearing aids so you can easily buy devices like Walker's Game Ear for around $200 at local sporting goods stores, or go to *www.walkersgameear.com*.

A hearing test by an audiologist can help you find the best match the first time. Some dealers suggest you send them a copy of your hearing test to help them program your aid to meet your needs.

Ask the sellers about their warranty and return policies. Most give you a 30- or 60-day trial period to decide if the hearing aid meets your needs. Call your state Attorney General or local Better Business Bureau and ask about any hearing aid dealer you are thinking of buying from. These agencies can tell you how many complaints a business has received and whether they are licensed to sell hearing aids in your state.

Home buying

Barter for a better price

A seller may list his house at a certain price, but you don't have to pay that. Negotiating can knock thousands off the cost of your next home. Sharpen your edge with this advice.

- Assume everyone is willing to bargain. Don't be afraid to negotiate when it comes to buying a home. You have nothing to lose except money.

- Decide what you want to pay rather than letting the seller set the price. Keep a reasonable figure in mind, and don't go above it.

- Build a relationship with the seller. It's hard to say no to someone you know and like.

- Compromise. Try not to think of negotiating as a win-lose situation where each side tries to best the other. Work together to find a price that makes both parties happy.

- Stay flexible. For example, offer to close when it's most convenient for the seller, and they may bargain more in other areas.

- Be willing to walk away. It's the most powerful weapon you have. If the seller knows you have fallen in love with the place, he may think it's only a matter of time until you cave in.

Keep these tactics in mind as you go through the home buying process. A little haggling goes a long way.

Move next to, not into, a mansion

Tired of being on the outside looking in? Buy the cheapest house in the best neighborhood and live better for less. You get all the benefits of a good neighborhood without the high price tag.

It's more than a home — it's a wise investment. Your house may not outshine the others, but the expensive homes around you will eventually raise its value. Keep in mind that improvements and repairs could offset your savings.

Avoid overpaying for your next home

Deciding how much money to offer for a home is part art and part science. What people consider a "fair price" largely depends on the cost of similar homes in the same neighborhood.

Called comparables, these homes act as valuable guidelines in the negotiating process. Just a little preparation could save you a lot of money. You are less likely to overpay for the house you want when you know what comparable ones recently sold for. You can dig up this information several ways.

- View selling prices yourself in the newspaper or track them down at your local town hall. Focus on sales in the last year to get the most accurate feel for the market.

- Real estate agents can give you a list of comparable home prices. Speak to a few who specialize in the neighborhood that interests you.

- Look up comparables on Internet Web sites. But beware — some make you pay for outdated information. You will find useful, free facts online at *www.domania.com*. Search its Home Price Check to get the sales price for any address in the United States from 1987 to the present.

Of course, the market can't predict how much your next house will cost, but it can give you a rough idea of how much you should spend.

Numbers aren't everything, though. Keep in mind a home's layout, location, age, condition, and other factors like who paid closing costs also play a role in the final price.

Check out these 16 super Web sites for home listings and buying advice.

- *www.realestateabc.com*
- *www.realtor.com*
- *www.mlsonline.com*
- *www.century21.com*
- *www.coldwellbanker.com*
- *www.remax.com*
- *www.domania.com*
- *www.buyowner.com*
- *www.forsalebyowner.com*
- *www.fsbocentral.com*
- *www.homeclassifieds. com*
- *www.homeswatch.com*
- *www.homegain.com*
- *www.homescape.com*
- *www.myhomeplans.com*
- *www.real-estate.com*

Insider's guide to buying foreclosures

Another person's loss could be your gain. Foreclosed homes make great opportunities to buy more for less.

Foreclosures occur when the owner can no longer make the mortgage payments or fails to pay property taxes. Then the lender or tax authorities take back the home and sell it, usually for much less than it's worth just to get rid of it.

It's easy to take advantage of these deals.

- Call the bank's loan officer in charge of foreclosures and make an offer. The bank may also hire a real estate agent to sell the house.

- Ask your county tax collector's office how they dispose of foreclosed property. Often, you can buy it in a public auction.

- Contact federal agencies, like the Internal Revenue Service (IRS) and Federal Housing Authority (FHA), that provide free lists of foreclosures for sale.

- Make a bid for a Housing and Urban Development (HUD) home by submitting a sealed bid through a real estate agent. Go online to *www.hud.gov* for more information and a listing of available homes, or call the HUD office in your state.

- Write to the clerk of the federal court in your area and ask for a free listing of bankruptcy sales.

These homes can be a steal. You can sometimes buy them with little or no money down, get preferred loan terms from the lender, and even score tax breaks from government agencies eager to unload the property.

But some you don't want. The really cheap homes are often in disrepair or in unstable communities. And you have to buy all foreclosures "as is." Get a home inspection before you sign on the dotted line, or you may find yourself stuck with expensive repairs.

Find a fixer-upper for less

If you're handy, you can save big on the cost of a home. Just look for a house priced well below market value that needs a little work.

The perfect "fixer-upper" will be good as new with a few minor repairs, cosmetic improvements, and some paint. However, stay away from homes that need major structural work unless you are very talented.

Make sure you take into account the cost of any repairs the house will need before buying it. It's no bargain if you have to spend a small fortune.

Score real deals at real estate auctions

"Going once, going twice … sold!" Those words could mean you're a homeowner. Real estate auctions are fast becoming a popular way to buy and sell houses.

No wonder. A recent study of a HUD auction in Florida found people paid much less for these homes than they were worth on the market, up to 21.5 percent less.

Auction prices vary depending on the neighborhood and condition of the homes, but good deals abound. Call your state's office of Housing and Urban Development for information about upcoming auctions in your area.

Hammer out bargains with builder

Go right to the source when shopping for your next home — the builder. Buying direct from a builder can shave money not only off the cost of the home itself but also off real estate agent fees.

You will probably snag the best deal buying a model home or a finished home in a new development, but you can also haggle on one built from scratch.

Unlike banks, builders have the power to make creative trade-offs. Even if they refuse to lower the home's price, they may add a fireplace or throw in other extras. They might even pay the closing costs.

Watch for these other ways to save money.

- Stay below the builder's allowances for items like flooring and kitchen appliances where you have options, and make sure he reimburses you the difference. This can lower the final price.

- Try to find a cheaper supplier than the one the builder uses.

- Look for a lower-priced builder. You might get a better deal if they know you are shopping around. Be sure to choose one whose work and reputation are both excellent.

Slash debt for smaller payments

Here's another benefit of lowering your debt — it will help you buy a house. Without high credit card debt, you may qualify for a larger loan and a better interest rate on your mortgage.

As a rule of thumb, lenders say you should spend no more than 28 percent of your gross monthly income on a mortgage payment. The total of your mortgage plus other long-term debts, like those for cars or college, should not exceed 36 percent.

Dodge disaster with inspection

You've heard the expression, "It takes money to make money." Well, sometimes the same rule applies to saving it.

Spending a little money up front on a home inspection can save you an arm and a leg later on, when you have already committed to a money pit.

A skillful home inspector will point out both the good and bad aspects of a home, including potential problems, essential repairs, and necessary maintenance. Try this advice from the Better Business Bureau to find one you can trust.

- Ask friends and neighbors for recommendations.

- Make sure the inspector has experience with the type of home you're considering.

- Ask about his training and experience. How long has he been in business? Does he belong to a professional association, like the American Society of Home Inspectors?

- Avoid those with potential conflicts of interest. It's hard to trust someone who will benefit financially if you buy the house.

- Accompany him during the inspection and ask questions. A thorough assessment can take up to five hours, so set aside plenty of time.

- Ask when you will get a copy of the final written report. Look this over carefully before you commit to buying the home.

Contact the American Society of Home Inspectors at 800-743-2744 or visit their Web site at *www.ashi.org* to learn more and find a qualified inspector near you. You can also write to them at this address.

Contact: American Society of Home Inspectors, Inc.
             932 Lee Street, Suite 101
             Des Plaines, IL 60016

Make more money selling your home

How much is your home worth? That's crucial information if you plan to sell at the best possible price. Appraisers will tell you for a hefty fee, but you have another option.

Before selling your home, get a free appraisal — no Realtor necessary. Just visit the HomeGain Web site online at *www.homegain.com*. Then type in your street address, ZIP code,

Turn your getaway into a gold mine

A second home can be a first-rate investment. Just ask Bob and Kathy, whose vacation home at the Jersey shore is now worth more than six times what they paid for it.

In 1986, they bought a small vacation home in Cape May, New Jersey for $62,000. "Last year the same homes were selling at $375,000 and up!" Bob says. "That's in less than 20 years. Quite an investment, huh? Location, location, location."

Wonderful restaurants, quaint Victorian homes, and a relaxing atmosphere make Cape May an ideal vacation spot, one Bob and Kathy have enjoyed for years.

"In retrospect, it was the best investment we could have made to get that kind of return on our money," Bob says. "That is not why we bought it, however. It was only for a getaway. We had no idea the property would appreciate the way it has."

The house even helped pay for itself. "We rented it selectively for the first 15 years while we were paying off the mortgage. We rented it about four or five weeks a year to friends and colleagues," he explains.

Once they paid off the house, they did some renovations. They put on a new roof, bought a new furnace, installed new carpet and linoleum, and had the furniture reupholstered. Their efforts — and initial investment — should pay off handsomely if they ever decide to sell.

the number of bedrooms and baths, approximate square footage, acreage, and a few other details about your home.

HomeGain will give you a ballpark figure on how much your home is worth as well as recent selling prices for houses in your area. This can help you price your home more realistically, improving your chances of a quick sale.

This Web site offers other handy tools, too, such as:

- a glossary of real estate terms.

- calculators to help you figure out your profit and capital gains tax.

- a tool to compare the expense of moving versus improving your current home.

- free consumer guides, articles by real estate professionals, and other advice.

It can even help you find and compare real estate agents for the best rate. All in all, it's a great place to start when selling your home.

Home improvement

Projects that pay for themselves

Remodeling your home can bring big returns — a more comfortable lifestyle and a more valuable home when you decide to sell. Unfortunately, not all home improvements pay off at resale. Turn your home into your castle for next to nothing by choosing home improvement projects that pay for themselves at resale. Some projects could earn you 70 to 104 percent of your remodeling expenses back!

Some projects add more value to your home than others, because buyers will pay more for them. Adding a deck has the highest payoff, says *Remodeling* magazine's 2003 Cost vs. Value Report. Nationally, homeowners on average recoup the total cost of this job plus an extra 4 percent when they sell their house, so 104 percent of the total expense. See how these other popular projects add up.

- Putting in a nice extra bathroom nets you a 95 percent return on the money you spend.

- Remodeling an existing bathroom does almost as well, earning you 89 percent of your money back.

- Updating your kitchen with new paint, floors, and cabinets recoups on average 75 percent of its cost.

- Turning existing extra space into something usable generally offers high returns. Finishing an attic into a bedroom and bath suite garners a 93 percent return on your money at sale time.

- Finishing a basement into family living space will pay back 79 percent of its cost.

- A few outdoor improvements pay off, too. Replacing old siding with new vinyl siding nets a whopping 98 percent return.

Choosing one of these remodeling projects doesn't guarantee a good return. Your neighborhood, climate, and housing market also affect what buyers are willing to pay for your home. Consider what's happening in the neighborhood around you, and decide how long you plan to live there. Extensive or expensive renovations may not pay for themselves if you only plan to live there a few years.

Just remember — increasing your home's value can be worthwhile, but in the end, your happiness matters more than the money you make.

Make weak economy work for you

Plan to remodel or repair your home when the real estate market and the economy are slow. You'll pay less for labor and materials from contractors hungry for work. But during boom times they set the price, and you may end up with less skilled workers.

Tips for finding a quality contractor

If you're remodeling your home and you need a contractor, what's the best way to go about getting a good one? Here are a few tips to help you find a quality contractor to transform your home.

- Ask your friends and acquaintances. Ask anyone who has had work done recently and find out if they were happy with the results. If they were, get the contractor's name. You also might get in contact with real estate agents in your area. It's likely they'll know who's reliable and who's not.

- Make a list of what you need to have done, and be specific. Give model numbers and brand names of what you want installed. Write up the time frame you expect.

- Get bids from at least three different contractors. Get the contractors' license numbers. Make sure you get license numbers for subcontractors who might come into the picture later as well.

- Don't automatically go for the lowest bid. That contractor could be inexperienced or he may not know how to do the job correctly. Watch the high-end bids as well — they may be trying to take advantage of you. Do your research and you'll make the right choice.

> Making your own improvements gives you a certain sense of pride, but don't get carried away. Some jobs should always be left to professionals.
>
> - Don't mess with a home's structural support. Installing a window in a solid wall and other projects that affect the home's support system can cause major damage if done wrong, from sagging doors to a collapsing roof.
> - Never do your own electrical work. Improper wiring could make your home go up in smoke.
> - Amateur plumbing is just asking for trouble, from water damage to sewer gasses backing up in your home.

- Make a payment agreement before the work starts. For instance, you might put an initial deposit down of 30 to 40 percent.

- Make yourself available to answer questions the contractor might have. This will prevent delays in the
completion of the project. If things change during the
course of the work — put the changes and the agreements concerning compensation, etc., in writing. Keep
communication flowing and you'll end up with a result
you love.

DIY to S-A-V-E

Simple home improvements don't have to break your bank.
Thanks to do-it-yourself (DIY) Web sites, cable channels, and
classes, you no longer need to hire a handyman for every job.
Now you can lay your own tile, hang a door, reupholster a
chair, or refinish an old table.

Internet Web sites like the ones listed below often offer
detailed instructions on how to do a variety of projects as well
as lists of materials and trouble-shooting tips. If you don't
understand the instructions, look for the Contact Us link on
the Web site, then e-mail or call them with your questions.

- *www.homedepot.com*

- *www.diynet.com*

- *www.askthebuilder.com*

- *www.hgtv.com*

Major hardware stores often offer classes where experts teach
you how to use tools safely, lay tile yourself, apply special paint
techniques, and other tricks of the trade. And remember to
check bookstores and garage sales for how-to books with good
photographs and illustrations.

Discover a gold mine of supplies

Hunt down building supply auctions. They will usually offer surplus inventory from suppliers and distributors. You can find appliances, fixtures, flooring, tile, doors, cabinets, and hundreds of other items — a veritable gold mine. Just remember, auctions don't offer warranties or returns, and rarely deliver.

Find a great deal on carpeting

From buying to installing, these tips will guide you through the process of getting a great deal on new carpeting.

- Buy your carpet directly from the manufacturer. They beat retail prices by as much as 75 percent.

- Live too far from a carpet outlet? Telephone ordering services can still save you 50 to 80 percent off retail, and they deliver right to your door. Start with Bearden Brothers Carpet & Textile Corp. at 800-433-0074, S & S Mills at 800-241-4013, or Warehouse Carpets at 800-526-2229.

- Get the heaviest, most densely woven carpet you can afford. It will last much longer.

- Buy a little more carpet than you need. Seal the scraps in a plastic bag and use them later to replace damaged spots.

- Have an expert install your carpeting. Most manufacturers only honor their warranties if a professional does the job. Keep the installation receipt with your warranty papers.

- Hire your own installer instead of letting the carpet store do it for you. They will charge a hefty fee just for making a phone call.

- Demand a separate, flat-fee estimate for each extra service like moving your furniture or disposing of old carpet. They may overcharge you if they roll it into one job estimate.

- Ask family or neighborhood kids to help move your furniture. The carpet installer will charge a lot more.

- Put in your carpet during the summer or winter. Experts charge top dollar in spring and fall, their busy seasons.

Get more mileage from new carpet

Instead of buying costly floor coverings, invest in a high-quality carpet pad. It costs a lot less, lengthens the rug's life, and makes even inexpensive carpets feel luxurious. A good pad also cuts energy bills by better insulating the floor. The Carpet Cushion Council makes these recommendations.

- In high-traffic areas and rooms with heavy furniture, choose a heavy, high-density, but thin pad, no more than 3/8-inch thick.

- Put a thicker cushion in bedrooms, dens, and areas with less wear and tear, but still choose a highest-density pad.

- Don't scrimp too much. The carpet cushion is a better investment than the carpet itself, and you'll get more for your money.

Rainy day fund a blessing

Major repairs, like replacing the hot water heater, seem to happen suddenly and may wreak financial havoc. Ease the pain of repairs by stashing 1 percent of your monthly income into a special maintenance fund.

For instance, if you earn $2,000 a month, set aside just $20 as part of your monthly budget. It will add up fast and become a blessing when you most need it. By planning ahead, you'll protect your livelihood when costly problems crop up.

Quick fix for electrical woes

Did the lights go out in your bathroom or that old refrigerator suddenly stop working? Don't panic. Before you throw away the fridge or call the electrician, check the circuit breaker.

Overloaded circuits and other electrical problems trip the breaker to prevent fires. First, unplug everything in the powerless room, and turn off the lights. Then find the main circuit breaker box.

Look for labels telling you which room or appliance each switch controls, or look for a switch out of line with others, either in the "Off" position or stuck in the middle. Find one? Reset the circuit by flipping the switch to "Off" and then "On."

Turn on the lights or plug in the appliance to see if it works. If not, or if this same circuit trips often, call an electrician as it could signal a more serious problem.

The National Association of the Remodeling Industry (NARI) offers 10 ways to save on remodeling projects.

- Skip the structural changes — revamp a tired room with new paint.
- Use textured wallpaper or paint to cover damaged walls instead of replacing them.
- Keep old kitchen appliances and build new, standard-size cabinets around them.
- Leave appliances and light fixtures in the same spot to save electrical and plumbing expenses.
- Look for hardwood floors under old linoleum, and refinish them instead of replacing the vinyl.
- Reface, not replace, old cabinets for a fresh look.
- Steal space from the linen closet to enlarge a bathroom.
- Add a small bow window or skylight in cramped bathrooms.
- Reglaze your tub instead of getting a new one.
- Install cultured marble sheets or fiberglass around bathtubs instead of ceramic tile.

A little care goes a long way

Home maintenance is like housework — do a little often and you won't have to do it all at once. Stay on top of small problems, and you may not face expensive repairs down the road. Keep your house in tip-top shape with this basic maintenance plan.

Once a year:

- Change the batteries in your smoke alarm.

- Check water heater for signs of leaking or rust.

Each fall:

- Clean the chimney flue to get rid of flammable creosote build-up, and check the firebrick for cracks.

- Drain outdoor water lines and hoses. Reopen them in spring.

In both spring and fall:

- Clean out gutters and downspouts, and check them for leaks.

- Trim back trees, shrubs, and heavy vegetation against the house.

- Repair the caulk on the outside of doors, windows, and other exterior areas, and replace damaged weather strips.

Clean your castle for mere pennies

Long before stores sold aisles of fancy cleaning products, people made do with simple, even natural supplies. Get back to basics.

Rubbing alcohol shines chrome faucets and disinfects counter-tops, while lemon juice lifts rust stains and mineral deposits.

You probably know club soda cleans fresh carpet stains, but it also washes stainless steel sinks and even vinyl floors.

Ammonia, on the other hand, works wonders on windows and mirrors. Mix it with water first, and avoid using it near bleach.

Baking soda cleans just about everything gently. Try it on countertops, porcelain sinks, ceramic tiles, and bathtubs. Vinegar beats bathtub film and grout stains, and the two together unclog drains. Pour baking soda directly down sink and tub drains, then slowly add vinegar to bubble out built-up muck.

Sleuth out potential problems

Hire a home inspector every five years to catch little problems before they become bank-breaking headaches. They'll examine areas like attics, roofs, and crawl spaces; spot roof leaks before they become gaping holes; and catch other problems you can't see, hear, or smell.

Here are just a few things your inspector will check.

- foundation and structural supports

- heating and air conditioning systems

- plumbing and electrical systems

- windows and doors

- roof and gutters

- fireplace and chimney

- smoke detectors and other safety devices

- landscaping and drainage

- exterior of the house

- ventilation and insulation

Ask friends and neighbors to recommend a good inspector, and make sure he is licensed by a national organization such as the American Society of Home Inspectors (ASHI) or the National Association of Home Inspectors (NAHI).

Home insurance

Slash premium with simple strategy

Lower your homeowners insurance by more than 35 percent. This little-used option is available to everyone. Just raise your deductible, and your premium will plummet.

The higher you can afford to go, the bigger your savings. Instead of a standard $250 deductible, aim for $2,000 or even $5,000. You'll save an average of 37 to 40 percent.

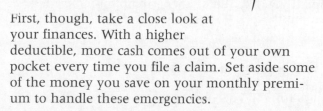

If those high numbers make you nervous, never fear. Any increase, even simply doubling it to $500, should shave a significant percentage off your premium. Talk to your insurance agent about adjusting your policy for maximum savings.

First, though, take a close look at your finances. With a higher deductible, more cash comes out of your own pocket every time you file a claim. Set aside some of the money you save on your monthly premium to handle these emergencies.

Make a policy of shopping around

You comparison shop for the best deals on groceries, clothing, cars, and electronics, so why not homeowners insurance?

Premiums can vary greatly from one company to another, so some deals are sure to be better than others. Follow these guidelines to find the best fit for you.

- Ask friends and neighbors for referrals, look in the Yellow Pages, or call your state insurance department.

- Get quotes from at least three insurance companies.

- Keep in mind that service counts just as much as price. Check each company's complaint record with the National Association of Insurance Commissioners online at *www.naic.org*, or call your state's insurance commissioner.

Bundle for best deals

Insurance policies are like guests at a party — the more, the merrier. Once you find a good homeowners policy, consider buying others through the same insurer, a practice known as bundling.

You might qualify for deep multiple-policy discounts. For example, you could save 10 to 15 percent just by getting your homeowners, automobile, and liability insurance from the same company. If you like them, it pays to do more business with them.

Discover little-known discounts

You may qualify for a discount on your homeowners insurance right now and not even realize it. Check out these underrated deals.

- Loyalty pays off. Many insurers give you a discount just for sticking with them — say 5 percent after three to five years and 10 percent after six.

- Age has its privileges. Being a retiree means you probably spend more time at home, where you can prevent fires and burglaries. Insurance companies may knock as much as 20 percent off your premium when you reach age 50.

- Just belonging to a group such as AAA, AARP, a professional organization, or an alumni association can save you money. Ask any groups you belong to if they have deals with an insurance company.

Play it safe for super savings

Put safety first, and savings will follow. Insurance companies reward you for better protecting your home.

In fact, a few simple improvements earn you a double benefit. Not only do they save you money, they might also save your home and family. Consider these smart, safe additions to slash your homeowners premium.

- Deadbolt locks

- Smoke alarms

- Burglar alarm

- Fire extinguishers

- Sprinkler system

- Monitored security system

- Storm or hurricane shutters

- Hurricane-resistant windows and doors

Not every upgrade will earn you big breaks, but they add up. Small steps like adding deadbolt locks might save you 2 percent, while a monitored home security system could take off another 20 percent. If no one in your home smokes, you might even qualify for a nonsmoking discount.

Tell your insurance company about any improvements you make so they know to lower your rates.

Recalculate your replacement value

Insure your home for its replacement value rather than what a real estate agent or appraiser tells you it is worth.

Replacement means how much it would cost to rebuild your house if something happened, whereas market value is what it would cost to buy it.

It's usually cheaper to rebuild than to buy because you only pay for the house, not for the land underneath it. You wouldn't need to "rebuild" the dirt. Market value, however, includes the

Premiums vary by state

Everything is bigger in Texas, including homeowners insurance premiums.

Texas ranks No. 1 on the list of most expensive states to insure your home with an average annual premium of $1,238 in 2002.

Other high-paying states include Louisiana ($840), Oklahoma ($800), and Florida ($786).

Some places are cheap. Wisconsin boasts the lowest rates with an average of $340. Idaho ($382), Delaware ($390), and Oregon ($398) are not far behind. The Insurance Information Institute says homeowners will pay an average premium of $677 in 2005.

value of the house plus the land. Insure your home at market value, and you'll be overinsured, paying more in premiums than you need.

Get an accurate estimate of your home's replacement cost and insure it for that amount. Contractors can give you rough estimates based on your home's square footage, materials used, and other details. Or work with your insurance company, which might even send a special appraiser.

Take inventory to limit your losses

Protect your personal property the same way Santa Claus prepares for Christmas — make a list and check it twice.

Take inventory of your possessions before they get destroyed, damaged, or stolen. This will help limit your losses and make sure you get the money you're owed next time you file a claim. Here's how.

- Use a regular camera or video camera to make a record of what you own. Go room by room and document every item. Open drawers, look in closets, go outdoors, and check your attic, garage, and outdoor storage.

- Insurers may also accept written lists, especially if you include such details as serial numbers, make, model, purchase date, and purchase price. Ask your insurer for a home inventory form to make the process easier.

- Every time you buy a valuable item, add it to your home inventory. Keep receipts so you know what you paid.

Stow your tape or list of items owned in a safe deposit box. With any luck, you'll never need it.

Check policy to trim costs

Take a fresh look at your homeowners policy every year. You just might discover you spend too much on insurance. Look for these ways to cut your coverage.

- If you got rid of any expensive items recently, drop them from your policy.

- Other items decrease in value over time, so you may want to reduce the amount of insurance you carry on them.

Updating your insurance to increase your coverage can also save you money and headaches in the long run. Have you made any major purchases or additions to your home? Make sure your policy covers them.

You may need to add a rider or extra insurance for expensive jewelry, computers, artwork, and other items not covered by a standard homeowners policy.

Pay less at your own peril

As W.C. Fields might say, being a homeowner is "fraught with peril." Luckily, your insurance protects you from many of these dangers.

Homeowners insurance offers three main types of coverage, each protecting you from more risks. Of course, the more perils your policy covers, the more you'll pay.

The basic kind, called HO-1, covers your home and property from fire, lightning, windstorm, hail, explosion, riot or civil commotion, aircraft, vehicles, smoke, vandalism or malicious mischief, theft, damage by glass or safety glazing material from a building, and volcanic eruption.

Sounds like a lot, but it's not everything. In fact, many home owners should consider upgrading to the next level, an HO-2 policy covering all of the above plus:

- water-related damage from home utilities or appliances.

- electrical surge damage.

- falling objects.

- weight of ice, snow, or sleet.

The last kind, HO-3, covers all perils, including the above, except for flood, earthquake, war, and nuclear accident. Talk to your insurance agent about the coverage you currently have and whether it's time to revamp your policy.

Avoid overinsuring

Homeowners insurance provides valuable peace of mind, but you can have too much of a good thing.

Make sure you don't overinsure — it just wastes money. For example, if your home is worth $100,000, and you insure it for $200,000, you will still only receive $100,000 if it gets destroyed.

Remember not to include the value of the land — which does not need to be replaced — when calculating the replacement cost of your home.

Pay premium only once a year

Like a spoonful of Castor oil, insurance payments are easier to swallow when you do it all at once.

Pay your premium annually rather than on a monthly payment plan. You will probably get a discount from the insurance company plus cut out billing fees and postage costs.

Cut down on small claims

It's reassuring to know the insurance company will handle any problem that crops up with your house, but you may pay a steep price for filing that claim. Frequent claims can trigger your insurer to raise your premium or even drop your coverage.

Don't file lots of ticky-tack claims. Pay for small repairs yourself, and only file for major emergencies. You will keep your premium low and may even merit a discount for having a claim-free history.

Clue to solving insurance mysteries

Supposedly, those who do not learn from history are doomed to repeat it. Similarly, those who do not learn the claims history of their homes may be doomed to pay outrageous insurance premiums.

Luckily, you have a clue to your home's mysterious past. Comprehensive Loss Underwriting Exchange (C.L.U.E.) tracks insurance claim histories for both people and properties.

Insurers use C.L.U.E. reports to determine the risk of insuring you and your home. Any claims made by you or the home's previous owner in the last five years can have serious consequences. For example, if your home has a history of water damage, you might have trouble finding affordable insurance or even selling the house.

Now you can know what your insurers know by ordering your own C.L.U.E. report from Choice Trust on their Web site *www.choicetrust.com*, or by calling toll-free 866-312-8076. You'll learn:

- potential problems before they affect your premiums or risk the sale of your home.

- how to correct or update your information.

It can also help when you buy a house. Buyers cannot order a C.L.U.E. report on the home they want — only the home's owner can. But you can ask her to give you a copy. Talk to your real estate agent about putting this request in the contract, so if the report shows any serious problems you can back out of the purchase.

Skip this costly coverage

Want to save money? Don't buy things you don't need, like mortgage-life insurance.

These policies pay off your mortgage if you die, so they really just protect your lender. Plus, they can cost three to five times as much as comparable term-life insurance.

It's cheaper and better to go with straight term insurance, which can be put toward any expenses when you die.

Home office

Hunt for bounty in your county

Don't pay top dollar for office furniture. Find a county surplus store near you. These stores sell used government merchandise at rock-bottom prices, everything from desks, chairs, and filing cabinets to sofas, bicycles, and computers,

Of course, you buy them "as is" without a warranty, but you'll find plenty of working items and sturdy furniture in good condition or in need of only minor refurbishing. Other items, such as unclaimed or seized property, may be barely used, even new.

Bid for big bargains

Enlist Uncle Sam to help furnish your office. Many government agencies hold auctions to get rid of surplus, seized, or forfeited property.

You can find office furniture, equipment, and a variety of other items at very reasonable prices. Get surplus printing, binding, and general office equipment from the Government Printing Office, or extra computers and office furniture from the United States Postal Service.

Keep your eyes open — it's easy to miss these deals. Look for advertisements for government auctions in the classified or business section of your local newspaper. Or check your local post office, town hall, or any other Federal government buildings. You'll also find lots of information on these Web sites.

Department	Web address
U.S. Department of Agriculture	www.usda.gov/da/property.html
Defense Reutilization and Marketing Service	www.drms.dla.mil
Federal Deposit Insurance Corporation	www.fdic.gov/buying/index.html
U.S. Department of Agriculture	www.usda.gov/da/property.html
Defense Reutilization and Marketing Service	www.drms.dla.mil
Federal Deposit Insurance Corporation	www.fdic.gov/buying/index.html
General Services Administration	www.gsaauctions.gov
Department of Justice	www.usdoj.gov/marshals
Small Business Administration	www.sba.gov/assets.html
Department of the Treasury	www.treas.gov/auctions
FirstGov.gov	www.firstgov.gov/shopping/shopping.shtml

Most sales are final, and you generally must pay by money order, certified check, or cash. Bidding procedures vary, and some special restrictions may apply. Contact the agency holding the auction for details.

Bag office supplies for a buck

Looking for savings on stationery and other office items? Look no further than your local dollar store where everything costs — you guessed it — $1. Stock your home office with envelopes, tape, pens, pencils, paper, post-it notes, and more. Dirt-cheap prices like this can make anyone feel like a tycoon.

Send free greeting cards

Perhaps you care enough to send the very best greeting card — but that can get very expensive. Stop paying through the nose for fancy cards and send an electronic one for free.

Electronic greeting cards, or e-cards, can be funny, sentimental, or even musical. You'll find one for any occasion or no special occasion at all. Just choose one you like, add a personal message, and e-mail it to that special someone.

Try these Web sites for free e-cards.

- *www.americangreetings.com*

- *www.bluemountain.com*

- *www.hallmark.com*

- *www.greeting-cards.com*

- *www.egreetings.com*

- *www.cardmaster.com*

- *www.mypostcards.com*

Some sites might ask you to join for a small yearly fee, but you can usually sample their free cards during a trial period. Plus, the fee is less than what you would spend on a year's supply of cards and stamps.

Home security

Trip up thieves with low-cost tips

Make your house more secure without spending thousands on a high-tech system. Just combine a basic burglar alarm with a few common sense strategies.

- Re-key the locks when you move into a new home.

- Give a spare key to a trusted neighbor instead of hiding it somewhere outside your home.

- Put deadbolt locks on all your doors. Door chains break too easily.

- Lock double-hung windows with key locks or pins.

- Use dowels, a broomstick, or locks to keep a sliding glass door from moving on its track.

- Even if you don't have a security system, post a sign announcing you do. It might deter burglars.

- Leave drapes and shades open in the day. Closed blinds point to an empty house and give a burglar the privacy to do his dirty work.

- Turn the TV or radio on when you leave so it sounds like someone is home.

- Install outdoor lights and leave them on at night, or install motion sensors for $20 to $50 to turn the lights on.

- Trim away bushes or trees that would allow someone to climb in an upstairs window or creep close to your house without being seen.

- Mow your lawn regularly and hire someone to do it when you go on vacation.

- Ask a friend or relative to housesit while you are out of town.

- Set timers to turn indoor lights on and off while you're away, or simply leave some lights on.

- Leave a car in your driveway or have a friend park there when you go out of town.

Shop shrewdly for a system

One in five homes has an alarm system. Americans spent a whopping $18.7 billion on professionally installed electronic security systems in 2001, says the National Burglar & Fire Alarm Association (NBFAA), and that number is only getting bigger.

Spend your money wisely. Follow these steps before you pay for an expensive alarm.

- Ask friends, neighbors, and your insurance agent for referrals.

- Make sure the security company's employees are trained and certified and have undergone background checks.

- Get an inspection and quote in writing from each company you are considering, and compare them.

Spot hidden security costs

In the rush to protect your home from burglars, don't get robbed by your security system's fine print.

- Beware of extra charges, such as a $25 fee every time the alarm company calls the police.

- Monthly payments to a 24-hour monitoring station can also add up. Consider less expensive systems that let you set your phone to dial a particular number when the alarm goes off.

- Hardwired security systems come with the high cost and bother of drilling into walls. Consider a wireless system instead.

Hospitals

Secret to free hospital care

Don't put off surgery or other necessary medical treatments because you're worried about the cost. Let Uncle Sam pay. A little-known government program could pay all your hospital and nursing home care.

Under the Hill-Burton program, the federal government says certain health facilities must give medical care away for free or at reduced costs. Here's why. In 1946, the government began giving money to some health care facilities. The hospitals, clinics, and nursing homes that get these funds must give something back in return — free or low-cost services to people in their communities.

Forget about Medicare limitations. Your eligibility is based on your income, but you don't have to be in the poorhouse to qualify. Hospitals, clinics, and other facilities may offer free or inexpensive services to people with an income up to twice the poverty level. And you may qualify for nursing home assistance even if your income is up to three times the poverty level.

Medicaid co-payments and spend-down amounts are eligible. This program won't, however, cover private doctor and private pharmacy charges. You can apply before or after you receive care, even if your bill has gone to a collections agency.

Find out if you can take advantage of this windfall. Call the Hill-Burton hotline toll-free at 800-638-0742 for more details and a list of hospitals, clinics, nursing homes, and other facilities in your area that participate in this special program.

Keep in mind that different facilities offer different services under Hill-Burton. Call or visit the facility and ask someone in the Admissions, Business, or Patient Accounts office about Hill-Burton assistance. They can tell you what services they offer and whether you qualify.

Comparison shop for the best deals

Shopping around never hurts, even when you're comparing hospitals. Surgery costs can vary dramatically from one hospital to another. Surprisingly, the best place for a certain procedure can also be the cheapest,

---

Here are four ways to find a quality hospital.

- Check to see if the hospital is accredited by the Joint Commission on Accreditation of Healthcare Organizations (JCAHO).
- Visit *www.quality check. org* on the Internet to see hospital performance ratings and comparisons, or call the JCAHO Customer Service Center at 630-792-5800 to request this report.
- Read more quality ratings from the Leapfrog Group online at *www.leapfrog group.org* and from Healthgrades at *www.healthgrades.com.*
- Ask your doctor or surgeon how many times the operation you need has been performed at that hospital. Check Leapfrog's Web site to see the minimum number they recommend.

and the most expensive hospital is not always the best. The difference could cost you thousands.

If you are lucky enough to have your choice of several hospitals for a particular procedure, call each of them and ask for estimates before you schedule the surgery. Ask your doctor which hospital is best for your operation and call them first.

Cut costs with outpatient surgery

Ask about outpatient options when your doctor breaks the news that you need surgery. Besides saving on the cost of the procedure, you'll avoid an expensive overnight hospital stay, which can add over $800 a day to your bill.

Some procedures require a hospital stay, but advances in medicine have helped doctors find less-invasive ways to perform many routine operations. Your doctor can tell you if you are a candidate for outpatient surgery.

Take a bite from emergency bills

Hospital emergency room workers waste huge amounts of time and money because many people use them to treat minor problems instead of serious emergencies.

Skip the hospital and find a good family doctor instead. A general practitioner can usually fit you in the same day if you wake up with a worrisome problem. That's better than spending four hours or more in a hospital waiting room. Plus, emergency room visits can easily cost twice as much as a regular doctor visit.

Call your family doctor first if you don't have a life-threatening problem. The doctor or nurse will tell you whether to come in or head to the emergency room. If you think you have a life-threatening condition, like a heart attack or stroke, don't delay — call 911 and ask to be transported to the hospital.

Shave hundreds off your hospital bill

You can save lots of money during your hospital stay just by bringing a few things from home. Hospitals charge ridiculous amounts for items that should be cheap. Consider bringing the following items with you:

- aspirin

- prescription drugs, if you take them regularly

- pillows

- gowns

- slippers

- robes

- tissues

- other basic items the hospital might try to provide

Call the billing department well in advance and tell them which items you plan to bring yourself. Make sure they understand you do not need the hospital to provide these things. Write down the name of the person you speak with, and double-check your bill on the way out. You'll see the savings when you read your itemized bill.

Tell the doctors taking care of you in the hospital if you brought any prescription drugs from home. These may interact with the medications they prescribe.

6 steps to spotting costly mistakes

Some experts say 90 percent of hospital bills contain errors, usually not in your favor. Grill your bill instead of coughing up the cash they claim you owe.

- Keep a pad and pen by your bedside and write down each test or procedure you have and when, as well as the names and dosages of every medication you receive, the names of each doctor you see, and any other item the hospital might charge you for. If you can't do this yourself, ask family or friends to help.

- Insist the hospital give you an itemized bill when you check out. They don't automatically do it, but they will if you make a special request beforehand.

- Is your bill just a jumble of computer codes and prices? Ask to speak with someone in Patient Accounts and have them explain each charge.

- Check your bill carefully against your own notes to make sure the quantities of medicine, tests, and other items are correct, along with the dates for each.

- Find an error? Either ask the hospital's in-house audit department to double-check your bill, or ask to speak with the supervisor in Patient Accounts. Ask them to investigate the error and to make a note of your call. Then write down their name and the date you talked with them.

- You can also have them put a 30- or 60-day hold on your account while they review it so the bill doesn't go to a collections agency.

Take advantage of free services

Help is just a phone call away for seniors who want to remain independent and in their own homes longer. The federal government's Older Americans Act (OAA) funds a variety of programs aimed at improving quality of life for older adults.

Here's one big way the OAA can serve you — a home health care service to help you recuperate at home instead of in a hospital or nursing home. It's not for people who need round-the-clock medical care, but it could be just what you need after an illness or surgery.

The Area Agencies on Aging (AAA) are your gateway to this and the other free services you need, including:

- transportation for errands and appointments

- basic housekeeping

- heavy chores

- home meal delivery

- home repair and renovation

- legal assistance

- state energy assistance

Call the AAA's Eldercare Locator toll-free at 800-677-1116, or visit their Web site at *www.eldercare.gov*. They can put you in touch with the services available in your community. Age, not income, is what counts — you must be at least age 60 to take advantage of this program.

Some agencies work on a first-come, first-served basis, but others may assess your needs so they can provide services to the people who need them most. Be aware that some programs provide services up to a set dollar limit.

Investments

How to find hidden treasure

The U.S. government may owe you money, and all you have to do is ask for it. More than $10 billion is waiting to be claimed. Here's how to find out what your share may be.

For example, more than 87,000 people are still owed nearly $73 million in tax refunds. Most can't be paid because the IRS doesn't have a correct address.

To find out if you're owed a refund, visit the National Taxpayer's Union Web site at *www.ntu.org,* and click on the block that says, "Find out if the IRS owes you money." Enter your last name and state, and click Submit. If your name appears, call the IRS toll free at 800-829-1040 to claim your refund. Be ready to give your new address and proof of identity.

If you've moved since you filed your last tax return but don't have Web access, call the IRS toll free at 800-829-3676 and request Form 8822, Change of Address. Fill out the form and mail it to the IRS, so they'll know where to send your refund if one is waiting.

State governments may also be holding money that is owed you. Visit *www.unclaimed.org* on the Web to check. Click on Owners and then Find Property. Search in each state where you or your family have lived. You might discover a refund from an old utility company, money from an escrow account, or something much more thrilling.

But that's not all. Visit *www.firstgov.gov/Citizen/Topics/Money_Owed.shtml* to discover more free money from the U.S. government. Click the links to find out what you may be owed, who to call, and what questions to ask.

Stash more cash with financial goals

Start setting financial and investment goals, and you may save even more money than you do now. In addition to saving for retirement or your child's college education, you can also set exciting goals like purchasing your dream house. Think about your wants and needs to help you list goals to set.

To turn a want or need into a goal, make it specific by answering these questions.

- Will this goal be short-term or long-term?

- How much time do I have to achieve this goal?

- How much will this goal cost? For goals like retirement, you can check online and in books to find calculators and worksheets to help.

- Will inflation make this goal cost even more — and if so, how much?

- How will I know for sure when I've achieved this goal?

Use your answers to define your goals and put them in writing. Make each goal as specific as possible and make sure it's reasonable. Then assign it a deadline. When all your goals are written, prioritize them. After all, raising enough money to meet every goal may be impossible, and you want to be sure you achieve the most important ones.

Next make a plan for meeting your goals. Figure out how much you'll need to save each month or how you'll need to invest to meet your goals on time. Chances are this will make you much more efficient at tracking your spending, eliminating unnecessary expenses, and saving more money.

Be prepared to re-evaluate your goals and set new ones, as needed. Do this any time your family experiences major personal, professional, or economic changes such as a pay increase, a new baby, or job change.

Tune in to your tolerance for risk

Say you have $500 to invest. Would you rather put the money in investments where you won't gain or lose more than $20 or where you could gain or lose $150? Your answer suggests how much risk you're willing to tolerate — and able to afford.

Buying investments outside your comfort zone may lead to panic and poor decisions that cost you. Protect your money instead by pinpointing how much risk you can stand. To start, decide which of these statements sounds like something you'd say.

The Certified Financial Planner (CFP) National Board of Standards suggests hiring a professional financial planner if one of these applies to you.

- You need financial expertise that you don't have, or you're facing a tough investment decision.
- You want professional help to improve how you manage finances.
- You want a professional to evaluate the financial plan you've developed.
- You never have time to do your own financial planning.
- You've been blindsided by an unexpected event such as an inheritance or serious illness.

- "I don't want to lose any money I invest. An investment that barely beats inflation is fine." If this sounds like you, you're a conservative investor and should pick low-risk investments like U.S. Treasury Bills.

- "My investment return should beat inflation by 2 percent, but I'll only accept a limited chance of losing the cash I invested. I can tolerate temporary drops in value if they give me a chance for higher rates of return than government bonds." Moderate investors like you should favor medium-risk investments like high-grade corporate bonds.

- "I want a higher return than the S&P 500 stock index, and I'll put my initial investment at high risk to get it. I have the faith to hold on to my investment even during years when its value may drop 25 percent or more." If this sounds like you, you're an aggressive investor and may prefer investments like stocks.

Avoid fees that gobble up gains

Investment fees are a lot like termites. You may not even know you have them, but their monthly nibbling can eat away at your finances. Dodge unnecessary fees with these tips.

- Before you purchase mutual fund shares, ask whether you'll be charged a commission or transaction fee each time you buy or sell. Favor mutual funds that don't charge these fees.

- Find out how long you must own a mutual fund before you can sell shares without being charged a penalty fee.

- Check whether the broker charges an order-handling fee along with the trading commission. Avoid brokers who do.

- Ask whether the broker or investment requires a minimum opening balance, and find out what it is.

- Find out if the broker or investment charges an inactivity fee or account maintenance fee. If so, ask how frequently you'd need to trade or how high an account balance you must carry to get that fee waived. If you can't easily meet the fee-waiving requirements, look elsewhere.

- Know the rates for Web trades, touch-tone phone trades, and live broker trades.

- Ask the broker whether she charges an IRA maintenance fee. Find a broker who doesn't charge this fee.

- Consider switching to a discount broker if you're comfortable handling your own investment research and decisions. Discount brokers may not charge high fees if you don't have a lot to invest.

- Check your monthly statement for fees. Some may lurk in the cash transactions section, and others may not appear every month.

Join forces to beat the stock market

Take a team approach to investing, and you may come out a winner in the stock market. By joining an investment club and pooling your money with other members, you can afford to buy more stock than if you invested alone. Plus, you benefit from the expertise of others who may have more knowledge and experience than you.

To discover clubs near you, contact the National Association of Investors Corporation (NAIC) or the American Association of Individual Investors (AAII). Also talk to friends, family, and colleagues to get recommendations.

Don't join a club until you've attended a meeting or two. Check out how they do research, whether they do more socializing than studying, and how well-informed the members are.

Members of an investment club pool their money, efforts, and knowledge to select and buy stocks. The money for stock purchases comes from the monthly club dues — usually between $50 and $100 per month. This system allows each member to benefit both individually and collectively.

"An investment club, hopefully, allows the investors to buy a whole bouquet of roses instead of a single rose," says the treasurer of the Southern Ladies Investment Club in Peachtree City, Georgia. "Pooling funds allows the purchase of more shares at a time — and the portfolio grows at a faster pace."

Of course, investments aren't guaranteed to grow, but that doesn't mean an investment club can't save you money, she explains. "The investment club is a good value because the costs associated with record keeping and trading fees — for buying and selling stock — is shared among all the members."

Find out how you can join the club as well as how easy it is to leave. And make sure you ask about the costs involved — including dues, fees, and expenses.

Try smart, convenient investing

Automate your investing, and you'll probably improve returns while trimming risk.

First, stop trying to predict when an investment price will hit bottom or peak. Instead, invest the same amount of money every month. You'll buy more units of an investment when it's cheap and fewer as the price rises.

You can arrange this "dollar-cost averaging" through a 401k, bank, or investment broker.

Max your 401k to save more

Putting more money in your 401k is like getting free extra money for retirement.

- If your company matches any part of your contribution, that's no-cost bonus money. Even better, some companies add up to 50 percent of what you put in. Just make sure your contribution is high enough to get those matching funds.

- The more dollars you put into a 401k, the fewer dollars you'll pay in taxes this year.

- You won't pay taxes on your gains from your 401k investments until after you retire — and then you might be in a lower tax bracket.

When an extra $100 goes to your 401k each month, your take-home salary only drops by $72. That means you've saved $28 that would have gone to taxes — a savings of $336 for the year. See the example in the table below.

	Per month	Per month
Salary before taxes	$2,000	$2,000
401k contribution	$100	$200
Taxable salary	$1,900	$1,800
Taxes at 28%	$532	$504
Take-home salary	$1,368	$1,296
Savings	$0	$28

Earn bigger returns with little risk

You may think your savings are safe in your passbook account. But it isn't truly risk free even though it has a lower rate of return than other investments.

Passbook savings face the risk of rising prices. After all, a $10 bill won't buy as many gallons of gas today as it did 20 years ago — because prices have risen nearly every year. In recent years, all prices have risen about 3 percent per year.

If your passbook savings earns less than that each year, your money won't buy as much in the future. That's why investments must grow faster than prices rise. In other words, your rate of return should beat the rate of inflation. To outshine passbook returns with only minimal risk, talk to your broker or bank about investments like these.

- Treasury bills are federally backed securities issued by the U.S. Treasury for one year or less. Treasury notes are similar but lock up your money for 2 to 10 years. U.S. Savings Bonds are also treasury backed.

- Shop around for the best deal on certificates of deposit (CDs) insured by the Federal Deposit Insurance Corporation.

- Many municipal bonds may provide state and federal income tax exemptions. Check the bond rating with Standard & Poor's before you buy.

- Money market mutual funds concentrate on short-term low-risk investments like CDs and federal government securities. But be wary of telemarketers and others who promise sky-high returns for little or no risk. This may be a sign of an investment scam. Ask your financial advisor, lawyer, or accountant to check out such offers before you pay a penny.

Diversify to strengthen investments

Whether you call it asset allocation or diversification, owning a mix of investments can help water down risk and avoid losses. After all, if you put all your money in one stock, you could lose it — just like many Enron stockholders did several years ago. Instead, divide your investment money among three types of assets — stocks, bonds, and cash-equivalents.

With stocks, you have a chance to make more money, but you run more risk of losing that money. You can counter that risk by putting some money into safer places such as bonds or money market accounts.

Mutual funds — groups of stocks, bonds, or a mix of investments — are another way to diversify. You can even diversify inside an asset category. For example, you can choose stocks from several different industries. Even if one industry has a horrible year, the other industries can help keep you afloat.

How should you divide up your investments? Conventional wisdom suggests the younger you are, the more stocks you need to help build up a nest egg. As you age, you should accumulate safer investments that produce income. Your risk tolerance, income, tax bracket, and other factors may also help determine the best way to "allocate" your investing. Experts recommend these general guidelines as a starting point.

- stocks and mutual funds — 40 to 80 percent

- bonds — 20 to 50 percent

- cash and equivalents (like money market accounts) — 10 to 25 percent

For more detailed guidelines, visit *www.myfico.com/CreditEducation/?fire=1* on the Internet. Click on Calculators, and then click Asset Allocator. But don't just depend on these guidelines. Talk to a financial advisor to find the best asset allocation strategy for you.

Get big advantages on a small budget

You may only have a small amount to invest every month, but you can own a diverse portfolio and have it managed by a professional investment manager. The key? Buy mutual funds.

A mutual fund is a company that gathers money from many investors. That results in a hefty pool of money that allows the fund to invest in a broad range of stocks, bonds, or other investments.

That means you don't need a ton of greenbacks to get started. Plus, the wide array of investments lowers your investment risk. Even better, mutual funds have managers and analysts who study and track the fund's individual investments so you don't have to.

To learn more about investing in mutual funds, visit *www.sec.gov* on the Web. Look below Investor Information and click Publications. Click on Mutual Funds, and then click Invest Wisely: An Introduction to Mutual Funds.

For more help in selecting good mutual funds, talk to a qualified financial advisor.

Keep good records to avoid mistakes

Staying organized will help you avoid costly mistakes — like paying too much in taxes. The best thing to do is create a practical system that gives each financial record its own place.

Set aside an area for it on your computer or in a file drawer, and decide which filing categories you'll need. These will probably include tax-deductible expenses, tax-related records, banking, savings, emergency money, investments, expenses, college funds, and retirement accounts.

In addition, consider making a separate file for each investment or each broker. You'll need a record of purchases and sales for tax purposes.

Drop commissions with DRIPs

Own just one share of a company's stock, and you can buy extra shares without paying commissions — thanks to a dividend reinvestment plan or DRIP.

Dividend-paying companies that offer a DRIP allow shareholders to automatically buy more stock with their dividend payouts. You pay no commission, and you usually don't need a lot of money to get started. Some companies even let you buy shares for up to 10 percent off. What's more, you'll benefit from dollar cost averaging.

Learn the savvy secrets of smart investing. Remember these 10 tips to get the most out of your money.

✓ Set goals, and adjust your financial plan accordingly.
✓ Know your acceptable risk level.
✓ Avoid investment fees.
✓ Get good advice from an advisor.
✓ Max out your 401k.
✓ Earn the highest rate of return at the lowest risk.
✓ Make your investments automatic.
✓ Diversify your assets.
✓ Invest in mutual funds.
✓ Keep good financial records.

Learn more about DRIPs at *www.investopedia.com*, and visit DripAdvisor.com to find out which companies offer this type of plan.

Lawn and garden

3 smart ways to beautify your yard

One key to a beautiful yard or garden is a good landscaping plan. There are several ways you can get a quality plan for little or no cost.

- Thumb through gardening books and magazines and save articles and pictures of things that might work for your particular layout. Look for ideas and instructions on Internet Web sites like *www.hgtv.com* or *www.diynet.com*. You can find millions of other possibilities with a search engine hunt for "landscaping."

- Check with your state or county extension office. They can give you advice or set you up with a trained Master Gardener volunteer. Or talk with an expert at your local nursery or garden center, which might offer formal planning services in addition to in-store advice. Fees may be discounted if you buy your plants from them.

- Inquire at a nearby college or university with a landscape design or horticulture program. You might find a student who will take on your project for free or at a reduced cost.

Sometimes — particularly in complex situations involving structures or earthmoving — you can save money by hiring a trained and certified professional. Get recommendations from garden centers or friends and neighbors with yards you admire. Look up members of the American Society of Landscape Architects at *www.asla.org* or the Association of Professional Landscape Designers at *www.apld.org*.

Where to get mulch for free

Gardeners can't seem to get enough mulch. This wonder material holds moisture in the soil, prevents weeds from sprouting, and helps improve the soil. Most organic mulch comes from ground up trees. When city or tree service workers feed branches into their big chippers, they're doing more than getting rid of the fallen limbs. They're also making mulch.

Sometimes it's free for the asking from the people with the chippers. Check with your municipal government or commercial tree trimmers. They might even leave some for you as they come through your neighborhood.

The downside to this kind of mulch is that it may still have pests and diseases from the trees it came from. Wood also robs the soil of nitrogen as it breaks down, so it's a good idea to add extra nitrogen when you use it.

Grass clippings and shredded leaves are another source of free mulch. It's a good idea to mix the two since grass clippings can mat together and prevent water from soaking through. Don't use grass that has been sprayed with weedkillers, and be aware it might contain weed seeds.

Tips for catalog shopping

The most avid gardeners shop from mail-order or Web-based suppliers. Convenience, unique merchandise, top quality, and reasonable prices are the biggest reasons people use these companies, but early ordering incentives, specials, and coupons can yield savings of up to 50 percent on flowers, bulbs, and seeds.

Always buy quality seeds. Many times cheaper seeds have low germination rates or purity. When that's the case, fewer seeds will develop into plants or the plants will not exactly match the variety description. You can also save by buying packets with fewer seeds. After all, there's no point in buying 100 seeds when you're only planting two 25-plant rows.

Another way you can save is by limiting the number of companies you use and orders you send in. Every order costs a few extra dollars for shipping and handling, and if you only order a few packets of seeds, it may cost more to send them than to pay for the seeds.

Spend less for long-lasting blooms

You'll spend less in the long run if you put perennials in your flower garden instead of cheaper annual bedding plants.

Many types of perennials are easy to grow. Once established, they don't need much watering and fertilizing because they have hearty root systems.

Properly planned, a bed of perennials will bloom all summer, with one variety budding out as another is dying back. The best time to plant perennials is in the fall, when the ground is warm and the air is cool.

Why you should plant in the fall

Fall is a good time for planting, especially if you want to go easy on your checkbook. In the fall, nurseries and garden centers want to clear out inventory for the winter. You could save as much as 50 percent off spring prices on trees and bushes.

Many lawn and garden experts recommend fall planting for another reason. You don't waste ideal spring growing conditions while your plants are recovering from transplant shock. They can go through that slow period during the winter, when they would naturally be dormant. By the time spring rolls around, they're ready to take off at full speed.

Keep your lawn green with less water

Chances are over half your water bill is for outdoor watering. But there's a good possibility you can water less and still keep a green lawn. Instead of watering sidewalks and driveways, or just spraying water into the air so it can evaporate, you need a simple way to give your lawn the water it needs, without the big expense of wasted water.

Depending on your climate, soil, and variety of plants in your yard, you may opt for an automatic sprinkler system, or you may find that the right hoses, timers, sprinklers, and drip systems will do the job just as well.

No matter what your system, wait until the top 6 inches of soil are dry before you water your lawn. Then water long enough to soak the soil below the root zone. Shallow watering encourages shallow root growth, which leads to drought damage and even more watering. It also lets weeds get started. Vegetables and flowers need water all the time, but deeper-rooted shrubs and trees don't need to be watered as often.

Sometimes you need extra help with yardwork. Here are some alternatives to an expensive lawn service.

- Hire neighborhood kids. If they don't come around looking for work, call and ask them.
- Swap work with friends. Offer to help them with something if they'll help you in the yard.
- Check with your church, school, or local 4-H and scout groups and help youths raise money for their projects.

Sometimes a professionally designed underground sprinkler system is the most efficient way to go — if you can justify the front-end expense. But if your growing season is short, your climate wet, or your yard less complex, you can go shopping for other equipment that is less expensive, but just as effective. Here are a few things to keep in mind.

- You can use timers to turn on the water early in the morning to avoid evaporation in the hot midday sun. Set them to start and stop the flow so water will soak in instead of puddling up and running off.

- When you buy a hose, remember that a larger diameter hose delivers more water.

- Look for sprinkler heads that will let you aim the stream where you want it to go. It's better to have a large-droplet spray because mists evaporate quickly.

- With soaker hoses and drip systems in your gardens and flower beds, you will use less water and do more good. You can also put timers on them. It's always a good idea to install a back-flow preventer to keep dirty water from backing up and polluting your tap water.

Life insurance

Insurance advice you need to know

Figure out exactly how much life insurance you need, and don't buy a penny more. That's the best way to ensure you're not wasting your hard-earned money.

So how much is enough? Some experts say it's equal to four times your annual salary, while others put it at 12 times your salary. Somewhere in the middle is probably about right.

Start with six times your salary, then add any other financial obligations you have, such as a mortgage payment or the cost of your children's education. Consider  how many dependents you have, how much money your spouse makes, and whether your spouse will have help raising the children.

If you have a computer, visit *www.myfico.com*, and check out the Life Insurance calculator in the Calculators section under Credit Education. It will give you a better idea of how much coverage you need. Once you have a figure in mind, buy only that amount of coverage. Stay away from any other features or products your insurance agent tries to sell you.

Check your employee benefits to see if you already have some life insurance coverage. If you do, buy any extra coverage through them since group premiums are so much lower. You can also check Web sites like *www.insweb.com* and *www.insure.com* to compare insurance quotes before you decide.

When to skip life insurance

Don't spend a lot of money on life insurance premiums if you are not married and don't have any children depending on you. You only need enough to cover the expenses of your funeral.

Even if you are married, you don't need life insurance if you both make a good income and have solid retirement plans. Children definitely don't need life insurance policies, and neither do pets. As a rule, you only need a policy if someone else depends on you for financial support.

If you do need and have life insurance, stay away from accidental death insurance that only covers death from car accidents or plane crashes. Your regular life insurance policy will cover you no matter how you go.

Refresh your policy for better rates

Get more coverage for less money by replacing your old life insurance policy with a new, cheaper one. Today's policies have lower rates because the mortality rate is lower than it was several years ago. Plus, as your kids get older, you don't need as much insurance, so your new plan can have less coverage, which will make it even less expensive.

Stick with the insurance you've got if your health is poor since you might not get a better policy. On the same note, if you're healthier than when you last applied for insurance, reapply for better rates.

Choose term for lower payments

Choose term life insurance over whole life, and you'll pay lower monthly premiums. It's cheaper because a term policy only offers insurance protection, while a whole-life policy also acts as a savings account that builds interest.

Term insurance is great if you're starting a family and have a tight budget. But if you're older, term insurance is not such a good deal. The premiums are higher for people in their 60s.

Also, since term policies only offer coverage for 10 or 20 years, they're not the right choice if you want to be covered for the rest of your life.

Lifelong protection that pays off

A term life insurance policy is the best choice if you only want to be covered for a certain time, but what if you want lifelong coverage? In that case, you're better off with a cash-value policy, like whole life. The premiums are higher, but they don't change, and you have coverage as long as you live.

The policy even acts like a savings account, where you earn interest on the money you put in. But make sure you keep a cash-value policy at least 15 years. It is a long-term investment, and canceling it too soon could cost you a lot of money.

Long-term care insurance

Think carefully about coverage

Long-term care (LTC) insurance is right for some people and not for others. The premiums can be more than $2,000 a year, and they increase regularly, so it's important to determine whether the investment is worth the future payoff. Before you sign up for a policy, make sure you really need it, and decide exactly how much coverage is necessary.

Statistics show only one out of three people over 65 will need nursing home care for more than three months. You may be one of those who don't need LTC insurance if you:

- qualify for Medicaid. If your income and assets are under a certain amount, Medicaid will cover your nursing-home expenses. Put any extra money you have into savings.

- already have enough money to retire. An impressive investment portfolio combined with Social Security income may be all the insurance you need.

- come from a family without a history of disease. Conditions like Alzheimer's and diabetes run in the family and will make long-term care necessary earlier.

- have a family member who can take you in later in life.

- are under 60 years old. Start any earlier and you could be paying for coverage you might never use.

Once you decide to open a policy, calculate how much assistance you'll need every year. For example, if the average cost is $70,000 a year, and you'll receive $35,000 per year in retirement money, you only need insurance for the remaining $35,000. Don't get any more than the minimum amount.

Choose cheaper insurance options

Long-term care insurance premiums are going through the roof. In recent years, some insurance companies have raised premiums as much as 40 percent. Either you drop coverage, tinker with your policy to save money, or pay up.

Luckily, you may have other options. Here are some cheaper alternatives.

- Federal Long-Term Care Insurance Program. Most current or retired federal and U.S. Postal Service employees or members of the uniformed services and their families are eligible for this plan. Learn more about it at *www.ltcfeds.com* or by calling 800-582-3337.

- AARP. Metropolitan Life Insurance Company and AARP have teamed to provide you with two attractive long-term care plans. Read about them at *www.metlife.com/aarp*. You can even talk to a long-term care consultant at 800-828-7472, ext. 689.

The National Association of Insurance Commissioners (NAIC) offers a free *Shopper's Guide to Long-Term Care Insurance* that can help you find the best policy. To order, go to *www.naic.org/consumer*, and click on Consumer Publications. You can also call 816-783-8300, or contact the NAIC at the address on the following page.

Contact:	NAIC Insurance Products and Services Division
	2301 McGee Street, Suite 800
	Kansas City, MO 64108

Compare online for best deal

A computer can help simplify the complicated process of shopping for long-term care insurance. By comparing companies online, you can find the lowest rates and save money.

Visit Long-Term Care Quote, an agency that researches and compares insurance policies, at *www.ltcq.net*. Fill out the questionnaires on the site to find out whether you need insurance and how much assistance you'll need.

Then compare prices and features of policies to decide which one is best for you. The site also lists the financial stability ratings of each company so you know your investment is sound.

For another resource, look at *www.ltc-info.com*. Click on Get a Quote, and fill out the survey to compare policies, coverage, prices, and ratings.

The National LTC Network posts a list of its members at *www.nltcn.com*. Click on Find a Network Member, and then select your region and state. You'll get a list of long-term care insurance agencies that provide coverage in your area, along with links to their Web sites for easy research.

Trim time to boost daily payout

You may prefer your leading man to be tall, dark, and handsome. But when it comes to long-term care insurance, short and fat can be attractive, too.

Instead of buying a lifetime policy with a small daily benefit, consider a short, fat policy — one with a bigger daily benefit for a shorter amount of time. In other words, instead of receiving $100 a day for your care for the rest of your life, you'll get $160 per day for four or five years.

You may pay a little more for your premium, but you'll get more bang for your buck. With the rising cost of care, that extra $60 a day can make a huge difference down the road if your policy includes inflation protection.

And you're not likely to need a longer benefit period. Almost 90 percent of people over age 65 who enter a nursing home stay fewer than five years. Currently, the average stay in a nursing home lasts two and a half years.

How to cut high premiums

Carrying a higher deductible helps lower premiums for your health, automobile, or homeowners insurance. Try the same approach for your long-term care insurance.

Protect yourself from inflation

When shopping for long-term care insurance, make sure to take inflation into account. Because of the rising costs of nursing homes, assisted-living facilities, and home care, today's daily benefit may not be worth much years from now when you actually need long-term care. That's where inflation protection comes in.

This feature keeps your daily benefit in step with rising costs. A recent AARP study found that a 5-percent compound inflation rider should be adequate for most people.

Although adding inflation protection makes your policy more expensive, it also makes it much more valuable.

Choose a longer elimination period — the period before your benefits kick in — and you'll pay a lower premium. For instance, boosting your elimination period from 30 days to 90 days can save you 10 percent to 20 percent. With the money you save, you can afford a bigger daily benefit or a longer period of coverage.

But remember, the full cost of the first 90 days of care will come out of your own pocket. Make sure you'll have enough money to handle that.

Because of the high cost of care, you probably don't want an elimination period longer than 90 days. In fact, some states don't allow it.

Take advantage of employer's plan

If your employer offers long-term care insurance, take it. Although most employers do not contribute to these plans, they're still a good deal. You'll pay more affordable premiums while you're still earning income. You also get the advantages of a group plan, rather than an individual policy.

While you're still working, make long-term care insurance work for you.

Medical care

Tame the high cost of medical care

Raise your hand to earn free health care, and get the satisfaction of knowing you could one day save lives. From leg braces to the latest breakthroughs in heart disease, volunteering in clinical trials can help you get the best treatment for next to nothing.

Researchers are always looking for volunteers to help them study new medicines and treatments or learn more about what causes an illness. You don't even have to be sick to participate. Many trials need healthy volunteers, as well.

The treatment being studied is generally free. Some studies even pay you for helping, anywhere from $5 to $100. In general, the more time you commit, the more the study will pay. Be sure to ask if the treatment is free, if the study will pay you for participating, how much time you will have to commit, and who will cover your transportation costs.

Check with these groups to find which studies in your area need volunteers and which ones you qualify for.

- Interested in alternative therapies? Then the National Center for Complementary and Alternative Medicine (NCCAM) is the place for you. Call the NCCAM Clearinghouse toll-free at 888-644-6226 to find which studies are recruiting in your areas of interest and where you live. You can also search their studies by therapy or disease online at *http://nccam.nih.gov/clinicaltrials*.

- CenterWatch lists information on industry-funded clinical trials, many of which test new drugs, devices, and treatments. Go to *www.centerwatch.com* and click on Trial Listings. You can even sign up to receive e-mail notices about new private studies by clicking on Notification Services from the main CenterWatch page.

- The National Library of Medicine keeps a huge up-to-date list of all the clinical trials the government sponsors. One day you will be able to search it by telephone, but for now, you need a computer. Visit *www.clinicaltrials.gov*. Search for trials by typing in keywords, such as "heart attack," or click on the link Browse by Condition to see studies organized by health problem. Don't have a computer? Ask for help at your doctor's office or local clinic.

- Researchers conduct more than 1,000 studies on-site at the National Institutes of Health Clinical Center in Bethesda, Md. To learn which trials you could participate in, go to *www.cc.nih.gov* and click on Search the Clinical Studies, or call the Patient Recruitment Office at 800-411-1222.

Take a look at new Medicare benefit

Medicare now covers a one-time "Welcome to Medicare" physical exam for people who enroll in Medicare Part B after January 1, 2005. You must get the physical within six months after joining or Medicare will not pay for it.

It's a great opportunity to get a thorough health exam and catch problems before they become serious. Your doctor will check your blood pressure, test your vision, give you an electrocardiogram (EKG), refer you for more tests or to another doctor if you need it, and make suggestions for managing any health problems.

Medicare pays for 80 percent of it after you meet your Part B deductible. If this is your first Medicare doctor's visit of the year, you may have to pay most of it out-of-pocket to reach your deductible.

Secret to getting free health tests

Here's a great way to make sure your heart and blood vessels are in tip-top shape — and the price is right. You can get a free cardiovascular screening if you qualify and if you joined Medicare Part B after January 1, 2005.

The new Medicare law pays for you to have a cardiovascular screening test once every five years to check your cholesterol, lipid, and triglyceride levels at no charge. Ask your doctor if you qualify for this free screening and how often you need it.

Medicare also now offers these services free for all its members under the new Part B plan. Talk with your doctor for details.

- diabetes screening test, up to twice a year if you need it

- yearly flu shot in the fall or winter

- one-time pneumococcal shot

Medicare will pay up to 80 percent of the cost of these services for people with Medicare. You will need to meet your Part B deductible for some of them, but not all.

- diabetes supplies, including monitors, test strips, lancets for people with diabetes

- training in how to manage your diabetes for diabetics at risk of complications

- screening tests for colorectal cancer for both men and women

- once-a-year mammogram for women over the age of 40

- pap test and pelvic exam every two years for women

- prostate cancer tests once a year for men over the age of 50

- bone mass measurement every two years for people at high risk of osteoporosis

- glaucoma tests every year for those at high risk of this disease

How to protect yourself from debt

Here are a few tips to help you avoid wracking up debt due to health problems.

- Have some insurance. Even if you can't afford the best policy, you should have something — even if the deductible is really high. At least you'll be covered for some of your costs if disaster or illness strikes.
- Talk to your insurer. Know what's covered and what's not — then try to fill the gaps in your coverage.

- Know your options. If you go to the hospital, ask to see the in-house financial counselor. Ask about special programs that might help you. Don't be embarrassed to ask. The programs are set up to help people with limited means.
- If you already have medical debt, find a lawyer or nonprofit counselor to be your advocate. Let that person help you sort through your options.

Simple ways to save on health care

You know the saying — an ounce of prevention is worth a pound of cure. Now see that in terms of dollars and cents. Out of over 1,200 people interviewed about their health care habits, three out of four said rising medical costs had led them to take better care of the health they have. Start by kicking these bad habits.

- smoking

- overeating or undereating

- drinking too much alcohol

Staying healthy will not only help you live a longer, higher quality of life. It will also lower your insurance premiums and slash the number of hospital and doctor visits.

Free health info at your fingertips

With the click of a mouse, you have access to free, reliable health information on the Internet. Some sites are easier to use and more trustworthy than others. Here's the cream of the crop — the best Web sites and who sponsors them.

- National Institutes of Health (NIH), Office of Dietary Supplements *http://dietary-supplements.info.nih.gov*

- Database from the NIH and U.S. National Library of Medicine *www.medlineplus.gov*

- The Harvard Center for Cancer Prevention *www.your diseaserisk.harvard.edu*

- Mayo Clinic *www.mayoclinic.com*

- NIH National Center for Complementary and Alternative Medicine *http://nccam.nih.gov*

- Med Help International *www.medhelp.org*

- Quackwatch *www.quackwatch.org*

- Centers for Disease Control and Prevention *www.cdc.gov*

- National Agricultural Library Food and Nutrition Information Center *www.nal.usda.gov/fnic*

- American Heart Association *www.americanheart.org*

- American Cancer Society *www.cancer.org*

- ConsumerLab.com *www.consumerlab.com*

- National Health Information Center's Health Finder *www.healthfinder.gov*

How can you tell the good sites from the bad? Government Web sites — anything ending in ".gov" — generally have the most conservative and reliable information. Beyond that, look for the Health on the Net Foundation (HON) seal of approval. This nonprofit organization has created a code of conduct to help ensure safe, top-quality health advice on the Internet.

Online health information can never replace your doctor's advice. Ask his opinion if you are concerned about a specific health problem and before trying a new treatment.

Steer clear of latest health scam

Imagine arriving at the emergency room only to find your health insurance won't cover your visit. You need the care, so you have to pay out of pocket.

Thanks to fraudulent and misleading discount health care cards, it happens to thousands of people every year. Many companies sell medical discount cards that seem like health insurance, but they're not.

For a fee, you get a card that supposedly guarantees you discounts on doctor visits, prescriptions, dental care, eye exams, hospital stays, and other treatments. Unfortunately, most pharmacies, doctors, and hospitals don't accept them.

Some legitimate discount health cards do exist, but they aren't particularly good deals. Most charge sizable monthly fees, up to $100 a month, for small discounts on health care services.

The Coalition Against Insurance Fraud offers this advice.

- Ask whether the card is insurance that covers your treatment or a discount card that gives you a reduced rate and leaves you responsible for most of the bill. The difference could cost you big bucks.

- Find out exactly which doctors, hospitals, pharmacies, or other services accept the card, and make sure it covers the ones you use.

- Check the prices it lists for services and drugs to see if you get a real discount over what you now pay. Comparison shop pharmacies and check the price of generic drugs. They may beat the discount deal.

- Call the providers it lists, or call your doctor and pharmacist, and ask if they will honor the card's discounts.

- Read the fine print for hidden fees. For instance, see if the company charges a fee every time you use the card. These can quickly eat up the money you save.

- Ask if they will refund your membership fee if you cancel, and if you can cancel your membership at any time without penalty.

Music

Orchestrate deals on the Internet

Remember the good old days when you could enjoy a song's smooth melody or its well-crafted lyrics? Thanks to CDs, you can easily recreate the soundtrack of your past.

Here's how to stock up on the music you love without breaking the bank — shop for CDs on the Internet. Not only will you usually pay less than you would at a retail store, you'll also greatly improve your selection. And you can do it all from the comfort of your own home. Get going with these good Web sites.

- CD Universe features certain CDs at 30 percent off on its Web site *www.cduniverse.com*. You can browse by category like Jazz, Oldies, or Country or search by artist, album, or song title. It's easy to find what you want at a price you don't mind paying.

- CDconnection.com also includes a search option and features a Best Inexpensive CDs page with discs as low as $5.01. Check it out at *www.cdconnection.com*.

- The site *www.bestwebbuys.com* lets you compare prices from various sellers. Just plug in an artist or album title and see who is offering the best price. It even takes into account shipping and handling charges to give you an accurate comparison.

- Don't forget to check out *www.amazon.com* and retail Web sites like *www.barnesandnoble.com*, *www.towerrecords.com*, and *www.fye.com*. Often, you'll find great savings, including free shipping on orders over a certain amount.

Changing the way you shop for CDs will save you a bundle of money — and that should be music to your ears.

Join clubs with caution

Need to bulk up your compact disc (CD) collection? Join a club. Perks include a big selection, the convenience of shopping from home, and several free CDs. The catch — shipping and handling charges and the commitment to buy more CDs, at steep prices, in the future. See how the two main music clubs measure up.

Columbia House is great for instant gratification — but it comes with a price.

- You get 12 free CDs right away when you join and the chance to buy another disc for just $5.99.

- Unfortunately, you also pay $2.79 a CD for shipping and processing.

- You must buy five more CDs at regular club prices, starting at $14.98 apiece, over the next two years.

- A Selection of the Month comes automatically unless you opt out of it by mail or online at *www.columbiahouse.com*.

BMG Music's current offer might be a better deal.

- You get seven CDs right away for free, plus shipping and handling, when you join.

- You must then buy one regularly priced CD, starting at $14.98, within a year.

- After that, you can choose four more free discs and pay shipping and handling charges.

- Like Columbia House, you will receive a monthly Featured Selection unless you decline it through the mail or online at *www.bmgmusic.com*.

Both clubs let you send back the monthly selection within 10 days of receiving it at no cost. Keep your eyes open for CD specials, like buy-one-get-two-free, that maximize your full-price purchases. You can quit the club once you fulfill your membership requirements.

Downsize spending with downloads

Have you ever bought an entire album just for one song? Talk about a waste of money. Thanks to the latest technology, those days are over. Now you can download individual songs from the Internet for 99 cents or less. That way, your collection contains only the tunes you want — and doesn't cost a fortune to assemble.

You may have heard all the fuss about kids illegally downloading music from the Internet. Well, you can also do it legally. Check these places for cheap music.

- Napster made downloading popular but ran into legal trouble. It's back in business and above-board, featuring over 1 million songs from 60,000 artists at *www.napster.com*. For $9.95 a month you get unlimited downloads, although you must stay a member to access the music.

- Emusic has three different subscription plans at *www.emusic.com*. Pay a monthly fee of $9.99, $14.99, or $19.99 for 40, 65, or 90 downloads per month, respectively.

- Other sites like the iTunes Music Store at *www.itunes.com* and the Musicmatch Music Store at *www.musicmatch.com* charge just 99 cents per song.

It's easy to find the music you want at any of these sites — just search by artist, album, or song. Most let you preview songs before buying. You may have to download special software to access the music, but it's free and easy to do if you follow the

	Monthly charge	Song charge/ limits	Download card/gift certificate	Free trial
Napster *www.napster.com*	$9.95	Unlimited	$14.85 (15 songs)	14 days
iTunes *www.itunes.com*	None	99 cents	$15, $25, or $50	No
MusicNow *www.musicnow.com*	$9.95	99 cents	$10 or $20	7 days
Musicmatch *www.musicmatch.com*	None	99 cents	$10 to $100	No
Emusic *www.emusic.com*	$9.99- $19.99	40 to 90 songs/ month	$29.97- $119.88 (3 to 12 months)	14 days

instructions. Many services also sell gift certificates and prepaid download cards that make great gifts.

Beware of file-sharing networks like Kazaa, Morpheus, Gnutella, and Grokster. You can download unlimited songs, but you might run into the same legal troubles Napster experienced if you swap copyrighted material. For a good explanation of downloading music and links to legal sites, check out *www.whatsthedownload.com*.

Rummage for retail discounts

Don't dismiss large retail stores while hunting for music bargains. Although their wares are often overpriced, they offer their share of good deals, too.

- Look through any bargain bins for low-priced, high-quality CDs.

- Pay attention to sales, too. Stores sometimes feature lower prices for a certain label or type of music. For example, all Blue Note albums or jazz CDs might be 25 percent off.

- Check for resale deals. Some big chains have a used CD section where you can find albums at a fraction of their retail price.

Play it again for peanuts

Why pay full price for new CDs and records? Buying used can save you a bundle. You'll find rare and out-of-print gems, long-lost favorites, and great deals on otherwise expensive albums.

Browse for bargains at used CD or record stores, garage sales, and thrift shops. Keep your eye open for CD and record conventions, where a small entry fee lets you dig for deals all day.

Before you buy, make sure the right CD is in the case. If you are looking for Bing Crosby, you don't want to end up with Metallica. Examine the disc for scratches or other blemishes. Some stores even let you listen before you buy, and many guarantee their merchandise.

Make a bid for online savings

You can buy almost anything on eBay at a good price — even elusive albums you thought you would never hear again.

The selection of CDs, records, and cassettes from around the world will amaze you. And you'll never pay more than you want for any item. Best of all, it's easy to use. Just go to *www.ebay.com* on the Internet and follow these simple instructions.

- Search for a specific album or browse the music categories.

- Find what you're looking for? Check the feedback for each merchant to see how satisfied other buyers were.

- Either buy the item immediately at a set price or make a bid on it.

- Bidding? Set a maximum, the most you are willing to pay for the item, and eBay will do the bidding for you.

- Pay the seller if you win the auction, and the item is yours. Most sellers accept PayPal, a safe way to shop online.

- Make sure to account for shipping when figuring the price.

Auction sites present a good chance to make money, too. If you find a CD, cassette, or record priced far below its value, you can buy it then turn around and sell it for a profit. In fact, many people make a living doing just that.

When Josh Ferko lost his job as a record store manager, he put his musical knowledge to work. Now he makes a living buying and selling albums on Internet auctions.

"Web sites like eBay give you access to collectors throughout the world whom you might not reach through stores, record shows, or private auctions." Many will pay top dollar for an album they want, he explains. "My best recent score was a rockabilly 45 by Lafayette Yarbrough which I picked up at a flea market for 50 cents and sold for $800 on eBay," far more than it was actually worth.

Do your homework, Ferko says. That's the key to spotting good bargains and selling them online. "You need to know as much as you can about labels, producers, writers, original pressings, and out-of-print items." For example, an original pressing or out-of-print record will fetch more. A record's label, producer, or writer can also affect its value.

Search the auction site to see what similar items are selling for, then price yours accordingly. Also, see how many other people are selling what you have. "Don't waste your time on common items," he advises. They simply won't bring you enough money.

As a buyer, you can snag deals on great records or CDs — just don't expect a steal on a rare gem. Too many dealers and collectors will compete for it, warns Ferko. "Again, run searches and be patient, and you can get good deals on just about anything."

Tune in for free tunes

Maybe you don't need to own the music you listen to — you just want to enjoy it. Do so for free with Internet radio. All you need is a computer with a fast broadband Internet connection.

You'll find stations from all over the world, playing every imaginable type of music from every decade. Whether you like big band, bluegrass, blues, jazz, R&B, folk, country, reggae, or classical, there's an online station for you. Plus, you get a break from the wacky disc jockeys and obnoxious commercials you hear on local radio stations.

Visit these Web sites to search for Internet radio stations.

- *www.radio-locator.com*

- *www.radiotower.com*

- *www.virtualtuner.com*

- *www.live-radio.net*

- *www.live365.com*

Search by musical genre, city, state, country, or call letters. Then sit back, put on your headphones or turn on your speakers, and enjoy the free music. CDs offer better sound quality, but you can't beat the price of Internet radio.

Check out music at no charge

You probably associate libraries with silence, where noise is a strict no-no. Ironically, they are one of the best places to hear great music at the perfect price — free.

In addition to books, many libraries lend out compact discs. The librarian may even let you listen to music on the premises — with headphones, of course. It's a great way to hear a wide variety of music without hurting your budget. Just make sure not to rack up any late fees.

Make new melodies with old tools

Just because it's secondhand doesn't mean it's second-rate. High-quality used instruments often sell at very low prices. Here's how to get the most for your money.

- Learn all you can before buying. Talk to experts, do some reading on the subject, or bring along a knowledgeable friend.

- Check classified ads, estate sales, school systems, piano dealers, pawn shops, and eBay or other online auctions for great buys on used musical instruments.

- Examine the piece closely yourself and play it to make sure it works. You may want to hire a professional to look over expensive instruments, like pianos.

Some old pieces, like pre-World War II grand pianos, actually appreciate in value. Think of your purchase as an investment as well as a bargain.

Save cents when you rent

Before you buy an instrument, give renting a try. It's a low-cost, low-risk way to explore the world of music, especially for beginners. You need less cash up front, and you get a chance to learn more about your chosen instrument. Plus, when you're ready to buy you will already know what to look for. Here's the scoop on this sweet-sounding option.

- You pay by the month with most rental plans.

- Many stores offer repair coverage in case something happens to the instrument.

- Talk to musicians, music teachers, and shop owners about brands, models, and construction. Then try their recommendations for yourself.

- You don't have to limit your choices to easily portable instruments — you can even rent pianos. To learn how, check the Internet or your local Yellow Pages, or ask at a music store.

- You are under no obligation to buy, but ask about rent-to-own programs. Many stores let you apply your rental payments toward buying the instrument.

Check out Music & Arts Centers, a national chain that rents band and orchestra instruments, including trumpets, trombones, flutes, and clarinets. Visit their Web site at *www.musicarts.com* and click on Instrument Rentals. You can even plug in your ZIP code to find a store near you.

Phones

Hang up on phone fraud

Telephone companies come at you from all directions with "money-saving" schemes, but they could have you spending needlessly. Hidden charges on your phone bill can jack up the price far beyond what you thought you would pay.

Don't let them nickel and dime you to death. Eliminate those hidden fees with a few simple tips that will save you money. Look for these common ways the phone company slips extra fees in on you, and learn how to avoid them.

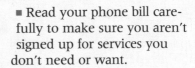

- Read your phone bill carefully to make sure you aren't signed up for services you don't need or want.

- Look closely for charges you don't understand and vendors you don't recognize, and call the company that billed them. Two common frauds — slamming, when a phone company switches your service without your permission, and cramming, where they charge you for services you didn't order.

These shady business practices are bad enough, but real phone-line thieves can rob you clean without ever entering your home. For instance, sneaky telemarketers may call you collect, and crooks who steal your calling card number can stick you with long-distance charges. Stop these scammers in their tracks by taking a few precautions.

- Don't accept collect calls from people you don't know.

- Look up unknown area codes before you dial them. Some international codes look just like United States area codes. Call them and you could rack up serious charges. First ask the operator where the code would call.

- Refuse to give out your calling card, bank account, social security, and other sensitive numbers over the phone. It's your right.

You may not recognize a scam until you get your phone bill, so check it carefully each month. The Federal Communications Commission offers more advice and warnings on its Web site *www.fcc.gov/cgb/information_directory.html*.

Trounce telemarketing scams

Put the kibosh on telephone scamsters. Telephone fraud is a $40 billion a year industry. Here's how to tell the legitimate telemarketers from the con artists.

- Be suspicious when you hear "You must act now," "this offer is about to expire," or "there are only a few left." Check with the Better Business Bureau first. Today's offer should be just as good tomorrow.

- Any legitimate organization will send you literature about their program, but scammers scramble to avoid it. Don't buy excuses like "It's a brand new offer and print-ed material isn't available yet" or "There isn't time to mail information."

- Be skeptical if a telemarketer tells you "You've won a fab-ulous prize!" when you haven't entered any contests. Also question statements like "You only have to pay taxes, shipping, and handling fees!" Real prizes shouldn't cost you a penny.

- Never give your credit card, calling card, bank account, or social security number to someone who calls you unsolicited. They do not need it to verify your identity or secure your prize.

- Be leery of claims like "You can't afford to miss this high-profit, no-risk offer!" No venture is risk-free. Discuss big investments with a financial advisor or a trusted friend first.

- Before you dial a number, check its area code. Some can rack up shocking international charges. For example, avoid calls to 809 (the Dominican Republic), 758 (St. Lucia), or 664 (Montserrat). Ask the operator where the code would call, or look it up online at *www.consumer.att.com* and click on Directory Assistance.

Trim the fat from telephone bills

Basic telephone service shouldn't cost a fortune, but yours might thanks to features you never use. Take a close look at your last three months of phone bills and ask yourself if you really need all the services you pay for.

- Extra features like call waiting, call forwarding, conference calling, and caller ID are wonderful, but each could cost an extra $40 to $85 a year. Decide which bells and whistles you can do without.

- Newer phones often have speed dial and an answering machine built in. If so, you shouldn't buy the same service from the phone company.

- Directory service, automatic callback, and repeat dialing of busy numbers almost always mean extra fees. Use these conveniences sparingly.

- Ask your phone provider what package deals they offer. You might be paying for several single services that come cheaper together.

- On the other hand, if you have a plan and don't use all the extras, you might be better off buying them separately. Compare the price of single services versus packages.

Phone companies offer specials all the time, so check with them occasionally to see how you could save.

Look for a better long-distance deal

Long-distance companies keep cropping up, giving you lots of opportunities to land a better rate. Gather up your old phone bills and put together your personal calling profile. Write down:

- the number and length of in-state, out-of-state, and international calls you make.

- what time of day you make each long-distance call and whether it's on a weekend.

- the rate you pay, whether a per-minute rate, a per-call charge, or a flat monthly fee.

Try these 12 clever ways to cut down your phone bill.

✓ Check your bill for questionable charges.
✓ Cancel any unnecessary features.
✓ Choose a long-distance carrier that suits your needs.
✓ Make long-distance calls with a prepaid phone card.
✓ Use a 10-10 dial-around plan.
✓ Write e-mails instead of calling long-distance.
✓ Get phone service through your Internet connection.
✓ Call on a cell phone with free nationwide coverage.
✓ Compare home phone and cellular rates on the Internet.
✓ Don't buy more mobile minutes than you need.
✓ Stay within your limit on mobile minutes.
✓ Sign up for a prepaid cell phone plan.

Now, go on the Internet and compare your present needs to what's available. Consider long-distance companies separate from your local provider as well as packages that combine local and long-distance. Some deals offer unlimited long-distance for a set monthly fee. Combo packages often bundle home phone, cell phones, high-speed Internet, and cable TV. Start with these Web sites.

- *www.smartprice.com*

- *www.consumersearch.com*

- *www.attitude-long-distance.com*

- *http://trac.org*

Dial around for extra dollars

10-10 services let you "dial around" your regular long-distance provider and hook you up to a discount carrier, instead. They might save you a buck — or not.

You've probably heard about their super-low rates, typically 3 to 5 cents per minute. That's much better than the 7 cents and up charged by many big phone companies for basic interstate calls.

You could save even more if you dial overseas often. For instance, if the phone company charges you 15 cents a minute to call Mexico but a dial-around service only charges 5, you save $10 for every 100 minutes you talk.

The devil's in the details, though. The connection fee on 10-10 services could run anywhere from 29 cents to more than $1 per call. A 10-minute call on regular long-distance at 7 cents a minute and no connection fee would cost 70 cents. The same call using a dial-around service at 3 cents a minute with a 50-cent hookup charge would cost 80 cents — no savings at all. The Internet Web site *10-10-phonerates.com* can help you decide if dial-around is right for you.

Prepaid cards cut call costs

Whether traveling or at home, prepaid phone cards are a cheap way to pay for long-distance service, charging just pennies per minute for national and international phone calls.

Travelers, students, and people who call overseas love them because they cost less and are more convenient than collect calls, credit card calls, or charges to your home phone. In fact, some people use prepaid cards for all their long-distance needs.

You pay for the card and a set number of minutes up front. A computer system keeps track of how many minutes you use and gives you the option of "recharging," or buying more, when you run out.

You can buy them everywhere these days, from newsstands to discount stores, and even on the Internet. But the rates and fees vary wildly. The cards also face common complaints like access numbers and PINs that don't work, cards that expire unexpectedly, and unforeseen charges.

- Get recommendations from friends and family who have had good luck with a certain card issuer.

- Read the fine print. Make sure you understand the rates and instructions on the card you buy.

- Start off buying the minimum amount of minutes to keep your losses small if it doesn't work out.

Free means to keep in contact

Back before telephones and long-distance, people kept in touch writing letters. It's still a good way to get a grip on steep phone bills, and it's even easier and cheaper today thanks to computers.

E-mail doesn't cost a thing. You can quickly write and send a letter without stamps, envelopes, or a trip to the post office.

You don't have to worry about catching someone at a convenient time, and you might even get an immediate reply.

Climb on the broadband wagon

Internet telephone service may very well be the way of the future. VoIP, or Voice over Internet Protocol, gives you total telephone service — local, long-distance, and all the extras — for as little as $20 a month. That's one-third what the average American pays for traditional phone service.

You need a broadband, or high-speed, Internet connection to use it. VoIP converts your telephone's voice signal into a digital signal and sends it over the Internet.

Businesses and telephone companies have had this fancy technology for years, and now people like you can, too. In fact, researchers say a million people used VoIP in 2004, up from just 131,000 in 2003. By 2008, they estimate more than 17.5 million people will subscribe to VoIP phone service.

Many VoIP providers let you call other VoIP customers free, but you will have to pay to talk to people with regular telephone service. Price plans change constantly, but most run $10 to $40 a month. They range from a set number of minutes for local and long-distance calls to unlimited calling, even overseas.

Interested in the concept but skeptical about how well it works? Sign up for one of the free VoIP services and still keep your regular telephone company for a while.

Dump long-distance for good

Do away with long-distance charges by going mobile. More and more cell phone plans offer free long-distance, and more and more people are making the switch.

Of course, some limits apply. Try this advice to get the most mileage from cellular calls.

- Find a plan that doesn't charge extra for long-distance.

- Choose one with enough minutes to meet your calling needs.

- Most carriers give you unlimited talk time on nights and weekends, but check the contract.

- Some carriers let you make free calls to any of their customers. Consider signing up with the same company your children, relatives, and friends use.

Surf for cell phone specials

When you're ready for a new mobile phone or extra equipment like headsets and batteries, it pays to surf around. Electronics stores and service providers usually sell at list price, but many Web sites offer discounts and special deals on both phones and accessories.

Different carriers and service plans use different, unique phones. Before buying a new phone, first choose your cell phone company and price plan. Then shop around, starting with these Web sites.

- *www.letstalk.com*

- *www.phonedog.com*

- *www.myphonefinder.com*

- *www.intelenetwireless.com*

- *www.easycellphones.com*

You can also visit the Web site of each wireless carrier. They often offer online deals on their phones, accessories, and plans not available in stores.

Study bill for cell phone savings

You probably pay for far more mobile minutes than you actually use. On average people only use 60 percent of the cell phone minutes they buy, according to J.D. Power and Associates. That leaves lots of room to trim your bill.

Figure out when, where, and how much you use your phone. Then look at different plans and pick one that gives you only what you need.

- Where you call from could cost you. Some plans charge outrageous roaming fees when you make or receive calls outside a designated area. Buy broader coverage. It costs more with most companies, but you'll need it if you use your phone for anything except local calls.

- Whom you call matters, too. Some plans charge extra for long-distance, some don't. Features like free calls to customers using the same cellular company can save you money if they fit your calling habits.

- When you call makes a difference. "Anytime" (daytime) minutes cost much more than "Off-peak" (night and weekend) minutes. Sometimes off-peak minutes even come free with your service plan. If you make most calls after-hours, you'll need fewer of the expensive anytime minutes. Consider a plan with fewer anytime minutes but with unlimited nights and weekends.

- Don't short yourself on minutes, either. Use more mobile minutes than your plan allots you, and you will pay dearly, around 40 cents for each additional minute. If you talk for 350 minutes on a $30, 300-minutes-a-month plan, you would actually owe $50. You'd be better off with a 600-minute plan for $40 a month.

- If you have several cell phones in your household and you all talk a lot, look into a family plan that gives you multiple lines and a "bucket" of shared minutes.

Avoid pricey over-the-limit minutes

Use more minutes than your cellular plan allots you, and you will pay dearly — as much as 40 cents per minute. A little care keeping track of how much you talk can go a long way.

Some cell phone carriers let you call to check how many minutes you have left, others let you look it up on their Internet Web site.

Now a few third-party companies will keep track for you and alert you when you are about to go over.

Several Web sites will give you all the information you need to find a cell phone plan that's right for you. They provide side-by-side comparisons so you can check the pros and cons of each plan. Some sites to try:

- *www.myrateplan.com*
- *www.wirelessadvisor.com*
- *www.letstalk.com*

- Your bank, credit card company, or Internet service provider may offer this service free to its customers. Call and ask.

- Go online to *www.minutecheck.com* to sign up for a free 60-day trial of their service or to buy it for $24 a year. A few minutes now could save you more than time later.

Sharp shoppers prepay to save

Want a cell phone for emergencies but don't plan to use it often? A pre-paid phone could serve you best.

Regular cellular plans make you sign a yearlong contract, cost $30 or more a month, and can leave you with loads of left-over minutes.

Prepaid phones, however, work a lot like prepaid phone cards, and cost about $20 every three months. You pay for a certain number of minutes which you have to use or lose in a certain amount of time. Once you use them up, you simply buy more.

The downsides — the per-minute rate is higher than with regular cell phone plans, and prepaid phones come with fewer bells and whistles. Weigh the pros and cons, then decide for yourself.

Prescriptions

Cut your prescription costs in half

Splitting pills, a clever and perfectly legal trick, has become a popular cost-cutting method with patients, doctors, and insurance companies. For instance, a 10-milligram (mg) pill may only cost a few cents more than the 5-mg size. When you split it, you get two doses for almost the price of one.

Many tablets come with score marks or lines on the pill to make it break easier. And many drugstores sell inexpensive pill splitters. Talk with your doctor about prescribing higher-dose tablets you can cut in half.

Just be sure to clear it with your pharmacist. Pill splitting is not a good idea for all medications. You should never try to cut extended-release tablets or shiny, enteric-coated pills. And think twice before splitting a pill without a score mark. It may not break in half evenly, giving you too much or too little of the medicine, which could worsen side effects or lessen its effectiveness.

If the pill tends to crumble when split, or if it's critically important you take just the right dose, play it safe and don't split the pill. Finally, if you have trouble splitting pills, ask your pharmacist or someone else to help you.

Studies suggest the following pills are generally safe and cost effective to split. Ask your pharmacist about others.

- atorvastatin (Lipitor)

- citalopram (Celexa)

- clonazepam (Klonopin)

- doxazosin (Cardura)

- lisinopril (Zestril)

- nefazodone (Serzone)

- olanzapine (Zyprexa)

- paroxetine (Paxil)

- pravastatin (Pravachol)

- sertraline (Zoloft)

- sildenafil (Viagra)

Buy more and pay less

Managing a chronic condition is hard enough. Paying for it can send you to the poorhouse. But mail-order pharmacies might offer the perfect solution, filling prescriptions for as much as 50 percent below retail and delivering them to your door.

Buying by mail does not make sense for all medications because you have to buy in bulk, but it's just what the doctor ordered for prescriptions you take daily. Unfortunately, not all mail-order companies are equal. Some actually charge more than you would pay at your favorite drugstore. Others offer genuinely good deals.

Call several mail-order pharmacies and ask them to give you a price quote on your medication, then compare this to what you pay at your local pharmacy. Most do not charge membership fees, but look out for shipping and handling charges. Ask them to include those in the price quote.

Check out these mail-order pharmacies and ask your doctor if he can recommend any others.

Advantage Health Services *www.advantagerx.com*	800-682-8283
DrugPlace *www.drugplace.com*	800-881-6325

Some medications get damaged by high heat, the kind mail-order drugs are sometimes exposed to during shipping. Talk with your doctor first about whether it's safe to order your medication through the mail.

How to pinch pennies at the drugstore

Sometimes you save more on the same drug just by buying in bulk. When you go to the grocery store, the big box of detergent costs less per ounce than the small box. The same discount pricing often applies to prescription drugs.

Ask your pharmacist if it's cheaper to buy your medication in bulk and if your insurance will cover the larger quantity. If so, talk with your doctor about writing a prescription for a larger quantity.

Sometimes it's best to stick with small amounts. Don't try to buy antibiotics or controlled substances, like narcotic pain medications, in bulk. And if you are filling a prescription for the first time, get the smaller quantity just in case it doesn't work or causes serious side effects.

4 painless ways to switch to generics

There's no sense paying outrageous prices for prescription drugs. Generic drugs could save you 50 percent or more on the prescription drugs you buy. These medications are just as effective as higher priced ones, only you pay less.

Generic drugs must be approved by the Food and Drug Administration (FDA), and they are subject to the same strict guidelines for safety, quality, and effectiveness. They must contain the same active ingredients in the same strength and have the same effect in your body as their brand-name counterparts. The only differences are how they look, the inactive ingredients they contain, and the price.

Generics in the United States may even be cheaper than Canadian drugs. The FDA compared the costs of the seven best-selling generic drugs for chronic conditions in the United States with the price of their brand-name twins in Canada. Six of the seven generics were cheaper than the Canadian brand names, and five of the seven were cheaper than the Canadian generic versions.

Don't wait to go generic

Eight in 10 people are fighting the rising cost of drugs by substituting generics for brand names — but not seniors. While more than half the prescriptions filled in the United States are for generic drugs, older adults use them less often.

Why the hesitation? On average, generics cost 70 percent less than their brand-name equivalents. You could pay even less by using a Medicare drug discount card, 39 to 65 percent less than other people pay for generic prescriptions, and up to 92 percent less than what you would pay for the name-brand version.

Switch to generics and consider enrolling in a Medicare drug discount card program while you're at it.

Here's how you can make the switch to generics:

- Tell your doctor you are on a limited budget and ask if she can prescribe a generic version of the brand-name drug she usually prescribes.

- Ask your pharmacist if a generic substitute of your prescription is available. The pharmacist may know of generic drugs your doctor doesn't and can consult with your doctor about changing your prescription.

- Visit Blue Cross Blue Shield of Michigan's Web site at *www.theunadvertisedbrand.com* to look up generic equivalents of your brand-name drugs and tally up your potential savings.

- Check with Medicare. People enrolled in Medicare's drug discount card program can find out if generics are available for their brand-name prescriptions, as well as how much they can save, by calling Medicare toll-free at 800-MEDICARE or visiting their Web site at *www.medicare.gov*.

Save a fortune with freebies

Always ask your doctor for free drug samples whenever he writes a prescription for you. It could save you hundreds of dollars, especially on new prescriptions, by allowing you to test drive them first. You'll discover which ones don't work or cause terrible side effects before you spend a fortune at the pharmacy.

Samples also give you time to comparison shop for the best prices. And don't feel a bit guilty for asking — drug companies want you to use these freebies. They give loads of prescription and nonprescription samples to doctors just so they can pass them along to you.

Great sites for comparison shopping

Drug prices can vary dramatically, even online. Fortunately, a few reputable Web sites take the guesswork out of comparison shopping.

Compare prescription drug prices at a variety of Internet pharmacies with a single click of your mouse at *www.pharmacychecker.com*. The site also researches mail order and Internet pharmacies, then ranks them by safety and online security, among other criteria.

The Web sites *www.pillbot.com* and *www.destinationrx.com* help you compare costs among Internet pharmacies, as well.

Wherever you shop, watch out for hidden fees, like expensive shipping and handling charges. These quickly add up, turning a fantastic bargain into an expensive nightmare.

Safety tip for buying Rx online

Forty-five percent of American adults take prescription drugs on a regular basis. Twenty-six percent of Americans have looked for information about prescription drugs online. Yet, most people are afraid to buy medications, or anything else, on the Internet. Sixty-two percent of Americans think buying prescription drugs online is not as safe as buying drugs at a pharmacy — and perhaps with good reason.

Worries about identity theft, medicine quality, and the trustworthiness of Internet dealers would give anyone pause. At the same time, the savings and convenience of shopping online are hard to beat. Internet pharmacies have fewer overhead costs than drugstores, so they often offer better deals on prescriptions. You can also compare prices more easily at your computer than by driving store-to-store or calling around.

Filling your prescriptions online can be safe, if you know what to look for. Start by searching for the VIPPS (Verified Internet Pharmacy Practice Sites) seal on an Internet pharmacy's Web site. It shows that the pharmacy is licensed by the states in which it operates and has passed the National Association of Boards of Pharmacy (NABP) requirements for quality and security. To see an updated list of VIPPS certified Internet pharmacies, go to the NABP Web site at *www.nabp.net* or call 847-391-4406.

The following online pharmacies have received VIPPS certification:

- Accurate Pharmacy (*www.accuratepharmacy.com*)

- Advance Rx (*www.advancerx.com*)

- Anthem Prescription (*www.anthemprescription.com*)

- Caremark, Inc. (*www.caremark.com*)

- Click Pharmacy (*www.clickpharmacy.com*)

- CVS Pharmacy (*www.cvs.com*)

- Drugstore.com (*www.drugstore.com*)

- Familymeds (*www.familymeds.com*)

- Medco Health Solutions, Inc. (*www.medcohealth.com*)

- Care for Life (*www.careforlife.com*)

- RxWEST (*www.rxwest.com*)

- CIGNA Tel-Drug (*www.teldrug.com*)

- Walgreens.com (*www.walgreens.co*m)

Many of these Web sites offer information on side effects and possible drug interactions. They should also give you a phone number to call if you need to speak with a pharmacist. Don't shop on any sites that don't offer these services.

Smart ways to spend less on drugs

Membership in a club or program can save you big money on prescription drugs, especially if you are uninsured. You may have to pay a small membership fee to receive a discount on medications and devices, but the upfront cost could well be worth it.

For instance, joining AARP for $12.50 a year gives you access to their drug discount program, MembeRx Choice. As an AARP member, you can enroll in MembeRx Choice for an additional yearly fee of $19.95, then use your special membership card to discover discount prices on brand-name drugs at participating pharmacies or through AARP's Pharmacy Service.

You'll save up to 53 percent on top-selling prescriptions and rack up savings of 30 to 50 percent by buying generic instead of brand-name drugs. Not a bad return on a small investment. Learn more about this program by calling toll-free 877-231-6015.

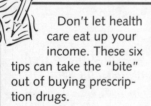

Don't let health care eat up your income. These six tips can take the "bite" out of buying prescription drugs.

- ✓ split the pills
- ✓ buy drugs in bulk
- ✓ request generic substitutes
- ✓ ask your doctor for free samples
- ✓ shop reputable online pharmacies
- ✓ use your membership in an organization for drug discounts

AARP's program is only one of many, and some may save you more. You won't believe the savings through MatureRx, a Caremark program for uninsured and underinsured older adults. You can get both brand-name and generic prescription drugs for up to 65 percent off at participating pharmacies.

You'll save even more when you purchase preferred medications. Enrollment in the program is free. Just call 800-511-1314. Once you receive your membership card, present it at participating pharmacies to earn your instant discount.

Membership in other groups, such as AAA, Costco, and Sam's Club, can also pay off with special deals on prescriptions. Think about all the memberships you already have and find out if they offer drug discounts.

Mistake to avoid when cutting costs

Cutting back on medications you need won't cut costs. A recent study funded by the National Institutes of Health looked at the health habits of more than 7,000 adults over the age of 51.

People with heart disease who skipped drug doses because of cost were 50 percent more likely to suffer a heart attack, stroke, or angina than those who took their medication as prescribed. While you may save money this way, you'll spend much more on trips to the hospital, not to mention the tremendous cost to your health, life span, and quality of life.

Save on drugs north of the border

Canadian drugs can be 50 to 80 percent cheaper than the same medications at your local pharmacy. The challenge comes in knowing how to buy them and who to buy them from. Not all imported drugs are safe or effective and not all sellers claiming to be Canadian pharmacies truly are.

Traveling to Canada is the safest way to fill your prescriptions. Go on your own or with a group, like the Minnesota Senior Federation. You get to see for yourself where your medicine comes from, visit a real brick-and-mortar Canadian pharmacy, and speak in person with a pharmacist about your medications, side effects, and drug interactions.

A Canadian doctor may need to rewrite your prescription before the pharmacy will fill it. Call the store in advance and ask. If so, ask them to recommend a Canadian doctor or visit a border doctor before going. Some doctors practicing near the

Import drugs at your own risk

Buying drugs from Canada or any foreign country is illegal, and the Food and Drug Administration (FDA) worries these medications may not be safe. Regardless, more and more people order their prescriptions from Canadian pharmacies because they cannot afford them any other way. A few states do it, too, and some members of Congress hope to pass laws allowing people to import their medicine legally.

For now, the practice remains illegal, but the government is deeply divided — lawmakers don't want to prosecute people because they understand the tough choices seniors face. So far, the FDA has not pursued individuals or groups for illegally buying foreign drugs. Instead, it has gone after the businesses selling them, like Canadian pharmacies.

But that may only be a matter of time. You should understand if you buy your medications from any foreign pharmacy — whether online, by mail, or across the border — you risk a run-in with the law, until and unless Congress changes the rules.

border are licensed in both Canada and the United States, and they can write a prescription for either country.

You can buy online or by phone. Internet and mail-order pharmacies fill prescriptions written by your doctor and ship the drugs to you.

Unfortunately, not every store claiming to be a Canadian pharmacy really is. Dealers from China, India, and other countries often advertise themselves as Canadian, but the drugs they sell are not subject to strict Canadian laws on safety and quality. You could pay with your health.

Look for Internet and mail-order pharmacies that:

- have a working toll-free phone number manned by live operators, not an answering service.

- have a physical street address in Canada instead of just a P.O. Box.

- require a prescription. No legitimate dealer will sell drugs to you without a prescription.

- are approved by either the Internet and Mail-order Pharmacy Accreditation Commission (IMPAC) or the Canadian International Pharmacy Association (CIPA). Look for their seals of approval on the pharmacy's Web site.

The reputable pharmacies generally have a Canadian doctor review your prescriptions and medical history before signing off on the sale. Some stores charge a fee for this — some don't, so factor in the cost. Shop around for the best deal on shipping and handling, too.

Here are just a few recommended Internet and mail-order pharmacies.

CrossBorderPharmacy.com *www.crossborderpharmacy.com*	888-626-0696
LePharmacy.com *www.lepharmacy.com*	888-453-6275
UniversalDrugstore.com *www.universaldrugstore.com*	866-456-2456
AffordableRx *www.affordablerx.com*	800-351-3035

You can find many other dependable pharmacies at *www.pharmacychecker.com*. This company reviews each store and ranks it on a scale of one to five. Don't buy from a source that scores less than five.

Make the most of tax deductions

Your medications could bring you big tax savings, but not if you get them from Canada. You can deduct your drug costs as medical expenses when you file your taxes each year, according to the IRS. But drugs ordered or shipped from other countries generally don't count. That's because you can only deduct medications obtained legally, and right now buying most drugs from Canada is illegal. Congress may change this in the future, but in the meantime, keep in mind the money you save buying over the border could be lost at tax time.

How to choose the best programs

Finding your way through the maze of drug discounts and government programs no longer has to be a Herculean task. Now you can do it with the click of a mouse. The National Council on the Aging and the Access to Benefits coalition have joined forces to help you choose the best combination of drug discount plans and cards.

Just visit *www.benefitscheckup.org* on the Internet. From here, you can get information on either prescription drug programs using BenefitsCheckUpRx or Medicare drug discount cards with the Medicare Card Finder. Then click on the Start button under the topic you want to research. In both cases, you'll fill out a short questionnaire about where you live, your income, what prescriptions you take, and date of birth. Rest assured all the information will be kept confidential.

This electronic service is free. In less than 10 minutes, you'll find out what combination of programs or which discount card will save you the most money based on your specific needs. The computer will even print out application forms for each of the programs you choose. Fill them out, mail them in, and you're enrolled. It's that simple.

Making sense of Medicare drug cards

Medicare-approved drug discount cards can help pay for your medication until the full Medicare prescription drug plan starts in 2006.

Right now you can choose from dozens of cards and plans, each offering different discounts on different drugs at different pharmacies. This guide makes it easy to choose the card that's right for you. Here are the general rules.

- You can only sign up for one card, so choose carefully.

- Each Medicare-approved drug discount card charges an annual fee, up to $30 a year.

- Medicare may pay the enrollment fee and grant a $600 credit for low-income adults — single people who earn less than $12,569 and couples earning less than $16,862 a year.

- The cards save you about 20 percent on the retail price of prescriptions, although you will get bigger discounts on certain drugs.

The best advice — look for a card that gives you the best deal on the prescriptions you need and lets you use the pharmacy you want. Talk with your pharmacist and check out these resources to help you decide which one fits you best.

- Benefits CheckUp, a service of The National Council on the Aging, at *www.benefitscheckup.org*

- Medicare Customer Service representatives at 800-MEDICARE or 800-633-4227

Seniors' drug benefits will change as the new Medicare program comes into full effect. Here's what you can expect.

- You will have a choice of either signing up for prescription drug coverage with a private company or using private health insurance to pay for medications and other health care.
- You will pay a $35 monthly premium for the prescription drug policy with a $250 annual deductible.
- Medicare will cover 75 percent of your medication costs as long as you spend less than $2,250 total.
- Medicare will not pay any of the cost if you spend more than $2,250 but less than $3,600 a year on drugs.
- Spend more than $3,600 on medicine, and Medicare will reimburse you for 95 percent of the cost.

Low-income seniors who earn a little too much to qualify for Medicaid are a special case under the new plan. They may be able to enroll in the Medicare prescription drug policy but not have to pay monthly premiums or a deductible. They may also get incredible discounts on their medication.

These guidelines could change again before the plan kicks in. Your best bet for up-to-date information is to discuss the Medicare plan with your doctor, or contact your local Area Agencies on Aging (AAA). You can find your local AAA in the blue pages of your phone book or by calling the national Eldercare Locator toll-free at 800-677-1116.

For all the card's help, you may save more buying via mail order or on the Internet. An employer's insurance plan, Veteran's coverage, supplemental insurance, or a Medigap policy may also beat the Medicare cards' deals. And don't forget about generic drugs. Choose the card that best meets your needs and then compare the savings.

You don't have to get a drug discount card. The program is voluntary. But if you want one, you must sign up by December 31, 2005.

The government rolls out the next phase of its revised Medicare coverage — prescription drug plans — in late 2005. You can sign up as early as November 15, 2005. Your discount drug card will expire May 15, 2006, or when you join a prescription plan, whichever comes first. You won't be able to use both.

Find out if you qualify for assistance

People without prescription drug coverage through insurance or a government program, like Medicaid, might qualify for free medication from private drug assistance programs.

Volunteers at The Medicine Program match people of all ages with private assistance programs based on their specific needs. Income limits vary, but generally you qualify if the cost of your medication makes it a financial hardship to take it, even if you earn $60,000 a year.

Start claiming your free medication. Applying is simple. Visit *www.themedicineprogram.com* and print out an application, or write a letter and include the following information:

- name of the medicine

- name, address, and phone number of the person who takes the medicine

- name of the doctor who prescribes it

- a processing fee of $5 payable to The Medicine Program

Mail your letter or application, along with the $5 fee, to the address on the following page.

Contact:	The Medicine Program
	P.O. Box 515
	Doniphan, MO 63935-0515

You can also call 573-996-7300 and ask them to mail a free brochure and application to you. Once you apply, The Medicine Program will mail a packet to you including a letter addressed to your doctor. Read it, sign it, and send it to your doctor immediately to get the ball rolling.

Send a separate application or letter and $5 fee for each medication you need. This processing fee is fully refundable if you don't qualify for assistance, but you must request the refund in writing within 90 days after applying to The Medicine Program. You must also include a copy of the letter from the drug manufacturer indicating that you are ineligible for assistance.

How drug companies help you save

Uninsured people younger than age 65 now have help paying for medications. Ten big-name drug companies have teamed up to offer the Together Rx Access Card, a super-sized drug discount card independent of the Medicare discount card program.

The savings can be big, as much as 25 to 40 percent off the retail price of both brand-name and generic drugs. Most pharmacies around the nation will honor the card, but it's a good idea to check with your pharmacy first.

Like most drug assistance programs, you have to meet certain requirements to qualify for the Together Rx Access card. You must:

- be under age 65 and a legal U.S. resident

- not be eligible for Medicare

- earn less than $30,000 a year if you are single, or $40,000 a year for a family of two

- have no other public or private prescription drug coverage

To enroll in the program for free, call 800-444-4106 or sign up on their Web site at *www.togetherrxaccess.com*. Your doctor and pharmacist may also have applications and more information about the program.

Some drug companies offer their own discount cards just for their medications. Contact these companies for more details.

Merck *www.merckhelps.com*	800-506-3725
Pfizer *www.pfizerhelpfulanswers.com*	866-776-3700

Lifesaver for people with low incomes

Patient Assistance Programs (PAPs) can help you get the medications you need absolutely free if you face true financial hardship, regardless of age.

Drug companies offer these programs to people living on very low incomes. Generally, you may qualify if you earn less than $18,000 a year as a single person or $24,000 as a couple and are not eligible for other assistance programs. If you qualify, you'll receive the medications you need free of charge.

Your doctor or another medical staff person will have to fill out the forms on your behalf and send them to the pharmaceutical company. You will have to apply separately for each medication you take. You won't know for several weeks whether or not you qualify, so don't wait to fill prescriptions you need right away.

Your doctor, pharmacist, senior center, or local government assistance program can help you learn which PAPs could work for you and help you apply.

You can find out more on your own by visiting these Web sites.

- Volunteers in Health Care *www.rxassist.org*

- HelpingPatients.org *www.helpingpatients.org*

- Needymeds.com *www.needymeds.com*

Taxes

■ Personal

Use free online tax service

Prepare your federal taxes for free with a Web version of popular tax software and electronic filing available through the IRS. Here's how.

- Visit *www.irs.gov*.

- Click Free File, then the Start Now button.

- When the Free File page displays, determine which companies' software you're eligible to use. Review the entire list to find your best choices. For more information, click the More Details links.

- If the eligibility summaries don't help, click the Guide Me to a Service button. You'll fill out a questionnaire to pinpoint which companies may provide free services for you.

- When you find a free service you're eligible for, click the company's name to go to its Web site.

- Use the company's online software to prepare your income tax return. When done, you can e-file it. You'll get an e-mail notifying you whether the return was accepted or rejected.

Some of the drawbacks to this program you should consider:

- If you don't access the free service through the IRS Web site, the companies may charge you.

- Free online software and electronic filing are usually not available for state tax returns.

- This program may not be appropriate for high income taxpayers who have complicated returns.

- Companies who provide the free services can change eligibility requirements during the filing season.

Prepare taxes without paying a penny

You may be missing out on free help from IRS-trained tax preparers. Find out when to use one, how to learn more about a free preparer, and how to snatch up this money-saving deal.

If you're worried about qualifications, be sure to ask how long they have been preparing taxes and what their background is. Tax preparers who can provide references or are members of a professional association are probably the best choices.

With those concerns out of the way, you have at least two ways to get your taxes prepared without paying a penny.

- If you're 60 or older, the Tax Counseling for the Elderly (TCE) program offers help preparing basic returns.

- Under the Volunteer Income Tax Assistance (VITA) program, volunteers taught by the IRS are available to help you fill out basic tax returns if your income is under $35,000.

To find out where to go locally for TCE or VITA, call the IRS toll-free at 800-829-1040.

Remember that signing your tax return means you agree with everything on it. Before you sign, review the return, and ask questions until you understand its contents.

Try tax help that saves millions

Taxpayers who use the free AARP Tax-Aide program save more than $40 million in tax preparation fees every year — and you can save, too. What's more, you may discover extra tax deductions and tax credits you never knew you could take.

AARP Tax-Aide aims to help middle and low-income taxpayers — especially those age 60 and up. You can meet with trained AARP Tax-Aide volunteers or get tax counseling online. Visit *www.aarp.org/money/taxaide/* or call toll-free 888-227-7669 to learn more and find an AARP Tax-Aide site near you.

Take a bite out of income taxes

Learn more about income that can't be taxed, and you may get thousands of dollars tax-free. This is money you can use any way you want. Consider these examples.

- some contributions to health savings accounts

- some scholarships and fellowships

- interest on municipal and state bonds

- part of the profit from selling your home

- most social security payments

- most life insurance proceeds

- worker's compensation

- court-awarded compensatory damages for personal injury or illness

Remember, IRS rules change yearly and many have exceptions, so check with a tax professional for details on what is tax-free.

Cut taxes with smart deductions

Deductions are the expenses the IRS lets you subtract from your taxable income. If you're not listing all you can on your tax return, you're probably losing money. The IRS suggests you may benefit from itemizing if any of these apply to you.

- Your total itemized deductions exceed the standard deduction you're allowed. The current standard deduction for married filing jointly is $9,700, but it's $10,650 if one of you is 65 or older, or $11,600 if both of you are. Compare that to the total itemized deductions you're allowed on Schedule A.

- You only qualify for a limited standard deduction.

- You paid interest and taxes on your home.

- You had sizable unreimbursed employee business expenses.

- You had hefty uninsured casualty or theft losses.

- You made large contributions to qualified charities.

- You've had large uninsured medical and dental expenses during the year. Itemizing these may be especially wise for older adults because medical expenses usually rise as you age. Medical expenses must be more than 7.5 percent of adjusted gross income to qualify for the deduction, so take a careful look at all your medical costs.

Keep in mind the IRS limits the amount of itemized deductions for married filing jointly if adjusted gross income is over a certain limit — $142,700 for 2004.

Benefit from home improvements

You can keep more of the profits from selling your home if you provide the right records to the IRS. Receipts for those home improvements that increase the value of your home — like adding a fence around the yard — are your ticket to tax deductions. Save those receipts until after you sell the house. Then you can deduct the home improvement cost from your profits so you pay lower capital gains taxes on the sale.

Nab unexpected tax reductions

Don't miss out on these tax shrinkers.

- Buying a hybrid car or truck may merit a deduction. Investment expenses and tax preparation costs might, too.

- If your county or town was declared a federal disaster area, your loss might qualify for a deduction.

- If you paid points to refinance your home, find out how much you can deduct this year.

Discover sources of medical tax deductions you may not know about. If soaring medical expenses equal more than 7.5 percent of adjusted gross income on your tax return, these deductions might help slash your taxes.

- Acupuncture
- Dental fillings, X-rays, and dentures
- LASIK or other corrective eye surgery
- Gasoline when you use a car for medical reasons
- Reconstructive breast surgery after cancer treatment
- Chiropractor services
- Weight-loss program for treating a medical condition like heart disease or obesity

- Check whether you're eligible for a tax credit on money contributed to a retirement account.

- Get a receipt for the value of items donated to charity to take a deduction.

- If you're self-employed, check whether health insurance premium costs are deductible.

- Teachers who qualify can deduct some school supply costs.

For more information, talk to your tax professional, visit *www.irs.gov*, or call the IRS tax assistance line toll-free at 800-829-1040.

Grandparents can get child tax credit

You can qualify for a child tax credit even if you're not the parent of the child you care for. You could be eligible for a tax credit of up to $1,000 for each child that meets these four requirements:

- under age 17 at the end of the tax year

- U.S. citizen or resident

- can be claimed as your dependent

- is your son, daughter, adopted child, stepchild, or a descendant of any of them — or your brother, sister, stepbrother, stepsister, or a descendant — as long as you care for them like your own child.

Visit *www.irs.gov* to learn more about claiming this tax credit.

Lower taxes while raising grandkids

Grandparents raising a grandchild may claim the Earned Income Tax Credit (EITC) with a qualifying child. Unless they're disabled, children must either be under age 19 or full-time college students under age 24 to qualify. They also must be U.S. citizens or residents with a valid social security number.

Not only can children and grandchildren qualify, but also stepchildren, adopted kids, siblings, step-siblings, and even some foster children — as long as you care for the child or children as your own.

For more details on qualifying children and eligibility for the EITC, call 800-829-3676 and request Publication 596, or visit *www.irs.gov,* and search for EITC Assistant.

Put more money in your pocket

A large tax refund every year could mean you're missing out on bonus bucks. After all, think how much that tax refund could have earned if it had been in your bank account or money market account for the last six months.

If you've been getting substantial tax refunds for several years, your withholding may be set too high. Consider increasing exemptions to have less tax taken out of your paycheck. Then

Don't give government an interest-free loan

"I see an awful lot of refunds that are in the $3,000 range," says Jim Churchill, a tax practitioner with Jackson Hewitt Tax Service in Newnan, Georgia. *"That includes getting some of their withholding back, earned income credit, and the additional child tax credit."*

But even regular taxpayers who don't qualify for tax credits get large refunds. *"We just try and advise our clients not to have more withheld than you would need withheld to get $1,000 back,"* Churchill says. *"The reason is that it's an interest-free loan to the government. That's your money. You should be able to do with it as you please."*

make sure you put the extra money where it can earn extra for you.

Just be careful not to trim too much. You don't want to be caught by surprise next year and have to pay.

Rescue IRA from harsh penalties

Don't let the Internal Revenue Service (IRS) take part of your hard-earned IRA money. Make sure you take your distribution on time, and make sure it's high enough — so the IRS won't charge you a 50 percent penalty on that year's distribution.

According to the IRS, you must take the first distribution by April 1 of the year following the year in which you turn 70 1/2. But you also must take minimum withdrawals each year after that — before Dec. 31. This applies to traditional IRAs, not Roth IRAs, unless you inherited your Roth.

Contact the custodian of your IRA to find out how much you must withdraw to meet the minimum distribution rules.

Avoid late tax-return fees

Send in your tax return just one month late, and you'll pay a penalty that's at least 5 1/2 percent of the taxes you owe. And, with each passing month, another 5 1/2 percent penalty — or more — gets added on. That's like giving money away.

If you've only missed the deadline by a few days, file right away by mail — not electronically. Because the IRS is deluged with returns around April 15, they may not notice a paper return is late, suggests the National Association of Tax Professionals. At the very least, the penalties won't continue to pile up.

■ Property

Legal way to delay paying tax

Get your next tax break on the house — literally. All 50 states have property tax relief programs, but the District of Columbia and 24 states offer a legal way to put off paying property tax for seniors.

Under these programs, senior citizens can defer property tax payments until the home is sold. Then the accumulated taxes come out of the sale proceeds. Interest on the total deferred property tax amount may be taken out of the proceeds as well.

Be sure to call your county tax assessor's office or state Department of Revenue to find out whether property tax deferral for senior citizens is available, what the requirements are, and how to apply.

Find exemptions you deserve

You may be surprised at what kinds of exemptions can lower your property taxes. Homestead exemptions and tax reductions may be waiting for older adults, those with disabilities, folks with low income, and veterans. Energy-conserving homes and historic buildings may qualify for property tax reductions, too.

Exemptions and reductions vary by state and so do their eligibility requirements. To learn about tax exemptions available to you, contact your local and state tax assessor, tax collector, or department of revenue.

Older adults can also visit *www.benefitscheckup.org* to fill out the BenefitsCheckup questionnaire. Its results will show government services and some — if not all — of the property tax breaks you can get.

Appeal to slash property taxes

Getting your property taxes reduced may be easier than you think. Follow these steps to help appeal an assessment that's too high so you won't risk overpaying property taxes.

- Find out deadlines from your local assessor's office. How many days do you have to appeal, or when is the appeal deadline?

- Determine if you have grounds for appeal. You must either find an error in the assessment or show your assessment isn't consistent with others on similar homes.

- Check the assessment for errors. Up to 60 percent of properties may be over-assessed, according to one estimate. If you find an error, gather evidence — like photos, blueprints, and surveys — to prove the information is wrong.

- Compare the assessed value of your home with the assessed value of houses in your neighborhood. Visit the assessor's office, and ask to see the assessment cards for each of them. Compare the figures to see if your assessment is consistent with the others.

- If your assessment has errors or is out of line with similar homes, request an informal meeting with the assessor so you can make your case. For best results, assume any problems with your assessment were unintentional. The assessor may sign a written agreement with your application that will ensure a property tax reduction.

If you strike out with the assessor, get ready to appeal. Find out what forms to fill out, what procedures to follow, and when to provide copies of your evidence.

Calculate the tax reduction you think you should get. Put it in writing, along with your supporting reasons. Then, sit in on someone else's appeal hearing so you'll know how the hearings work. On the day of your hearing, you'll be ready to present your case and make recommendations for your property tax reduction.

Trim taxes with veteran's exemptions

Cut your taxes to the bone with special exemptions for veterans and their spouses. IRS approved! For example, veterans who live in Laramie County, Wyoming can qualify for tax exemptions on their county property tax and license plate fees.

To help find out what exemptions may be available to you, contact your local Veterans Affairs office. If you can't find an office near you, contact the national headquarters.

Contact: Department of Veterans Affairs Headquarters
             810 Vermont Ave NW
             Washington, D.C. 20420
             www.va.gov

Tires

How to find a bargain

When it's time to replace your tires, the road to finding a bargain can be rough. Since the tire market is so competitive, the difference between the lowest and highest prices on a particular tire may only be $10.

But sales do happen. Some of the best deals are offered on discontinued styles. They're often the tires featured at "closeout" prices. Other sales are seasonal. Manufacturers' promotions often correspond with car races like the Indy and Daytona 500s or driving holidays like Christmas and Memorial Day. Those are good times to watch for sales and savings.

When it comes to Internet and catalog specials, make sure you figure your total cost. You may find these tires are deeply discounted, but by the time they're shipped and mounted, you may end up paying what you'd have paid at a local dealership. Some Internet sites you may want to try are *www.tirerack.com* and *www.tires.com*.

When choosing a tire dealership, keep in mind you may get more experienced installers and better service at an independent shop rather than a discount giant. But wherever you go, ask if they offer lifetime balancing and rotation on their tires. This standard service will help reduce the overall cost of your tires.

Be a smart, thrifty tire buyer

Your car's tires are like your shoes. Only a certain size fits. Without the right size, performance suffers. Follow these tips to be sure you have a smooth, safe ride.

- Stick with the prescribed size found in your owner's manual.

- Match your tire type with how and where you drive — performance, off-road, touring, around-town, rain, or snow. All-season radials are usually a safe bet.

- Be sure you're comparing apples with apples. Compare tires with nearly equal ratings on the three T's — tread wear, temperature, and traction. The "grade" for each of these is embossed on the tire's sidewall.

You won't have to buy new tires as often if you take good care of the ones you have. Do these things regularly, and you'll find a little preventive maintenance will go a long way.

✓ pressure check
✓ alignment
✓ balancing
✓ rotation

- Call around to compare prices. Once you've talked with several tire centers, pick one that is conveniently located and has quality tires at decent prices.

Buy used for a great deal

Used tires. Second-rate? Worn out? Unsafe? Not necessarily. Used tires can be high quality, safe, and economical buys.

If you're in the market, check with tire dealers to see if they have any "practically new" tires on hand. Sometimes, people accessorize their new cars with custom tires — something snazzier than the all-season radials it came with. If your timing is right, you may be able to buy their "old" tires at a great discount.

You can also look for tire dealers that specialize in used-tire sales. They grade the tires based on their quality and condition and sell them to you at bargain prices.

Retreaded tires are also an option. You may have heard urban legends that make you afraid to try them. But take the time to look at the facts.

- New treads are attached to tires through a process similar to new-tire construction. Only tires that meet industry quality standards are allowed to be sold. Up to 85 percent of passenger tires don't even pass the initial inspection to become retreads.

- Retreads cost 30 to 50 percent less than new tires.

- Retreads are friendlier to the environment, requiring 15 fewer gallons of oil per tire to manufacture than new tires.

- Emergency vehicles, taxi fleets, and race cars all put their faith in the safety of retreaded tires.

You can get more information from the Tire Retread Information Bureau (TRIB), a non-profit association dedicated to tire recycling. Check out its Web site at *www.retread.org*, or call toll-free 888-473-8732. You can also write to the following address.

Contact:	Tire Retread Information Bureau
	900 Weldon Grove
	Pacific Grove, CA 93950

Toys

Dig up deep discounts

Treasure hunting at yard sales, consignment shops, flea markets, and swap meets is the best way to get a good deal on toys. You can find gently used and sometimes even brand new toys for a fraction of retail cost.

If you find a used bargain, protect your loved ones and your purchase by following a few precautions.

- Try to buy toys in their original box. It has model numbers you may need to check for recalls.

- Look up toy recalls on the U.S. Consumer Product Safety Commission Web site at *www.cpsc.gov*.

- Open the box and make sure it has all the pieces. You may be able to order missing parts from the manufacturer.

- Look for any instruction manuals or warranties that should come with the toy.

- Plug it in or test it with batteries before you take it home.

- Wash and disinfect toys for small children.

- Never buy used items like play "doctor" kits or kid cosmetics. For safety's sake, only get them new.

Test drive before you buy

Don't spend big bucks on a hot new toy only to have your little one get bored after 5 minutes. Find out if a toy has staying power before you shell out your cash. Let her play with it at a friend's house or at a store with opened toys on display. Some libraries even loan them out just like books. Call yours and ask. You'll save money and put a smile on a child's face.

Find missing parts for favorite toys

You don't have to buy a brand new toy or game set just to replace a missing piece. Most manufacturers will replace parts for a small charge.

Make a complete list of parts you need, including the color of missing pieces and edition of the game since some, like Monopoly and Trivial Pursuit, have come in different editions throughout the years. Then check the box to find out who makes it, and look for a customer service number to call. If you can't find one, start with these.

- Hasbro Games, Milton Bradley, and Parker Bros. 888-836-7025

- All other Hasbro products 800-327-8264

- Playskool 800-752-9755

- Tiger Electronics 800-844-3733

- Mattel, Inc. 310-252-2000

- Fisher-Price 716-687-3000

- American Girl 608-836-4848

■ Disney 800-328-0368

Be sure to ask how much the part will cost, including shipping and handling charges.

If the part costs more than you're willing to spend, shop garage sales for used versions of the same toy. Buying a 50-cent Scrabble game for a few letters probably beats the price of ordering replacement pieces.

Or, if you're Internet savvy, post a message to an online forum such as About.com's Board Games Forum at *www.BoardGames.About.com.* You can offer to buy or trade for that hard-to-find piece.

Travel

Stay in style without spending a dime

Home exchanging — it's an overlooked opportunity for free lodging for your next vacation, an ingenious solution to traveling almost anywhere your heart desires without having to pay any lodging costs.

House swapping started in Europe, when teachers in the Netherlands and Switzerland began trading homes during summer holidays. Basically, you switch houses with someone who lives in a place you want to visit. With a true exchange, they stay in your house at the same time you "borrow" theirs.

They have to want to visit where you live, too, though. Living near a tourist destination like New York City or Orlando helps draw interest in your home, but don't worry. You'll find plenty of rental deals as well as swaps on second homes.

With home exchanges, you get more than just free accommodations nearly anywhere you travel. You also have:

- the chance to stay in a neighborhood and meet local people.

- access to a kitchen, laundry, and other creature comforts of home.

- possibly even the use of a car.

You do not have maid service, so you are responsible for leaving the house neat and tidy.

Several exchanges and agencies put interested people in touch with each other. Most work exclusively on the Internet. In return for a membership fee, you get to list your home and view other people's listings.

Many listings are in Europe, but you will also see swap opportunities within your own country. You'll find a match faster if you are flexible with when and where you want to visit.

These Web sites can help you take advantage of available home exchange offers immediately. Phone numbers are given when available.

- *www.homelink.org*, 800-638-3841

- *www.exchangehomes.com*, 800-848-7927

- *www.homeexchange.com*, 800-877-8723

- *www.intervac-online.com*, 800-756-4663

- *www.seniorshomeexchange.com*

Make sure you have insurance coverage at both ends, and tuck valuables out of the way to avoid misunderstandings or accusations. Lastly, have a backup plan in case you arrive at your borrowed home only to discover the seaside villa is really a fisherman's shack.

Here's a look at how much money a couple on a two-week vacation could save with a home exchange instead of a hotel room.

	Expense	Hotel	Home Exchange
Airfare (2 @ $350 each)		$700	$700
Hotel (14 nights @ $90 each)		$1,260	0
Car Rental (2 weeks @ $175 a week)		$350	0
Eating out (14 days @ $35 a day per person)		$980	0
Groceries		0	$250
Sightseeing		$160	$160
Total		$3,450	$1,110
Savings			$2,340

Never pay full fare again

You'll never have to pay full fare again for airline tickets, cruises, and vacation packages — once you pass your 50th birthday. You can join AARP and get far better than normal "over 50" discounts and savings.

Among AARP's benefits is the AARP Passport, which is like a travel agency and search engine combined to help you find the best deals. You can use it either online or over the telephone to:

- simplify your hunt for the cheapest airfares available

- get special deals on cruises

- take advantage of AARP vacation package discounts

There are also regular AARP benefits for hotel stays and car rentals. Discounts range from 10 to 50 percent, depending on the hotel chain. You can make reservations either direct or through AARP. Be sure to have your membership number handy to get the discount. Car rentals work the same way.

AARP isn't the only organization that can save you money. An increasing number of membership associations, like AAA, offer travel agency and discount services. If you sign up with one of these groups, it works best to use them when you make your reservations. If for some reason you decide to book a ticket or room directly with a provider company, ask if they give a discount for the membership you have.

If you're active duty or retired military, here are some of the ways you can save on travel. Remember to always ask about a military discount for any expense, including admission tickets.

- Space Available Flight
- armed forces recreation centers
- on-base lodging
- discounted airfares
- discounted car rentals
- discounted hotels and time shares

Get airfare refunds when prices drop

You thought you had a good price when you bought your plane tickets, but you see an ad for an even better deal in this morning's paper. Chances are, you can still snag the lower price if:

- the airline offering the cheaper fare is the same one you bought your original ticket from.

- you meet the new fare's advance purchase and other requirements.

- you plan to keep the same destination, travel date, and time.

It's up to the airline which issued the ticket, so check with them or your travel agent about getting a refund for the difference.

'Blind' travel offers bargains

Are you willing to let a stranger decide your travel details, like which airline to fly and what time to leave? If so, you have a 50 percent chance of booking a bargain on your next flight or hotel room by using a "blind" travel Web site.

Blind sites don't tell you the name of the airline, hotel, or car rental company — or even when your flight will depart and arrive — until you pay for the reservation. Plus, bookings are non-refundable and usually don't earn you frequent flier miles.

But they do tend to offer the best travel deals. Consumer WebWatch compared Priceline and Hotwire, the two leading blind sites, to the top three regular travel sites — Orbitz, Expedia, and Travelocity. Priceline offered the lowest rates 47 percent of the time.

Still, lots of people don't like buying blind. Sometimes, the uncertainty and inconvenience are not worth the savings.

At *www.priceline.com*, you bid for bargains. You say where you want to go, what days, and how much you are willing to pay. The Web site either accepts your bid or asks you to change your offer. The site *www.hotwire.com* gives you an upfront price on discounted tickets, but both sites make you pay before they tell you the full details of your trip.

Here are some tips for using a blind Web site.

- Check regular travel Web sites like *www.expedia.com*, *www.orbitz.com*, *www.travelocity.com*, and *www.hotels.com* to see what deals they offer before booking on a blind site.

- Find the lowest fare for your trip on a regular site before visiting *www.priceline.com*, then use this amount as a benchmark for making just the right bid.

- Make sure you understand all the terms, conditions, and fees of each Web site.

- Double-check your travel information before buying so you don't get stuck with a non-refundable ticket for the wrong trip.

Online auction nets great vacation

Paula Rubel couldn't believe it. "A friend found a five-day cruise out of Miami on eBay and asked if we wanted to go," she recalls. "We said 'yes', and at the end of the auction, we got four cruises for about $100 apiece. The port fees cost more than the cruise!"

Buying vacations from online auctions is another way to get a great deal — if you're willing to do some homework. "There's always a fear factor, because you're not sure what you are getting into," Rubel says. "I've gotten some good deals and some bad deals. You have to do a lot more research."

When bidding for a bargain, you are bound to find a downside. Don't be afraid to ask questions and check details, and the ups should outweigh the downs. Try these tips to make your winning bid worthwhile.

- Find out details about the place you want to go. Is a hotel in the Bronx the same as a hotel in Manhattan?

- Talk to others who have been there. Did they have a good time?

- Read the fine print on travel deals. What are the taxes and extra fees? Exactly what is and is not included? When can you go?

Besides www.eBay.com, you can also bid on travel packages at www.SkyAuction.com, www.bid4vacations.com, and www.Priceline.com.

- Always pay by credit card. It offers you more consumer protections than a debit card.

A quick guide to consolidator fares

One of the basic rules of commerce is to "buy at wholesale and sell at retail." Travel consolidators must have missed that day at business school because their philosophy seems to be "buy wholesale and sell wholesale." That's why they can offer low, low airline tickets, hotel rooms with discounts up to 65 percent, and the finest hotels at more than half off. They contract for groups of airline seats and hotel rooms at deeply discounted prices and then resell them to the public at markups that are still less than the going rate.

This practice is particularly common in the airline business, but you can also book hotels, cruises, rental cars, and even complete vacations. It works because once the cabin door is closed the revenue from an empty airplane seat is lost forever. The same goes for a hotel bed, cabin on a cruise ship, or rental car. At the end of the day, any revenue is better than an empty seat or bed, so airlines and hotels sell off their excess capacity for any price they can get.

Airlines have been able to charge anything they want for a ticket since they were deregulated in 1983. Most publish a multi-layered fee schedule that charges many different prices for riding on the same airplane. They also have another set of fares for customers who buy tickets online. Corporations, tour operators, and consolidators negotiate for the leftovers. Prices and availability of these tickets depend on how many empty seats the airline expects for any particular flight.

Since there are many different prices for tickets and rooms, depending on when you book and what discount you can find, it's sometimes hard to know just what percent off you're really getting. If you want to make sure you have a bargain price, get quotes from several different places so you have a good idea what your deal is really worth. Get as many details as you can, too. Consolidators get good prices because they buy tickets that are hard to sell any other way. Departure times, connection details, even the airline you travel on may not be the best. Decide before you pay how much convenience you're willing to give up in exchange for the cheaper price.

Sign up for exceptional offers

Many travel Web sites will e-mail free newsletters to you with their latest news, tips, and special deals. You can even sign up to get an e-mail whenever a new low fare or special rate comes up for a special destination.

Most airlines send out regular newsletters with travel tips and special offers. You may have to belong to their frequent flier program, or you may just have to register on their Web site. They will set you up for special e-mail alerts on sale fares and last-minute deals, which may not be available anywhere else.

Online travel agents offer a variety of services. Travelocity's FareWatcher tracks the best fares for up to five city pairs of your choice. Visit their Web site at *www.travelocity.com* for more information. Expedia's e-mail travel deals are also customized to your preferences. Go to *www.expedia.com* to sign up. Most last-minute deal Web sites have some sort of e-mail notification or newsletter system.

Travel guide publisher Frommer's, at *www.frommers.com*, has a variety of e-mail newsletters, as do many other publishers and travel agents. All you have to do is sign up. But be selective so you don't get more information than your inbox can handle.

Free guides for planning trips

Travel brochures take the sting out of planning top-notch trips and vacations. You can find one for almost anywhere — every state, many cities and regions, individual attractions, hotels, even some restaurants — and they're almost always free.

- Go to the library and ask for The Americas Chambers of Commerce Directory and the Toll-free Travel/Vacation Phone Directory. Use these to look up specific tourist sites and send for brochures.

- The Internet features a wealth of information on virtually every destination. You can even learn how to send for hardcopy pamphlets. Start with the Web sites *www.seeamerica.org*, *www.24-7Vacations.com*, and *www.travelbrochurecenter.com*.

- Look for brochures at hotels, restaurants, and local tourist information centers to gather ideas for your next visit.

- Stop at the big information centers at state lines. In addition to a wealth of pamphlets, you can pick up a free official state map and visit a clean restroom.

Brochures help you track your trip once you return home, too. Their pictures are usually far better than any snapshot, cost less than postcards, and have written descriptions that help you remember why you liked being there so much. Paste them in your travel journal, or mail them to friends in lieu of postcards.

Keep cruise costs under control

The reputation of a cruise as a bargain comes because everything is included — food, room, entertainment, and travel to exciting ports of call. But an affordable cruise vacation can quickly turn into a wallet-devouring monster thanks to attractive extras. Follow these steps for cruise cost control.

- Shop around. Check with several travel agents, individual cruise lines, and Internet Web sites for specials on trips going when, where, and for how much you want.

- If you have a trusted travel agent, ask him to keep an eye out until he finds exactly what you want.

- After you book it, keep an eye on the price of your trip. If it drops, you may be able to get it for the lower price.

- Most advertised prices are for inside — not ocean view or balcony — cabins. Think twice before you upgrade. Will you really spend that much time in your room?

- The shore excursions cruise lines offer are usually expensive. Compare them closely with tours you can book through an independent company.

- Do it yourself. You may see plenty of sights just walking around town or renting a car. Remember, though, the ship will wait if a cruise excursion is late, but it won't if you are late on your own.

- Alcoholic beverages cost extra. You have to pay for that drink with dinner, so consider those costs, too.

- Many ships also have casinos. If you like to gamble, budget accordingly.

- Some shipboard activities are complimentary while others are not. Make sure you know what a spa session, Pilates class, or golf lesson will cost before signing up.

- Port charges and transportation to and from the ship are unavoidable expenses. Some cruises include airfare, but as a rule you can get a better price on your own.

Stock your stay with cheap meals

Avoid high-priced meals by sticking snack packs and small pop-top cans of fruit in your purse or carry-on bag. Pack napkins and plastic utensils in a sealable bag, too, and check the grocery store for other individually wrapped foods.

Eat them while you wait at the airport or to offset expensive restaurant food on vacation. Use the microwave oven in your hotel room for a cheap, easy, do-it-yourself meal.

Ban surprises on hotel bills

Hotel bills are often much higher than you expect just because of room occupancy taxes. You can't help those, but you can help charges for tempting extras like mini-bars, pay-per-view movies, in-house laundry, and room service. Other luxuries add up, too. Try these tips for limiting extra charges.

- Keep a prepaid phone card with you to avoid hotel long-distance charges.

- Look for public parking lots near big-city downtown hotels instead of paying the inflated rates for hotel parking.

- Watch for automatic gratuity charges where the hotel automatically adds a tip amount to your bill. Don't tip twice.

Rough it for real vacation values

Camping means a tent, a sleeping bag, and a camping stove, not hitting the road in a $100,000 recreational vehicle. The basic equipment costs very little, and you can stay free or for dollars a day most places. Plus, the scenery can't be beat for sheer beauty.

Take the Grand Canyon, for instance. You can rent a campsite on the south rim for $15 a night. National Park lodges, on the other hand, range from $66 for a cabin to $123 for a full service hotel. Commercial motel rates run even higher, from $60 to $210 per night.

Camping is catching on again. The Travel Industry Association of America says one-third of American adults have camped on vacation in the last five years — and only 6 percent didn't like it. Find out which camp you're in.

Great way to see the national parks

The Americans with Disabilities Act of 1990 made it easier for disabled people to travel. Special discounts or free admissions for disabled travelers are another big help. Just remember you usually have to ask for them.

One such deal is the Golden Access Passport, a lifetime pass to all U.S. National Parks. It works the same as the Golden Age Passport, which you can buy for $10 after age 62, except it's free for people with disabilities. For more information, call toll-free 888-GO-PARKS.

More tips to stretch your travel funds

Make your money go farther the next time you travel with more handy hints.

- Use local coupons. Look for them in newspapers, at the hotel's front desk or concierge, at tourist information centers, and in the local yellow pages. The phone book is also a good source of maps.

- Shop for gifts at supermarkets and department stores. You'll find cheaper, more authentic local food and clothing there than in souvenir shops.

- Buy your own beach chair if you plan to be seaside more than a couple of days. You'll spend less than if you rent and can simply give it away or discard it when you leave.

- Take your own headphones on the airplane. Usually, the music and the movie are free, but you have to buy or rent the airline's headphones, at outrageous prices, to listen.

Utilities

■ Electricity and gas

Insulate yourself from high heat cost

You may grumble about electricity, oil, and gas bills but accept them as a necessary price for a comfortable home. It doesn't have to be that way, though. You can bring down your heating and cooling bills and at the same time make your house even more comfortable than it is now. The secret is insulation.

The U.S. Department of Energy says much of the country's housing is not insulated as well as it should be. Older homes are most likely to come up short, but even new homes can benefit. Depending on each individual situation, adding insulation will save enough money in reduced bills to pay for itself within a few years.

Your attic should be your top priority for insulation. The recommended level for most attics is to insulate to R-38 or about 10 to 14 inches deep, depending on the insulation type. A quick way to tell if you've got enough is to see if the floor joists are visible. If you can see the joists, you probably need more insulation.

You'll also want to plug the gaps found around plumbing, light, and electrical fixtures, chimneys, and under the eaves. Sealing up these leaks helps the insulation work better and also adds to your comfort.

After taking care of the attic, work on getting enough insulation under floors above unheated spaces and around walls in heated basements or unventilated crawl spaces. Make sure exterior walls were insulated to the recommended level when your house was built. If not, you should upgrade your wall insulation the next time you remodel or re-side your house.

Use candle to discover air leaks

You can save up to 10 percent on your heating bill just by stopping air leaks around windows, doors, ducts, plumbing, and electrical openings. Find out where your warm air is going by holding a lit candle next to a suspected air leak. Horizontal smoke means you have a draft, and you need to apply caulk or weatherstripping. Smoke drifting to the ceiling means nothing is blowing in, and you'll stay warm and cozy.

Program your thermostat for savings

A programmable thermostat is an amazing little device that can slash your utility bills — gas and electric — by up to 30 percent. Setting the temperature back when you're asleep or not at home uses less energy and lowers your heating and cooling costs. It takes much less energy to heat a house than it does to keep it heated over a period of time.

You can set it to lower the temperature around bedtime in the winter and then have the heat start back up just before the alarm goes off in the morning. In the summer, let your house warm up during the day when no one is home, and cool it off again about a half-hour before anyone is due back.

Exact savings will depend on how hot or cold outside temperatures get, the normal temperature you set inside your house, and how long your setback periods are.

Programmable thermostats average about $100, not including installation. Buy them at hardware, home improvement, or heating and air conditioning stores. Be sure to get one that will handle your particular heating and cooling system. If you're not sure, check with your service repairman.

AC cover stops winter drafts

Don't let your window air conditioner keep cooling your house during the winter. Get an indoor cover to keep chilly drafts from that idle unit from making you uncomfortable and overworking your heating system. A simple fabric cover with a wind-block insulating liner and a roll of removable tape costs less than $15. Ask your heating and cooling dealer, or order one from *www.energyguide.com*.

Clip power bill with filter checks

You may be surprised at how much you can save by checking the filters in your heating and air conditioning systems once a month. A heater or air conditioner with a clogged filter must work harder to pull air through the filter. That's wasted money. So check your filters every month — even the ones in room air conditioners — and replace them as often as needed.

Check for utility discounts

Some states give older adults a break on their gas or electric bills. Specific qualifications depend on the state and utility company. Most senior discounts also have a maximum income level. In Georgia, for instance, customers over age 65 with an annual income under $12,000 don't have to pay the base serv-ice charge — $10.50 for gas and $7 for electric. Some low-income assistance programs have an additional discount for seniors. Call your gas or electric service provider or the state utilities commission to find out.

Get help with heating costs

Federal programs are available to help low-income families with heating and cooling costs. The government supplies money for these programs, but they are run by individual state and local agencies.

Pay your bills with PIPP

A Percentage of Income Payment Plan (PIPP) is one way to keep up with util-ity bills. With this plan, a fixed percentage of your income takes care of your total ener-gy bill. PIPPs are designed to help low-income households, and — like LIHEAPs — each separate plan has its own rules and requirements.

A typical plan requires you to pay 15 percent of your income for all your gas and electricity. If you make enough money that it's cheaper to pay the regular bill, then a PIPP is not for you.

As a general guideline, your income must fall below 150 percent of the national poverty level, which is about $19,000 for a family of two. But each state or local agency sets its own rules, so check their requirements.

- The Low-Income Home Energy Assistance Program (LIHEAP) provides money to pay regular heating and cooling bills and also helps with shutoff or other energy crisis situations. Requirements and levels of assistance vary, but they usually give priority to homes where the health or safety of the elderly, disabled, or children under 6 years is at risk.

- The U.S. Department of Energy's Weatherization Assistance Program reduces utility bills by making homes more energy efficient. They do an analysis of your house and the work necessary to cut your gas and electric bills. On average, weatherization has reduced heating bills by 31 percent and overall energy bills by $274 per year.

To apply for either of these programs, get in touch with the agency that runs them in your area. Or check with your state social or human services office. You can also call the National Energy Assistance Referral (NEAR) project at 866-674-6327, or visit its Web site at *www.energynear.org*.

Low lighting saves energy

Light bulbs can use a lot of electricity. Here are some ways you can keep them from burning up so much energy.

- Turn off unused lights. With today's technology, bulbs don't use extra energy when turned back on.

- Replace any bulbs over 100 watts with 60- or 75-watt bulbs to reduce your electric bill.

- Install timers, photo cells, or motion detectors instead of leaving lights on all day so you don't come home to darkness.

- Use task lighting — like under-cabinet fixtures for countertops — to focus light where you need it instead of lighting up the entire room. Use three-way bulbs and dimmer switches to keep light low when bright isn't necessary.

- Open your blinds to let in the daylight, and decorate with lighter colors that reflect daylight better.

Long-lasting light bulb a winner

A new type of light bulb called the compact fluorescent light (CFL) bulb uses only one-fourth the energy, lasts 10 times longer, and gives off the same amount of light as an incandescent bulb.

The downside is this bulb costs more. But you save because it lasts longer and burns less electricity. You can see by this chart

	Incandescent	CFL
Watts	100	23
Life	750 hours	10,000 hours
Price	$.75	$11
Bulbs needed	6 for 3 yrs	1 for 6.8 yrs
Cost of bulbs	$4.50	$11
Cost of electricity	$35.04	$8.06
Total 3-yr cost	$39.54	$19.06
Savings		$20.48

you'll save more than $20 over three years, and the bulb will still last another three years. If electric rates go up, you'll save even more. You'll also help save natural resources. It takes nearly 500 pounds of coal to generate the electricity saved by using a 20-watt CFL instead of a 75-watt bulb.

Maybe the nicest thing about CFLs is that new technology has eliminated the buzz and flicker you hated with older fluorescent tubes. They come with a screw base, and the tubes are folded over so they fit in places designed for incandescent bulbs. You can even buy CFLs now that can be used with dimmer switches.

Since light bulbs cost more to run than to buy, you won't save a lot by replacing bulbs in seldom-used fixtures. But you can cut your energy bill for lighting in half if you replace 25 percent of your lights in high-use areas with fluorescents.

If you have any halogen-bulb torchiere lamps, though, consider replacing them no matter how much you use them. Halogen bulbs don't cost much, but they use 300 to 500 watts of electricity and can put off up to 1,200 degrees of heat. They are actually a fire hazard and can cost you double by making your air conditioner work harder when they're on. Energy-efficient torchieres that use CFL bulbs are now available.

When you shop for compact fluorescent lights, make sure they have the government's ENERGY STAR label. In the past, CFLs of questionable quality have been imported and sold in the United States, and people have been unhappy with their performance.

Save with energy-efficient appliances

You may be better off buying a new kitchen appliance even though there's nothing wrong with the old one. It all has to do with energy efficiency — how much it costs to operate that appliance. You can pay much more for the electricity a refrigerator or dishwasher uses over its lifetime than you did to buy it in the first place.

National energy conservation laws set standards for appliance efficiency, and the U.S. Department of Energy keeps them up-to-date. Every few years, technology improves, the bar is raised, and manufacturers begin producing equipment that runs better on even less juice.

For instance, a typical refrigerator sold in 1973 used more than 1,800 kwh of electricity a year. The typical model today uses less than 500 kwh. More insulation, tighter door seals, larger cooling coils, and better compressors and motors make the difference.

So when you buy a new refrigerator, it's probably better to recycle your old one instead of moving it to the garage or base-ment. One big refrigerator is generally cheaper to own and operate than two small ones. If you want an extra refrigerator just for beverages and snacks, try an energy-efficient compact model instead of your energy-guzzling old one.

Efficient dishwashers, like clothes washers, use less hot water and save the energy needed to heat it. Virtually all dishwashers available today have booster heaters to take water to higher temperatures. Set your hot water heater at 120 degrees, and you'll save even more water-heating dollars.

For information on which models are the most energy effi-cient, go to Consumer Resources on the American Council for an Energy-Efficient Economy's Web site at *www.aceee.org*, or call 202-429-0063 to order one of their publications.

Get paid to improve your home

A new energy-efficient furnace will save you enough in utility bills to pay for itself in just a few years. The problem is, the furnace company wants the $5,000 cost of the new unit now, not in a few years.

That's why the government came up with Energy Efficient Mortgage (EEM) loans to cover the cost of energy efficiency upgrades. Energy Improvement Mortgages (EIMs) are for remodeling projects and are a type of EEM.

The money from an EEM is added to your regular mortgage. Your improvements must cut your utility bill more than the loan adds to your monthly payment. The three main benefits of EEM are:

- You are allowed to go over traditional loan limits.

- You don't have to qualify for the additional funds.

- You can finance 100 percent of the improvements.

You have no out-of-pocket expenses, and even though your mortgage goes up somewhat, your utility bills go down. So it's almost like getting paid to improve your home.

The Federal Housing Authority (FHA) and Department of Veterans Affairs (VA) secure the loans. You can get them from many private secondary mortgage lenders and some private mortgage companies.

Other state programs help finance energy improvements as well. The Alliance to Save Energy has a database of more than 60 energy efficiency funds and programs on its Web site. Log on to *www.ase.org/section/topic/financingee for more information.*

Save up to $400 a year

ENERGY STAR is a government program that can help you save up to $400 a year on energy costs. To earn that label, a product has to meet strict guidelines set by the Environmental Protection Agency (EPA) and the U.S. Department of Energy.

The average American family spends around $1,300 per year on energy costs, and the EPA estimates you can save about 30 percent of that by using energy-efficient equipment. If you live somewhere with higher than average energy costs or more severe weather, you could save even more. ENERGY STAR currently saves businesses and consumers more than $8 billion a year.

It's not unusual for ENERGY STAR products to perform 20 percent better, and in some cases, up to 75 percent better. The purchase price will probably be more, so you have to do some figuring on what your total cost over the life of the equipment will be. In some cases, the more efficient product will be expected to last longer.

Look for a big, yellow tag called the EnergyGuide on new appliances to tell you how much energy it will use compared to other models, along with its estimated yearly operating cost.

The ENERGY STAR program has specific standards for more than 40 product categories, including windows, refrigerators, and electronic equipment. A program also exists for newly constructed homes to earn the ENERGY STAR label. Get more information on ENERGY STAR and how it can help you save money by logging on to *www.energystar.gov* or by calling 888-STAR-YES (782-7937).

Enjoy double savings with ENERGY STAR

Buy an ENERGY STAR appliance, and you may enjoy double savings. On top of the lower operating cost, sometimes you can also get rebates on certain appliances.

Private financing companies also may offer longer terms and better interest rates for ENERGY STAR heating and cooling equipment compared to conditions for standard appliances. Be sure and ask for better terms if you take out a loan.

Sometimes local utilities give cash rebates when you buy ENERGY STAR appliances. These rebates may range from $50 on a dishwasher or washing machine to $100 on a refrigerator to $300 or more on air conditioners or heat pumps. You might even get credit on your bill when you buy ENERGY STAR-rated light bulbs.

A quick check for rebates in your area is the Web site *www.energystar.gov*. Click on Special Offers in the Products category. Funds for these programs may be limited, so ask your utility company about future rebates if you can't find any current ones.

Choose a top-notch washer

Wouldn't you like to have a washing machine that uses 40 percent less water, 50 percent less energy, and is gentle on your clothes? Try a horizontal axis washing machine, better known as a front-loader.

These washers, common in commercial laundries and in Europe, have only recently started showing up in American homes. If you're ready for a new machine, it's the thing to get.

Front-loaders tumble clothes in a small pool of water. They take less water — especially important because of the energy it takes to heat the water — and don't have to work as hard while they're washing. The spin cycle takes more water out of the clothes, so your dryer uses less energy, too. The savings just continue to build up, because you also use less soap and your clothes last longer.

A typical top-loading machine uses about 40 gallons of water per load. A full-size horizontal axis washer uses between 20 and 25 gallons. If you average a load of wash a day, that's a savings of somewhere around 7,000 gallons of hot water a year. Since front-loaders are usually the newest models, you can expect them to have the latest technology, too.

If you don't need a new washing machine or don't want to pay the higher price for a front-loader, here are some other ways you can have an energy-efficient laundry.

- Use warm or cold water.

- Wait for a full load instead of washing small loads.

- Use shorter wash cycles for lightly soiled clothes.

Plug in late for lower electric bill

Check with your electric company to see if you can get credit for plugging in after hours. Many utilities now have special off-peak or time-of-use pricing programs.

Some of these programs offer substantial discounts for electricity used when the demand is low — 3 to 5 cents per kilowatt-hour as opposed to 12 to 15 cents for peak usage. Others pay extra if you agree to shut down certain appliances during peak times.

If your electric company has a program, you may have to sign up for it and get special equipment in order to participate. Peak hours and seasons when the special rates are in effect vary depending on the climate in your state.

Off-peak power solves problems

A power plant can generate only a certain amount of electricity. When customers try to use more than that, they experience brownouts and outages. Then the electric company has to buy power somewhere else or build a new plant in order to keep up.

When those peak load demands can be shifted to off-peak times, it solves several problems. The power stays on, electricity that would otherwise be wasted gets used, and the need for costly new construction is put off a little longer.

Some examples of these programs include:

- A company in Minnesota lets you hook up water heaters, certain electric heat devices, pool pumps, spas, and air conditioners to an interruptible power line in exchange for low off-peak rates.

- "Time of Use" plans in Arizona and Alabama charge higher rates during the afternoon and lower rates at night. A special meter keeps track of how much juice you use during both peak and off-peak times.

- Georgia Power will pay you to install a radio-controlled switch on your air conditioner. When hot summer days push up load demands, they activate the switch, which limits how long your air conditioner runs at one time. They also pay you every time they turn on the switch.

Control your natural gas price

You can control the price you pay for natural gas if you live in a state that has deregulated those prices.

Under deregulation, you can choose between several marketing companies instead of just one regulated provider. Most of these

Understand what you pay for

If you've been around a while, you're probably used to seeing the term "CCF" on your natural gas bill. But many gas companies now charge for "therms" instead.

Your gas meter registers the volume of gas you use, measured in cubic feet. A CCF is 100 cubic feet. A therm, however, is an amount of energy roughly equivalent to one CCF. The energy content of natural gas varies slightly, so your gas bill converts CCF to therms. You pay for the energy you receive instead of the amount of gas.

companies then offer different pricing plans. For example, recent gas prices in Ohio ranged from a variable rate of 91.5 cents per hundred cubic feet to a one-year fixed rate of $1.08.

Once you research the different plans, you can decide which company and which pricing plan to lock into for the long run.

Smart game plan for savings

A home energy audit is like a game plan to help you save money. It shows you improvements for your home that will cut hundreds of dollars off heating and air conditioning costs every year. The charge for one session ranges from $300 to $500, but you'll get that money back after just a year or two.

Your electric or gas company may conduct home energy audits for a low fee. If their price is not acceptable, ask them for names of local companies that perform the service. Or look for auditors in the phone book in the "Energy" section of the yellow pages. The local energy office can also recommend auditors in your area.

When the auditor arrives, have a list of any problems and copies of past annual energy bills. The auditor will walk through the house looking for air leaks and problems with insulation. He may use an infrared camera, surface thermometer, and blower door, which is actually a giant fan. The process generally takes four to eight hours.

The auditor may also examine your heating and cooling equipment. If you've had the unit more than 15 years, you might need to replace it. He may also give you suggestions on energy-efficient lighting.

Stay cool with the right room AC size

Prevent skyrocketing power bills and rooms that feel like Death Valley. Before you buy your next room air conditioning unit, figure out how much cooling power your next room air conditioner needs so you — and your wallet — will feel better this summer.

The right amount of cooling power for your unit will be measured in British Thermal Units (BTU) per hour. To figure out how much your room needs, measure the length and width of the room. Then multiply the length by the width to get the room's total square footage. For example a 10-foot by 9-foot room would be 90 square feet.

Now find the appropriate BTU for your room on the chart below.

Square Footage	BTU Per Hour
100-150	5,000
150-250	6,000
250-350	7,000
350-400	9,000
400-450	10,000
450-550	12,000

You may need to adjust this figure a little bit depending on how you use the room and how sunny it gets.

- If the room is very sunny, you'll need about 10 percent more cooling power.

- If the room is a kitchen, add at least another 4000 BTU to your total.

For an even more accurate estimate, visit Energy Guide at *www.energyguide.com*, and click the link for Room AC Calculator.

■ Plumbing

11 easy tips to trim water bills

Saving water means saving money, and these ideas can help you do both.

- Take quick showers instead of baths so you don't have to fill the entire tub with water.

- Catch the cold water with a bucket while you wait for it to warm up, then use it later for pets, plants, or cooking.

- Buy a showerhead with an on/off switch so you can turn the water down to a trickle while you shampoo or soap up. This little gadget will halve the amount of water you use.

- Scrape dishes instead of rinsing them before putting them in the dishwasher.

- Only run the dishwasher when it has a full load of dishes. The same goes for loads of laundry.

- Put a shut-off nozzle on your hose when you water plants or wash your car.

- Water your lawn during the coolest part of the day, around early morning.

- Point your sprinklers so they water the lawn, not sidewalks, streets, or passersby.

- Use soaker hoses or a trickle irrigation system to send water from gutters and drains to plants and trees, or catch it in a barrel and water plants later.

- Sweep the garage, driveway, or sidewalk with a broom instead of rinsing off leaves and twigs with a hose.

- Fix any leaks you find coming from toilets, faucets, pipes, and hoses. A leaky toilet can lose more than 40 gallons of wasted water a day.

Lower the flow

Want to drop your hot water bill by $150 a year? Put flow restrictors on all your faucets and showerheads.

Low-flow showerheads reduce the amount of water coming through the pipes. You won't even notice the difference until you get your water bill. A family of four conserves almost 15,000 gallons of water a year using flow restrictors and cuts 25 to 35 percent off their water-heating bill each month. You can buy these devices at any hardware store, and they're easy to install.

Set your heater to save money

Save 30 percent on your heating bill by setting your hot water heater to a timer. Most heaters run constantly to keep the water hot all day long. A timer turns it on and off at the hours you choose, so it only runs part of the day. You'll use much less energy and reap smaller bills in return.

Consider setting the heater to run at night so you have all the hot water you need the next morning. Or set it to turn off at night and back on in the morning, about an hour before you shower.

Hold the heat to cut down costs

Your hot water heater does more than give you hot water. It also gives off heat to the air around it. You pay for that heat along with all the hot water you get.

Wrap the heater in an insulation blanket to trap the heat, and you will save more than $20 a year on your heating bill. Hardware and home improvement stores like Home Depot and Lowe's sell these blankets for under $20, so it pays for itself in less than a year.

Energy ratings mean greater savings

The next time you buy a hot water heater, get one that costs less to operate.

- First, decide whether you want a gas or electric heater. Gas units are cheaper to run in most places, so factor that in to your decision.

- Next, look for the model with the highest Energy Factor (EF) rating. This measures how efficiently the water heater works. The higher the number, the better. A perfect unit that never lost any energy would have an EF of 1.0. Most gas heaters score between 0.60 and 0.70.

The more efficient, the more you'll save over the unit's lifetime, even if it costs more to install in the beginning.

Here's an example. A hot water heater with an EF of 0.90 will cost a little more than one with a 0.8 EF. However, you'll spend around $390 a year to run the heater with the 0.80 EF, compared to $351 for the 0.90 EF. After 30 years, the heater that cost more to buy has saved you $1,170.

Vision

How to get free eye care

You won't believe your eyes. You can get a free eye exam once a year, as well as free eye care — even for serious conditions like cataracts or glaucoma. Since 1986, the National Eye Care Project (NECP) has connected more than half a million seniors with free eye care from ophthalmologists volunteering in the program. You qualify if you:

- are a U.S. citizen or legal resident.

- are at least 65 years old.

- have not seen an ophthalmologist in the last three years.

- do not belong to an HMO or have Veteran's vision care.

One phone call gets the ball rolling. Dial the toll-free help line at 800-222-3937 to get the name and phone number of a participating ophthalmologist near you. Then call the doctor's office to make an appointment. You'll receive a free eye exam, and the ophthalmologist will treat any condition he diagnoses at no charge to you.

If you need multiple treatments, NECP will cover them for up to one year. The doctor will accept

Medicare or whatever insurance you have as full payment with nothing more from you. Don't have insurance? Then your eye care is free.

Nab deep discounts on eyeglasses

You'll never pay full price again. Just buy your next pair of eyeglasses through AARP Eye Health Services, a benefit of AARP membership. Members land up to 55 percent off frames and lenses, even specialty options like scratch-resistant coating. All you have to do is show your AARP card at a participating optical store in Sears, Target, JC Penney, Pearle Vision, or one of thousands of independent optometrists. Go to AARP's Health Care Options Web site at *www.aarphealthcare.com* to find a participating provider or call toll-free 888-352-3924.

People who buy AARP's supplemental insurance get a slightly larger discount on standard lenses plus a discount certificate for a family member or friend on a pair of eyeglasses. Learn more by calling the same toll-free number.

You may hold other memberships offering eye care deals and not even know it. Contact the organizations you belong to and ask about membership benefits.

New law saves you money

The federal government recently passed a law requiring your eye doctor to give you a copy of your prescription for contacts or eyeglasses, even if you forget to ask for it. Before, only a few states required it. If yours didn't, then you may have had to buy your eye wear from the doctor's office — sometimes at substantially higher prices.

Thanks to the new law you have the right to shop around, as well as the time to do it. The law makes your prescription good for at least one year. You can get it filled anywhere you choose, whether a discount club, mail-order supplier, the

Internet, or the doctor's office. The choice is yours, and it could save you a bundle.

Help for low-income working people

Over 40 million working people cannot afford regular eye care or health insurance, but because they work they are often not eligible for government or private assistance.

Vision USA aims to help these families and their children. This nationwide, year-round program sponsored by the American Optometric Association provides free basic vision care to uninsured, low-income workers and their families. So far, 340,000 people have gotten free eye exams. The requirements vary in each state, but generally you must:

- have a job or live with someone who does.

- not have vision insurance.

- not have had an eye exam in the last two years.

- earn less than a certain amount, based on the size of your household.

You can apply by calling 800-766-4466 Monday through Friday, 7 a.m. to 9 p.m. Central Standard Time, or send off for an application by writing to the following address.

Contact:	Vision USA
	243 North Lindbergh Blvd.
	St. Louis, MO 63141

If you qualify, you will be referred to a local optometrist for a free comprehensive eye exam. In some states, you may even walk away with free or low-cost eyewear.

Receive the gift of sight from friends

The Gift of Sight program gave away over 100,000 pairs of new glasses in 2004 to people who needed them but couldn't afford them.

To find out if you qualify, contact your local senior center, Lions club, United Way agency, church, or other community organization and tell them you would like help through the Gift of Sight program. They can give you a voucher or a referral and send you to a participating optometrist, such as a local LensCrafters store.

Each group has its own financial eligibility requirements you will have to meet in order to get free glasses. Stumped about which organization to ask? Each LensCrafters location has a Gift of Sight store captain who works with these community groups. Call a nearby LensCrafters store, ask for the captain, and talk with him about which organizations he works with. Then contact those groups about getting glasses through the program.

Gift of Sight also has an OutReach program where optometrists visit nursing homes and hospitals, adjusting or fixing people's eyeglasses for free. The eye doctors may also be able to help residents get new glasses through Gift of Sight. Talk with the nursing home or hospital administrators about taking part.

Cataract surgery at no cost to you

Cataract surgery is expensive, and most people without health insurance can't afford it. Enter Mission Cataract USA, a unique program connecting people in need with surgeons who donate their time to perform cataract surgery.

The program began 14 years ago when a California doctor decided to give something back to his community. Since then, it has grown to a national program providing more than 10,000 free cataract surgeries.

To be eligible, you must be uninsured, not have Medicare or Medicaid, and have operable cataracts. Call Mission Cataract USA toll-free at 800-343-7265 and leave a message with your name, address, and phone number. A volunteer will call you back as soon as possible and help set up a free eye exam. If you have cataracts, the volunteer will tell you which surgeon to call to schedule your surgery. Most of the surgeries take place in May, but the date varies by state.

Unfortunately, not every state boasts a participating surgeon. Mission Cataract USA will find one closest to your home, although you may have to travel out of state for the operation. If so, you will have to pay your travel costs — but it's an unbeatable deal for free cataract removal.

Escape the menace of glaucoma

More than 3 million people have glaucoma. Yet, half of them don't know it because the disease often has no warning signs. Perhaps that's why it is one of the leading causes of blindness in the United States.

Now you have one more way to protect yourself. Through the Glaucoma EyeCare Program, you may be able to get a free glaucoma screening and initial treatment. The people who qualify:

- are U.S. citizens or legal residents.

- have not had an eye exam in at least 12 months.

- are at increased risk for glaucoma because of age, race, or family history.

- do not have HMO or Veteran's vision coverage.

Call toll-free 800-391-3937 to find out if you are eligible and to get a referral for treatment. If you have insurance, you are responsible for your co-payment. If you have no insurance, your exam and treatment are free.

Protect yourself from blindness

People with diabetes are 25 times more likely to become blind than other people. In fact, diabetes is the leading cause of new blindness in adults. But there's good news. Diabetic blindness is preventable when eye disease is caught early. Unfortunately, many people skip eye exams because they can't afford to pay for them. Now there's help.

EyeCare America sponsors a Diabetes EyeCare Program to help people with diabetes get affordable eye exams and treatment. If you qualify, you will get an eye exam and treatment for a year at no cost to you. You might be eligible if you:

- have diabetes.

- are at least 65 years old.

- do not have HMO or Veteran's vision coverage.

- have not seen an ophthalmologist in three or more years.

- are a U.S. citizen or legal resident.

Call 800-272-3937 to find out if you qualify. If so, you will get a referral to a participating ophthalmologist. Each doctor will accept your Medicare or other insurance as full payment for your visit, with no out-of-pocket expense for you.

5 ways to save on contacts

Your options grow every day when you're searching for a good deal on contacts. You can buy them directly from your eye doctor, shop online, order them over the phone, or even pick them up at your favorite discount store. To find the best price, do some comparison shopping. Here are a few tips to get you started.

- Ask at your eye doctor's office about their prices when you're fitted for contacts. They may offer competitive rates, particularly if you buy in bulk or bundle your services — for instance, get your eye exam, lenses, and eye care products there.

- Visit or call Target, BJ's, and Wal-Mart. Their lenses may cost less than many of their competitors'. Plus, you get in-person service instead of dealing with a telephone operator or faceless Web site.

- Decide how fast you need them. Some online or mail-order sellers may offer better discounts, but they may also take longer to ship your lenses because they have fewer in stock. Do you need them fast, or are you willing to wait to get a good deal?

- Check out dealers you have never used with the Better Business Bureau (BBB) before you buy from them. Call your local BBB or visit them online at *www.bbbonline.org*.

- Ask about return policies. You want to be able to return unopened boxes of contacts if you ordered in bulk. This is important if your prescription changes or you have a problem with the lenses.

Quick guide to LASIK surgery

LASIK eye surgery is the most common type of refractive surgery, which reduces or eliminates your need for contacts or glasses. Here are a few things to consider to help you decide if it's right for you.

First, understand the procedure. After numbing your eyes with special drops, the surgeon cuts a small flap in the outer layer of your eye. Then, using a laser, he zaps away some tissue from under the flap and puts the flap back in place. After several hours, your vision should improve drastically, but there's no guarantee. You may still have to wear glasses.

The procedure costs around $4,000 to $6,000 for both eyes, and insurance doesn't usually cover the cost. If you decide it's worth it, shop around for a doctor with a good price, but don't sacrifice expertise to save money. Only let an expert perform this surgery on your eyes.

Some people are good candidates for LASIK, while others are not. If you're over age 65, for example, LASIK may not be the best option. Find out if you're a good candidate by visiting *www.allaboutvision.com* and taking their free LASIK screening test. Then make an appointment with your eye doctor for more information.

Make it easier for kids to see the light

Sight for Students, a VSP charity, provides more than 50,000 needy children with eye exams and glasses every year. If you are raising a child and can't afford eye care, it could help you, too.

Income is the biggest qualifier. The family's annual income cannot be more than 200 percent of the federal poverty level. In general, that means no more than $24,980 for a family of two, $31,340 for a family of three, $37,700 for a family of four, and so on. In addition, the child:

- cannot be over 18 years old.

- must still be in school.

- must have a Social Security number, or have a parent who has one.

- must be a U.S. citizen or legal immigrant, or have a parent who is.

- cannot have Medicare or other vision insurance.

Local community partners, such as the YMCA and Boys and Girls clubs, help run Sight for Students. The parent or guardian applies through them and receives a gift certificate for either a free eye exam or glasses for the child.

To find a community partner where you live, call toll-free 888-290-4964. Be sure to ask for a list of participating doctors when you get your child's gift certificate. You will have to make the appointment yourself.

Index

selling 211-212
Hospitals
  billing 241-243
  fitness clubs at 160
  free services 243-244
  Hill-Burton program 239-240
  outpatient surgery 241
  selecting 240-241
Hot water heaters 360-361
Hotel, minimizing charges 342
Hotwire 336

I

Infomercials 158-159
Inspections
  auto 46-47
  home 209-210, 221-222
Instructors, fitness 160-161
Instruments, musical 283-284
  renting 284-285
Insulation 344-345
Insurance 56
  auto 56-60
  credit card 82-83
  Flexible Spending Account (FSA)
    200-202
  homeowner's 59, 223-231
  life 83, 261-263
  loan 95-96
  long-term care 264-268
  Medicare 270-272, 308-311
  mortgage-life 231
  rental car 54
  unemployment 96
Internet
  radio 282-283
  services 132-134
  telephone service. *See* Voice over
    Internet Protocol (VoIP)
Investments
  401k plans 251
  avoiding fees 248-249
  certificates of deposit (CDs) 252
  clubs 249-250

determining tolerance level 247-
  248
  diversifying 253
  Dividend Reinvestment Plan
    (DRIP) 255
  municipal bonds 252
  mutual funds 252-254
  organizing 254-255
  planning 246-247, 250
  refunds 245-246
  stocks 253
  treasury bills 252
IRAs, tax penalties and 322
iTunes 279

J

Junk mail, opting out 75

L

Landscaping 256-257. *See also*
  Gardening
  mulch 257
  watering 259-260
LASIK surgery 368-369
Lawns, watering 259-260
Lemon law 34-35
Library
  music and 283
  toys and 330
Life insurance 83, 261-263
  term vs. whole 263
Light bulbs, energy-efficient 348-
  350
Loans 85
  adjustable-rate mortgage (ARM)
    94-95
  auto 26-27, 95
  automatic deductions 91-92
  brokers 87
  comparing 89
  consolidating 85
  Energy Efficient Mortgage (EEM)
    351-352

O

P

R